VITAMINB

{ FOR BUSINESS }

ANDY BAILEY

VITAMINB

{ FOR BUSINESS }

Foreword by JOHN SPENCE

Advantage®

Published by Advantage, Charleston, South Carolina.
Member of Advantage Media Group.

ADVANTAGE is a registered trademark, and the Advantage colophon is a trademark of Advantage Media Group, Inc.

Printed in the United States of America.

10 9 8 7 6 5 4 3 2 1

ISBN: 978-1-64225-145-6
LCCN: 2019917464

Editing and design by the Bradford Group, Nashville, Tennessee.

This publication is designed to provide accurate and authoritative information in regard to the subject matter covered. It is sold with the understanding that the publisher is not engaged in rendering legal, accounting, or other professional services. If legal advice or other expert assistance is required, the services of a competent professional person should be sought.

Advantage Media Group is proud to be a part of the Tree Neutral® program. Tree Neutral offsets the number of trees consumed in the production and printing of this book by taking proactive steps such as planting trees in direct proportion to the number of trees used to print books. To learn more about Tree Neutral, please visit **www.treeneutral.com.**

Advantage Media Group is a publisher of business, self-improvement, and professional development books and online learning. We help entrepreneurs, business leaders, and professionals share their Stories, Passion, and Knowledge to help others Learn & Grow. Do you have a manuscript or book idea that you would like us to consider for publishing? Please visit **advantagefamily.com** or call **1.866.775.1696.**

Dedication

I have been the recipient of the good fortune of others for most of my life. The number of people who have poured their support, love and wisdom during my journey is seemingly endless. Without this, I never would have achieved any level of success, nor would I be in a position to pass along the healthy doses of Vitamin B in this book. I am grateful to everyone that has guided me and for the opportunity to share these insights with you.

I especially want to express my gratitude for the team at Petra Coach, who have shown me, in ways I've only begun to truly appreciate, what a true team can achieve. By banding together, weathering storms, celebrating like mad, pressing forward when it seemed impossible and, most of all, caring for one another, you give me the inspiration to fuel my own fire. Thank you – you define "No Try." **+10Mhb**

{ INTRODUCTION }

*"You'll never **change your life** until you **change something you do daily**. The secret of your success is found in your **daily routine**."* – John C. Maxwell

The B vitamin is essential for the health of your brain, nervous system and really the entire body. Similarly, *Vitamin B (For Business)* is vital for company leaders – improving the health of your organization with daily mental supplements.

As a lifelong entrepreneur, the idea of taking a small, effective action every day toward a goal has been the cornerstone of every one of my successes. I've spent my life listening to thought leaders, reading hundreds of books, attending countless events and working with hundreds of teams.

And it all boils down to this: *Take daily action on what you are learning. Nothing ever happens if you don't.*

I wrote this book with that goal in mind – to provide you with a daily dose of learning. Served in bite-size chunks, *Vitamin B (For Business)* gives you a simple formula that allows you to take what you read each day, write down an idea and take action.

If you have an ambitious goal and only accomplish 2 percent every week, that may seem like a small amount, but you could be done in a year! Now, I realize it doesn't always happen exactly like that. But big priorities can be broken down into small steps, which can be easily achieved when you put your mind to it.

The same is true for this book. Most people don't get excited about reading another business book, but reading one page every day? That's easily doable.

Start on whatever day works best for you. But once you start, I encourage you to **keep going.** The concepts on these pages work together to help you become a better leader, a better entrepreneur and a better person. Isn't that what we all want?

As a business coach, I am passionate – fanatical some may say – about helping leaders, entrepreneurs and businesses succeed. That's why I work hands-on with companies 100+ days a year, spending more than 1,000+ hours every year helping leaders and companies improve.

The result is that the organizations I work with are growing at a rapid pace. Their revenues and profits are increasing by more than 50% annually, in many cases, and their company cultures are exciting and engaging.

My coaching is built on the Rockefeller Habits, which are outlined in the books *Mastering the Rockefeller Habits* and *Scaling Up 2.0* from Verne Harnish. Verne is a highly respected author, entrepreneur and founder of the world-renowned Entrepreneurs' Organization, which has more than 14,000 members worldwide. The methodology centers on all members of an organization finding alignment in their purpose, strategies and priorities. It also sets up a system of positive accountability to ensure that everyone is completing tasks and working toward shared goals.

Here's what success looks like according to the Rockefeller Habits:

1. The executive team is healthy and aligned.
2. Everyone is aligned with the #1 thing that needs to be accomplished this quarter to move the company forward.
3. Communication rhythm is established and information moves through the organization accurately and quickly.
4. Every facet of the organization has a person assigned with accountability for ensuring goals are met.
5. Ongoing employee input is collected to identify obstacles and opportunities.
6. Reporting and analysis of customer feedback data is as frequent and accurate as financial data.
7. Core values and core purpose are "alive" in the organization.
8. Employees can articulate the key components of the company's strategy accurately (i.e. core customer, brand promises, elevator pitch, etc.)

9. All employees can answer quantitatively whether they had a good day or week.
10. The company's plans and performance are visible to everyone.

These form the basis for all of my business strategies and thought processes, and they will be touched upon frequently as you go through this year-long journey with me.

Many of the writings in this book came from articles I authored, which were published in *Forbes*, *Huffington Post*, *AllBusiness*, *SmallBizDaily* and other media outlets. Other writings are excerpted from my first book, *No Try, Only Do*. Additionally, I had some business coaches from my company, Petra Coach, contribute, as you will see noted. I have also included takeaways from books I have read or speakers I have heard. It is an amalgamation that provides a well-rounded guideline to become a better and more effective leader.

Effective leadership isn't one and done. It requires a daily effort and mindfulness. This book will help you become the leader you want to be.

"It's not what we do once in a while that shapes our lives. It's what we do consistently."
— Anthony Robbins

THE NEXT STEP IS YOURS. **GO DO SOMETHING!**

{ FOREWORD}
by John Spence

John Spence *is recognized as one of the top business thought leaders and leadership development experts in the world, and he was named by the American Management Association as one of America's Top 50 Leaders to Watch along with Sergey Brin and Larry Page of Google and Jeff Bezos of Amazon. John is the author of five books –* Excellence by Design: Leadership, Awesomely Simple, Letters to a CEO, Strategies for Success *and* The Keys to Referability *– and co-author of several more. He's also a business consultant, workshop facilitator, keynote speaker and executive coach with a client list that includes numerous Fortune 500 firms, as well as small businesses, professional associations and other organizations. He was the owner or CEO of six companies and currently serves as a board member or adviser to several organizations and executives.*

Recently, one of my coaching clients, the CEO of a multibillion-dollar organization, asked me if I could make a little time to talk to his two sons. He explained to me that whenever he met a person who he felt had important wisdom to share, he wanted to get his sons in front of them to learn everything they could. "I don't know how long I have on this earth, John," he said to me. "So, I try every day to expose my boys to new ideas, information and people that will help them become men of value." I told him it would be a privilege to spend time with them.

I don't have children and don't spend much time around young people, so I was a little nervous when his kids showed up to ask me questions. Their ages were 14 and 16, and they were both very bright and respectful young men. We sat down across from each other at the conference room table in huge leather chairs, and I started the conversation by saying,

"What would you like to know?" Although we were only supposed to talk for 15 or 20 minutes, an hour later, they were still peppering me with questions.

"What is the secret to success?"
"How do you become more confident?"
"How do you handle failure?"
"What was your biggest failure?"
"What does it mean to be successful?"
"What made you want to become a business person?"
"How can I be a better leader on my soccer team?"
"What will it take for me to become the best in the world at golf?"
And on and on.

I told them they were asking tough questions, and I did my best to give them candid and frank answers. When we finally reached the end of our time together, I asked them what they had learned from me, and they said I basically had told them the same things everyone else had. To which I responded, "Do you know why? Because it works."

This book is much the same. You're going to be exposed to timeless business wisdom from some of the smartest people in the world. Andy and his team have spent decades helping companies of every type and size to be more successful. He has worked shoulder to shoulder with incredibly talented leaders and entrepreneurs, and through that work, he has created proven frameworks and business concepts that help his clients dramatically increase their growth, revenues and profit.

Here's the challenge – it's called the Knowing-Doing Gap. As you work through this book, you're going to come across ideas that you've seen before, and as you read them you will nod your head in agreement and say to yourself, "That is a great idea." You KNOW it is a powerful idea – but are you DOING anything about it? Are you effectively and consistently executing on it every day? The answer is most probably no.

Realizing that there are all these wonderful ideas that you're not doing anything about can become overwhelming and a bit depressing, which is why I love the layout of this book. You don't try to conquer it all at once. You get a daily dose of practical business advice that you can use immediately to begin improving your leadership and business. Each day you can make a few small changes and execute them with discipline. The pace will be reasonable, and the progress might seem trivial, but as days turn into weeks, and the weeks into months, the positive change in your organization will be massive.

Like Andy, I have spent the last three decades of my life traveling upwards of 200 days a year worldwide helping people and businesses be more successful. As part of that quest I have read a minimum of 100 business books a year since 1989, and I have had the great opportunity to work with some of the most prominent business leaders of our lifetime. And through all of that, I have built my career around finding patterns. What do the best businesses do – and do consistently – that allows them to outperform all of their competitors? What are the models of extraordinary leadership? What is similar about all high-performance teams? What do companies with great cultures all have in common? It has taken me thousands of hours to discover the most critical patterns for business success. Luckily, Andy has laid them all out for you in this book.

You are fortunate to have the opportunity to learn from Andy and his team. Reading this book is the equivalent of having one of the premier business coaches in the world share his best ideas with you. Read it carefully. Take your time. And every time you come across an exciting idea, ask yourself these three questions:

1. What does this mean to me?
2. How can I use this idea?
3. What can I do right away?

If you will do that, this book has the potential to change your business and your life in many, many positive ways.

I wish you every possible happiness and success.

– John Spence
One of the top business and leadership experts in the world

JANUARY

{ VITAMIN B-1 }

*Vitamins are essential nutrients that drive
your body's energy and growth. The beginning of
a new year brings with it endless possibilities
to achieve new heights, so take advantage
of this time of dynamic development.*

JANUARY 1

{ IDENTIFY YOUR "WHY" }

The new year is indeed a new beginning. It is when businesses set their annual goals. And that process takes time because a good plan – one the business leader and the team will stick to – isn't created overnight.

That is also true for personal resolutions. Forty-five percent of people set resolutions. Of those, only 8 percent maintain and achieve their promises. Want to be among the 8 percent? Find your "why" – the real reason you want to accomplish your goal.

A few years ago I was coaching a man, let's call him Bob, who wanted to lose 40 pounds. I asked him why. He shrugged his shoulders nonchalantly and said it was because he wanted to get healthy.

"What's the real reason, Bob?" I asked. "Leading up to today, that reason hasn't inspired you to change."

"Um…to see my kids grow up?"

I looked at him unconvinced.

After a few minutes of prying, he let out a sigh, began to tear up and divulged that his father had died when Bob was only eight years old. His father led an unhealthy lifestyle. He was overweight, smoked and never exercised. Because of that, he left the world early. Bob didn't want his kids to live with the same pain of losing their father.

That year Bob fulfilled his resolution.

Bob proves that once you have your "why," you have the sturdy foundation to devise a plan that will actually work. Take a moment to think of one goal you may have set as a New Year's resolution and identify your "why" – it may be the secret to getting it accomplished!

TODAY'S ACTION ITEM

JANUARY 2

{ HOW'S YOUR TEAM HEALTH? }

The first month of the year is traditionally a time dedicated to setting goals to become a healthier you in the new year. But do you have goals in place to build a more robust company this year?

Today's workforce is craving a life where work isn't just something they do to pay the bills. They want work to be an essential part of their well-being, providing confidence, creativity and friendship. It's possible to achieve a reality where employees are more satisfied coming to work each day – with a little bit of effort and maybe a happy hour or two. Here are two main ways to improve your team's health:

Over-communicate.
Communication is so important to relationships, but how often do we communicate poorly with those we spend the most time with throughout the day? Make this the year you get into a regular meeting rhythm and encourage lines of communication (and doors) to stay open among team members. I often advise implementing communication habits into your business systems, like a daily huddle, two-week task meetings (Rocks) or a weekly standing team meeting to discuss any outstanding issues.

Encourage growth.
Companies go to great lengths to ensure they are hiring smart, friendly and trustworthy team members who will benefit their organization. But do we continue to put forth the time and effort to develop these individuals throughout their tenure? Maybe they want to grow as a leader, run a marathon, speak a new language, read more, learn a new skill or simply keep their desk more organized. No matter the specific goal, personal growth and achievement positively affect day-to-day emotions, drive and self-confidence. Hold your team members accountable for their own goals and help them succeed. Encourage your team to work toward something that matters to them and see their personal and professional growth soar!

TODAY'S ACTION ITEM

JANUARY 3

{ WHAT CAN YOU DO IN ONE YEAR? }

Bill Gates once said, "Most people overestimate what they can do in one year and underestimate what they can do in 10 years." If that's true, we need to be intentional about the ways we are planning for both.

The beginning of the year marks a clean slate, which is both exhilarating and terrifying. If you're anything like me, I relish in the opportunity to set lofty goals, but often fall victim to the dreaming instead of doing. Charting your one-year plan is the best way to ensure your dreams turn into reality. Here are two things to consider:

Clients: Most business owners see their clients like numbers – a pile of data, which determines the client's importance. Instead, be a reliable partner to your clients or customers regardless of their revenue or pocket size.

Priorities: The majority of businesses focus on the urgent, not the important – the day-to-day challenges that pop up and can cloud the bigger picture. With a little planning, you can systematize your daily operations. Then you will not be bogged down by the menial interruptions and can stay on your long-term course. When you set priorities, you can proactively grow your business instead of merely maintaining it.

TODAY'S ACTION ITEM

{ 4 WAYS TO HELP MAKE MEETINGS MATTER }

I don't know about you, but I am of the opinion that meetings suck. They're necessary to achieve the results you want, but they still suck.

Here's how I get over it: I use the SLED (Suck Less Every Day) philosophy for meetings. Day by day, meeting by meeting, work to improve productivity until your team is punctual, engaged and working together to generate results. Here are four helpful tips:

1. Establish a clear objective.
Don't waste valuable time at the start of each meeting to brief everyone on its purpose. Distribute an agenda beforehand, so attendees go into the meeting prepared with ideas and questions. Be extra bold and institute a "no agenda, no attenda" rule.

2. Invite wisely.
Limit attendance to team members whose participation will help produce results. It's easy, and sometimes a habit, to invite everyone in the office to a meeting, but that is an inefficient use of time. At a minimum, dismiss people after they are no longer needed.

3. Be timely.
Don't go outside the set time boundaries. Close the conference doors when the meeting is scheduled to begin, and end at the promised time. If you're the meeting leader, set a standard for meetings going forward.

4. Who, what, when.
The conclusion of each meeting ignites the start of the action. Always establish "who is going to do what by when" before adjourning each meeting.

There is no better time to start than now. Make your meetings more productive, and then they won't suck!

TODAY'S ACTION ITEM

JANUARY 5

{ APPRECIATE YOUR TEAM }

If you want to grow your business, you're going to need great employees. Want great employees? Treat them right!

Lack of appreciation is the number one reason that employees leave their jobs, according to the U.S. Department of Labor. It's not benefits, bonus structure or salary. People go because they feel like their hard work is not recognized or appreciated.

The next time team members do something well or go above and beyond what's expected, tell them how much you appreciate it. Here are the rules though:

- Be specific.
- Be genuine.
- Deliver it in-person, with enthusiasm.

Instead of sending an email that reads, "Good job today, Sam," go to Sam's office and say: "Hey, Sam, I appreciate all of the thought you put into that graphic. It enhanced that presentation and made the difference in our getting the business."

Believe me, Sam will not only continue to produce thoughtful graphics, but he will also escalate his all-around productivity. And he's more likely to report that he is feeling satisfied with his job because he knows that, without a doubt, his boss is confident in him and his work.

TODAY'S ACTION ITEM

JANUARY 6

{ THE SECRET TO LEAVING YOUR COMFORT ZONE }

Guest contribution from Petra Coach Marshall Martin

Early in my career, I was an executive in a nearly $2 billion company and had all I could ever want in a job. But it became too comfortable, and I didn't feel like I was continuing to grow personally. That's when an opportunity presented itself that would allow me to move into the C-suite at a software technology company that had less than $10 million in revenue and would require a move.

We are all creatures of habit and thrive on the predictable to minimize stress. Taking risks is not our immediate nature. But I knew one thing: If I chose to follow my fears and stick with only the familiar, I would be destined to fall behind everyone else willing to take a chance.

That's how I found my "zone of courage." Your zone of courage lies just outside your comfort zone. If you're not ready to take a big leap, take a baby step. You've got to start somewhere. The zone of courage contains much less predictability than your comfort zone, but it could also provide opportunities for personal and professional growth.

The key to success is finding that area outside your comfort zone but before the "zone of terror," where it is too overwhelming. The zone of courage is the sweet (but slightly uncomfortable) spot that allows you to move forward and grow without being paralyzed with fear.

When I took that leap of faith, every challenge that came after seemed far less stressful and made me a better person, personally and professionally.

TODAY'S ACTION ITEM

JANUARY 7

{ DEAL WITH THE "ROCKS" FIRST }

In my work with companies, one thing I always recommend is to implement bi-weekly, one-on-one meetings with each employee and his or her supervisor. I call these meetings "Rocks." They are an opportunity for supervisors to check in and see how employees are doing with work and in their personal lives. During the meeting, tasks and priorities are set for the next two weeks or until you meet again.

The concept of "Rocks" is based on the idea that, to best fill a jar, you need to put the big rocks in first so you know they will fit. Then, you can add the pebbles, sand, water or whatever else. If you change the order, the there won't be room for the rocks.

Related to the *Rock*-efeller Habits methodology (see what I did there?), set your biggest priorities and goals first so a proper plan of action can be put together. If you don't know where you are going, it's difficult to plan steps to get there.

Additionally, it makes sense to address the more significant issues first because they may be the cause of other smaller issues. Once those bigger "rocks" are resolved, it becomes a lot easier to deal with the pebbles.

Not only are these Rocks meetings part of a healthy system of communication and problem-solving, but they are also important for guiding team members through relevant and attainable goal-setting.

Even if you don't have the bandwidth to implement one-on-one meetings just yet, at least use this frame of reference when meeting with your team and planning for the future. It will guide you in the right direction.

TODAY'S ACTION ITEM

JANUARY 8

{ GREAT LEADERS DO EXIST }

What does the term "great leader" mean? What sets the genuinely great apart from the rest of the leadership pack?

The answers to these questions came into focus when I read *The Master Coach: Leading with Character, Building Connections, and Engaging in Extraordinary Conversations* by fellow entrepreneur and leadership author (and personal friend) Gregg Thompson.

In Gregg's bold opinion, great leaders don't really exist. They are just deeply committed men and women who work to improve every day and are committed to the development of their colleagues, success of their organization and strength of their relationships.

As a CEO and business coach myself, I have a lot of experience working with different types of leaders. And I agree that the title of "great leader" isn't some end goal or box you can check off at the end of a long, hard journey.

However, I *do* believe that great leaders exist because I've seen them in action.

Great leaders are specific and forward-thinking. They recognize that ideas like "strive for success" and "stay committed" are often too general to inspire real progress. They live by clear-cut day-to-day actions, timely priorities and measurable goals. They also have a relentless focus on the road ahead, paying no mind to what's happening in the periphery or rearview mirror.

And above all, great leaders are humble. They know they don't always have the right answers, and they accept honest feedback. They focus on their strengths and improve weaknesses. This combination of modesty and self-awareness enables leaders to move past obstacles.

Bottom line: Great leaders do exist, and you can learn to be one too.

TODAY'S ACTION ITEM

JANUARY 9

{ THE DIFFERENCE BETWEEN HAVING A JOB AND HAVING A BUSINESS }

Most business owners aren't in it just for the money. In fact, in many cases, they could earn more money, with fewer headaches, working for your average large corporation.

Instead, what attracts most of us to start a business is the need for more freedom. Unfortunately, many business owners end up simply harnessing themselves to another job.

I know because I've been there. I owned a wireless business for 18 years, and for the first nine years, I was working for this unmerciful jerk I saw in the mirror each morning. I had created myself a job, not a business. And in doing so, it made me miserable.

However, for the last nine years of my company, I worked on building a business with clear and sustainable processes that were led by very capable people. Not only was I much happier, but I was also able to create something I could sell and exit because it could run without me.

And that, my friends, is the difference between a job and a business. If it can run without you, you've built a business. If it can't, you've created another job for yourself.

TODAY'S ACTION ITEM

JANUARY 10

{ CHANGE THE PEOPLE }

You may have heard this common quote in business before: "If you can't change people, change the people."

The statement might seem harsh, but it's an important lesson: Sometimes, the answer is to replace team members with new people. After all, training can improve performance, but it's difficult to change attitudes.

Some leaders want to avoid looking at responsible parties directly and instead only patch problems in hopes that the issues will eventually go away. While it might work temporarily, this is neither a long-term fix nor an effective short-term solution.

Once you directly address team members' problematic behavior, if the conversation yields little to no improvement, part ways quickly. Keeping them hurts your company's culture and productivity.

That said, approach this change the right way: with communication and preparation. State the company's decision to let them go. Clearly but succinctly explain how their actions affected the business. If applicable, let them know that you can refer them to a different kind of job that may better suit them. Exiting team members have more respect for a past employer if leadership straightforwardly engages them.

You may feel a weight off your shoulders when they leave, but the rest of your team may not feel that relief. Ensure that no one is stressing about workloads or reflecting negatively about the way the change was handled.

By biting the bullet and letting someone go, you can improve the functionality of your team. Additionally, you will help people who aren't thriving in your organization find a better fit elsewhere.

TODAY'S ACTION ITEM

JANUARY 11

{ DON'T FORGET TO LOOK UP AND ENJOY THE VIEW }

I travel a lot in my work. But every morning when I'm home, I purposely set aside time to take a walk around "The Loop," a little stretch of land that starts in my backyard and winds along a grassy path in the town where I live.

The Loop is just a small slice of a local farm – a rare gem of a place that is the most significant historic farm associated with the modern Tennessee Walking Horse industry.

On my two-and-a-half-mile walk, I pass by a small lake filled with geese and ducks, several ramshackle barns spotted with a blue heron or two, a river lined with trees claimed by hawks (and, more rarely, an owl), wide-open pastures of green grass and a famous old horse barn where people come from miles around to take wedding and family photos.

Words can't do it justice. It's a breathtakingly beautiful place to walk, enjoy nature and be in the moment. Most of the other folks walking The Loop are with someone else and chatting, sometimes taking in their surroundings, sometimes not.

It was during one stroll that I saw another couple walking. The woman was strolling along, and the man was occupied with his phone and not looking up. He was missing the splendor of the scenery.

As simple as it may be, I urge you to look up today. Just look up. As we enter this new year, give yourself a renewed sense of beginning. We have yet another chance to "get it right," and be better than we have been in the past.

TODAY'S ACTION ITEM

JANUARY 12

{ PREVALENT PITFALLS AND HOW TO AVOID THEM }

Guest contribution from Petra Coach David Pierce

"Set a goal, make a plan, do the work."

In other words, figure out what your priorities are, outline the steps to get there, and then do it. But it is surprisingly difficult for many people to set and meet goals.

To improve your success ratio, make your goals reasonable and attainable – and avoid these typical errors:

Pitfall #1: Too many priorities

The human brain is wired to do only one thing at a time if that thing is to be done excellently. Studies are frequently questioning the validity of "multitasking," concluding it is nothing more than "task switching." With every switch, the lag time between tasks increases, and productivity declines considerably. The law of diminishing returns kicks in when focusing on more than 3-5 significant priorities for any given period.

Pitfall #2: Vague priorities

Unclear priorities that don't answer the five Ws – "who," "what," "when," "where," and "why" – are predisposed to failure, or at best, underachievement. A target you can't see is difficult to hit.

Plus, a priority must be measurable. If you can't measure it, you can't manage it. When your goals are quantified, you will be able to track your progress and know when they are completed.

Pitfall #3: Priorities without visibility and accountability

Being accountable to others creates an internal commitment to not let them down. It's like the "tree falls in a forest" concept: If no one else knows what you want to accomplish, who will know if your goal was met?

TODAY'S ACTION ITEM

JANUARY 13

{ KEEPING TABS ON YOUR TEAM }

People are the catalysts that make businesses perform, and people, not processes, determine whether or not companies will flourish or flounder. Even if you've heard it before, it's worth saying again: People are your greatest asset. Take the extra steps to hire the right people, fire the wrong people and heavily invest in those you have on board.

Here are three things I continue to assess when it comes to my team:

1. Do I have enough diversity?
Don't shy away from diversity. The experiences your team brings to your table are often invaluable, including skill sets, perspectives, ideas and strategy. Diversity fosters better and alternative approaches in the decision-making process.

2. Am I overloading my team?
At some point, an additional one percent is just too much. Avoid burnout and taking your team for granted. It's one thing to be efficient with human capital and another thing entirely to spread people too thin and take advantage of their capabilities. Successfully managing your team means continually monitoring your expectations, their workload and the resources they need to get the job done.

3. Is my company still the best fit for this person?
A-players want to work with other A-players for a multitude of reasons. To start, I firmly believe that people will rise to the standard that you set for them. Keeping C-players on the team to avoid conflict can ruin an organization because these employees bring the playing field down a notch. Set high expectations for your entire team and maintain those expectations by hiring like-minded professionals who bring tangible value to the table.

TODAY'S ACTION ITEM

JANUARY 14

{ CREATING YOUR COMPANY VALUES }

Every fingerprint is unique, and no two snowflakes are exactly alike. Similarly, each company has a particular set of core values that define every daily business decision, from how phone calls are answered to which technology is leveraged. Without clearly defined core values, an organization lingers in a constant state of an identity crisis. But classifying exactly what's most important to you and your company isn't always easy.

Ask yourself: What are the essential qualities every employee must possess? What drives your business decisions? Does everyone in your company share the same motivations and priorities? Are there certain fundamentals you're not willing to compromise on?

Brainstorm with your team.
This is one of the best insights into what's critical to your company. Write down whatever comes to mind with a "there are no wrong answers" attitude. Discuss other team members. What do you admire about them? Which of their attributes and behaviors exemplify the best elements of your company culture? Set a time limit to ensure you don't overthink – 15-30 minutes should do it.

Put all your ideas on the table (or wall).
Look at all your ideas and see what jumps out. Anything surprising that even you can't believe you wrote down? If possible, wallpaper the room with large sticky notes for everyone to see. Step back and take a look at your options from a different point of view.

Hold an auction.
Ask yourself, "If I had $4,000, and each value cost $1,000, where would I put my money?" You'll be amazed by how fast this narrows your choices and reveals what you value most.

Then, you'll be on the fast track to defining your company's core values.

TODAY'S ACTION ITEM

JANUARY 15

{ ACCOUNTABILITY DOES NOT MEAN RESPONSIBILITY OR AUTHORITY }

Although the words "accountability," "responsibility" and "authority" are used interchangeably in business, they shouldn't be. Verne Harnish explains their specific differences in his book *Scaling Up*.

Accountability is literally the person with "the ability to count." In other words, the accountable person is the one who is tracking the progress of a goal and making it known when there is no advancement.

This person is not necessarily the decision-maker. He or she is there to keep the horse moving. And as a general rule, there should be only one person accountable. As Harnish puts it, "If more than one person is accountable, then no one is accountable and that's when things fall through the cracks."

Responsibility is literally the person with "the ability to respond." That means they are the ones to proactively step in and support the team, especially to carry out specific processes or to work out certain issues.

Authority is the end-all-be-all decision-maker. This person holds the reins and makes the calls on how a process will be carried out, how an issue will be solved and who is responsible and accountable for them.

As you move up the ranks in a company, some of these lines start to blur a bit. For example, someone in the management might be both accountable for and responsible for a specific process. Depending on the role, this person also may have authority over the way the process is handled.

Make sure every person on your team knows what their role is on this spectrum, and you'd be surprised how much more gets done.

TODAY'S ACTION ITEM

JANUARY 16

{ PUSHING PAST PROBLEMS }

Everybody's got problems, and in the workplace, there's no shortage of them. I talk to business leaders every day about what's going wrong and how they've tried to make it right.

First, there is no "try" – only "do." (You'll hear this theme a lot in this book.) Second, you need to understand the difference between patching problems and eliminating them.

If you're dealing with the same problems over and over, delve into why. A lot of folks just put a Band-Aid on it because it's a quicker "fix." However, that temporary appeasement is not a fix at all, and you'll find yourself having the same conversation about the same problem a week later.

For example, if you're consistently hiring employees who underperform or aren't a good fit for your company, it's not enough to fire and rehire with the hope that you'll get it right next time. You have to figure out what you're doing wrong first.

Then ask, "Is there a way we could eliminate this?" If there's a task or issue that's repeatedly wasting valuable time, maybe there's another option. Asking the big question can be scary, but it could lead you to innovation and improvement. The discussion may break you out of your comfort zone, and it may require taking risks, but you may find a solution you hadn't previously considered.

Think about how much time you're wasting by "solving" the same issues over and over again. It's time to get back to your business and out of the business of patching problems. What challenges can you eliminate today?

TODAY'S ACTION ITEM

JANUARY 17

{ UNDERSTANDING AND BROADCASTING LEADING INDICATORS }

Getting leaders to think about where their business is heading and how they measure progress is one of the toughest challenges I face as a business coach. All too often, leaders fall back on looking at revenue and profit as the only benchmarks to evaluate how well they are doing.

The most successful business owners focus much of their attention on the priorities and tasks that will drive *future financial performance*. They treat these leading indicators – such as the number of upcoming sales calls or customer visits – as the benchmark that will help them achieve desired outcomes. Here's the approach I recommend:

1. Focus on three leading indicators.
While each business has its unique leading indicators, it's tempting to cast a wide net and measure too many. My advice to business leaders is to determine a few indicators (three is best) that will have the largest impact on your business. Then pay very close attention to them on a regular basis. Create space on your calendar to do these activities.

2. Educate everyone on your team.
Once you have your key indicators, teach everyone in your organization about them. More specifically, explain how they can help improve the numbers. People need to know how a business makes money and how they fit into that equation. If you educate team members around these simple numbers, they will begin to take ownership of them.

3. Make it public and post information so everyone can see it.
Think of it as your company scoreboard. You can use an online dashboard or a simple community whiteboard, but the data must be visual and right out in front for everyone to see.

TODAY'S ACTION ITEM

{ HIRE SMART, NOT FAST }

Nothing – I repeat – nothing will affect your business more than the people you add to your team.

There are two hiring philosophies. You can either hire smart or hire fast.

The first creates a team with A-players who can help drive your company to the next level; the latter just fills the seats.

After 20 years of hiring – and when necessary, firing – team members, I can tell you that taking time to find A-players is the only way to go if you want to grow your company.

A-players by definition are the top 10 percent of talent available for the job and dinero you're offering – the best at what you need for your business.

When I'm working with a business owner or leader, the first question I ask is: How much time, on average, do you spend interviewing, testing and researching candidates before you hire them? Most say five hours or fewer.

That's scary. In selecting a new team member, you're choosing a person you may spend more time with than members of your family. This is someone you'll spend thousands of dollars training and maintaining and who will influence your business's financial security.

If I haven't made my point yet, maybe this next one will hit home: In choosing a new team member, you're picking someone you may share a toilet seat with. Take your time!

Hiring the right team members is most often sidestepped, but it affects so much of your business. It's not easy finding A-players, but it's easier than being surrounded by a team of C-players, guaranteed.

TODAY'S ACTION ITEM

JANUARY 19

{ WHY YOU SHOULD CONDUCT A SWOT ANALYSIS }

Threats exist in every industry and every business. For every checkbook, there's a debit card. For every telegraph, there's an email. And for every pager, there's a cell phone. Business leaders need to recognize, discuss, debate and plan for upcoming threats to mitigate them.

It may be more critical now than ever to recognize threats because our technological world enables the quick transfer of information and ideas, which initiates change. I recently attended an event where the speaker talked about Moore's Law, which notes that the pace of computing technology doubles roughly every 18 months. That seems quick, but it's just slow enough that we don't notice it until it's too late to catch up. If consumers' wants and needs are changing quicker than your business structure can address, you're in trouble.

Do you know your strengths, weaknesses, opportunities and threats (SWOT)?

SWOT is an analyzation process that urges business leaders to gain a better understanding of their enterprise. By carving out time to consider your company's strengths, weaknesses, opportunities and threats, you will be able to recognize issues and tackle challenges (hopefully) before they arise. When is the last time you considered what is threatening your business? I would guess that you haven't thought about that at all in the past six months. Our world changes quickly, so you need to be hyper-aware of what may be lurking in the shadows ready to trip you up.

The entire SWOT process is designed to force you to think more in-depth about your business, which allows you to be proactive rather than reactive to threats.

While it may seem time-consuming to start, your forethought will reap rewards for your business in the future.

TODAY'S ACTION ITEM

JANUARY 20

{ THE CONCEPT OF COOL }

Guest contribution from Petra Coach JT Terrell

I often hear about the "cool" bosses who install arcade games in the office or host happy hours every Friday. But what does it *really* mean to be "cool"?

I was first introduced to the concept of "cool" by watching the show Happy Days in the 1970s. The coolest guy on TV was Arthur "The Fonz" Fonzarelli, played by the great Henry Winkler.

From a child's perspective, he had it all. Fonzie commanded respect, was seemingly invincible and got immediate results when he snapped his fingers. (It also helped that he rode a motorcycle.)

I was watching the show recently – for the sake of research, of course – and noticed some new things about my touchstone of cool that I didn't pick up on as a kid:

Fonzie isn't just strong, he also uses that strength to stand up for folks who need help. If a rival gang is threatening his friends, The Fonz intervenes and squashes the drama. If Joanie's upset, he always offers a hug and some kind words of encouragement. The Fonz cares deeply about his friends and family, and they know it.

He isn't just a result-oriented leader, he also mentors Richie to be the same. Sure, he could have just been the Cunninghams' neighbor and stayed out of Richie's life, but he gets real satisfaction from seeing him grow and become more assertive in his own right.

He isn't just cool with his peers, he also shares love and emotion with the elders on the show: Mr. and Mrs. Cunningham, Al at the diner and, more than anyone else, his mom.

Could such an influential figure also be vulnerable and humble? Answer: Yes, he can.

"Aaaaayyyyyyyyyy" (Thumbs up!)

TODAY'S ACTION ITEM

JANUARY 21

{ HOW TO MOTIVATE YOUR TEAM }

Let's face it. Entrepreneurs and business leaders often find it challenging to motivate team members. One reason is that leaders seldom lack self-motivation. It's so second nature to them that they get frustrated when a team member doesn't appear to have the same level of drive and ambition.

One of the most frequently asked questions I hear from business leaders is, "How can I motivate my team?" Imagine their surprise when I tell them, "You can't."

Business leaders must understand that team members will not always share their outlook, passion or motivation. So instead of forcing your will and drive on others, use these two approaches to inspire motivation in your team:

1. Lead by example.
Show your team members how it's done and dedicate yourself to showing your passion and motivation in everything you do. When your team sees your genuine excitement and enthusiasm, they'll be much more likely to increase their energy level and get on board.

2. Honesty is the best policy.
Be open and honest about the task at hand. Get your team members to understand why the project is so important to you personally and to the company. Not every goal, task or objective will foster the same amount of excitement and teamwork. If what you want is challenging or risky, let your team know. They'll respect your transparency and be more likely to trust you and your leadership.

TODAY'S ACTION ITEM

JANUARY 22

{ SETTING S.M.A.R.T. GOALS }

What most often stops people from actually achieving their goals?

They're not S.M.A.R.T.: specific, measurable, attainable, relevant and time-bound.

Specific – A specific goal has a much higher chance of being accomplished than a general goal. It must answer the six "W" questions: Who is involved? What do I want to accomplish? Where? When (timeframe)? Which requirements and constraints should be considered? Why?

Measurable – Establish concrete criteria for tracking progress toward the attainment of each goal you set. This helps you stay on track and motivates you to reach your goal.

Attainable – Avoid those "Climbing Mt. Everest" goals if you've never been climbing before. When identifying goals, be sure you can realistically make them come true based on your current attitudes, abilities, skills and financial capacity.

Relevant – The goal should be something that matters right now. It also should be an objective toward which you are both willing and able to work. Be sure that every goal represents substantial progress because the higher the goal, the more motivational force to reach it (assuming the goal is attainable). Some of the hardest jobs you ever accomplished seemed easy only because they were a labor of love.

Time-bound – A goal should be grounded within a time frame, or else there's no sense of urgency. If you want to lose 10 pounds, by when? "Someday" won't work. But if you anchor it within a timeframe – "by May 1st" – then you've set your mind in motion to begin working on the goal.

TODAY'S ACTION ITEM

JANUARY 23

{ TIME TO AUDIT YOUR APPOINTMENT CALENDAR? }

Effective time management ranks among the more challenging, and often exasperating, aspects of being a successful leader. It requires the flexibility to respond to unexpected challenges and the self-discipline to block out distractions and complete daily tasks.

In my experience as a business coach, I frequently hear leaders express frustration with how easily their well-planned days veer off course. They describe how demands from clients, colleagues and other constituencies take away precious time from their workday.

If you find you are having challenges managing your day, here's what you need to do: Audit your calendar. Sit down and review three months of activity. The data from the analysis will show where you spent your time (which projects, tasks and priorities demanded your attention) and with whom you collaborated to get the work done.

The audit will also reveal if the work you were doing is properly aligned with company goals and priorities. It will shed light on areas where you were distracted, where you were the most productive and which tasks/ projects took more time (or less) time than anticipated.

Face it – there will never be enough hours in the day to accomplish everything you need to do. But if you methodically review how you spend your days and instill focus and discipline while completing daily priorities, you will soon find more time to work on the long-term success of your business.

TODAY'S ACTION ITEM

JANUARY 24

{ DON'T BE AFRAID OF FEEDBACK }

As the leader of a company, it's not easy to take responsibility for the issues your company is having.

Most leaders are deeply and emotionally invested in what they do. If they say that any issues are their fault, it can mean admitting they made mistakes and opening themselves up to scrutiny. It is not easy. But it is a necessary step to begin the process of change.

One of my company's clients wasn't sure how to get to the heart of the issues it was having and transform them into something productive. The company's executive team decided to conduct a talent assessment, in which each leader "graded" one another on his or her performance. It was an opportunity to be very frank about what was working and what was not.

Once those concerns were voiced, it became a heck of a lot easier for them to take the feedback and turn it into actionable steps.

Each team member came away with an action plan to make changes, including key performance indicators (KPIs) to measure when goals have been reached and an accountability partner to make sure each person stays on the right track.

When the team made a process for sharing their feedback, it became a lot easier for them to be open about it.

Takeaway: Don't shy away from getting feedback, formally or informally. Just make sure it's used constructively rather than destructively.

TODAY'S ACTION ITEM

JANUARY 25

{ GET EVERYONE INVOLVED IN CHANGE }

One of the biggest lessons I drill into the teams I coach is that you can't *really* make changes in a company without the buy-in of the entire team.

You can be a dictator and roll out a bunch of new rules and policies without consulting anyone, but let's face it, how many eye-rolls will you produce from doing something like that?

Skip the looks of disdain and bring your ideas to the table first.

Get into the details of your plan – the who, what, when, where, why and how – so your team can get behind you and chip in. Make sure the whole group understands what the changes will look like in the big picture and what's being asked of them to get the company there.

I always say that your people are the most important thing to the success of your company, so they need a chance to play devil's advocate or build on your ideas, whichever it may be. It's good to have some dissent, but it needs to happen there in the room so it can be discussed openly. Have everyone agree that once all voices are heard and a decision is made, that should be the end of it – no grumbling or gossip later.

If that means bringing in a third party, like a coach or another trusted advisor, so be it. Sometimes a person on the outside can help facilitate this kind of discussion because they offer a broader, unbiased view.

When your team jumps on the bandwagon with you, you'll be working against a lot less push-back, and you may be surprised what they have to offer that you hadn't even thought of or didn't know you needed.

As they say, "Teamwork makes the dream work."

TODAY'S ACTION ITEM

{ VOICES IN MY HEAD: THE IMPORTANCE OF POSITIVE SELF TALK }

Each of us has a voice in our head. Self-talk is something we do throughout the day. Like the proverbial angel or devil on our shoulder, that voice can be either positive or negative.

Think about the number of times you criticize yourself each day. You'd be surprised how often it happens, and how destructive that kind of talk can be.

A negative internal monologue puts focus on unconstructive thoughts and will make them grow. The negative words we use in our self-talk affect our emotions and our interactions with colleagues, friends and family members.

We can overcome this destructive mindset by focusing on the words we choose in the inner dialogue we have with ourselves. When you feel yourself going toward the negative, positively reset your thought process and choose words that are affirmative, upbeat and supportive.

Master positive self-talk and make it a daily focus. That will keep you confident and motivated and put you and your team on a trajectory for success – instead of mired in the worry of what could go wrong.

TODAY'S ACTION ITEM

JANUARY 27

{ HOW I LEARN FROM HISTORY }

A year ago, I attended a leadership skills workshop in Washington D.C., where we did something more valuable and eye-opening than expected: We toured the Holocaust Museum.

The museum was heartbreaking and moving. And I was reminded that we must learn from history so that we do not repeat it. Here are some leadership skills I took away from my visit:

Evaluate yourself: Take your role as a people-builder seriously by being humble and working toward your continual improvement. Look in the mirror. Is there something you could do better? Do it.

Speak the truth: If you must mask your intentions or fluff up your delivery, you're most likely overcompensating or covering up deceit. Be genuine and upfront with your agenda and values. Give those following your lead the opportunity to know who they're following.

Walk the walk: Only delegate tasks you're willing to do yourself. Instructing someone else to do your dirty work does not relieve you of associated shame or responsibility.

Stand up: It is everyone's responsibility to keep leaders in check. Leadership is a privilege, not a right or a title. If you see an abuse of power, do something. Despite your fears of potential failure, step up and become a leader yourself.

The anniversary of Auschwitz's liberation is January 27. The UN has designated it International Holocaust Remembrance Day. We must all remember the terrors that occurred not so long ago so that they never happen again.

"How wonderful it is that nobody need wait a single moment before starting to improve the world." – Anne Frank

TODAY'S ACTION ITEM

JANUARY 28
{ YOU'RE NOT TACOS AND ICE CREAM }

Is that title confusing? Let me explain: What do tacos and ice cream have in common? They are both delicious and tend to make people happy.

But you are not tacos and ice cream (as much as we want to believe the "you are what you eat" principle), which means you cannot make everyone happy.

I repeat: Unless you are filled with cheese and salsa or topped with hot fudge and sprinkles, you cannot make everyone happy.

So don't hold yourself to that standard. Obviously, as a leader, it's your job to make sure your team is satisfied, healthy and supported. But when it comes down to making the hard choices, there will always be someone who disagrees with your decision – or at least isn't 100 percent happy about it.

The goal is to make those calls to the best of your ability based on what's best for the team as a whole.

The principle applies in other areas of your life, too, such as your schedule. You only have 24 hours in your day, so don't say "yes" if you genuinely don't have time to take on that new thing. Sometimes you have to turn down a task or an opportunity if you don't have the capacity for it. The asker may be disappointed, but they'll understand if you're honest with them.

When you put your all into pleasing others, you most likely will trade in your happiness, and it becomes a vicious cycle.

While your happiness and others' happiness are equally important, leave the "always happy" heavy lifting for tacos and ice cream. They can handle it.

TODAY'S ACTION ITEM

JANUARY 29

{ PUSHING FOR MORE }

Everyone wants to be on top. But what happens once you get there? The first instinct for many entrepreneurs is to put on the bathrobe of success and just get comfortable. It may feel good for a little while, cozy even, until comfort leads to complacency, and complacency leads to crashing and burning.

The only way to stay on top is to keep improving, but the problem you face as a successful entrepreneur is that it takes a lot of motivation to improve from great to even better.

Here are three simple tips to motivate you to continue to push for more:

1. Go to a bigger pond.
There is always more to conquer. If you are on top of the citywide competition, that means it's time to move your company to a bigger arena. Take on the county, the state and the nation – create a growth plan that takes you out of your comfort zone and keeps raising that glass ceiling.

2. Remember your competition.
The top spot is always yours to lose. The moment you decide you have enough of a lead to slow down, competitors will start moving faster to catch up. Remember: Your competition is not comfortable; they have a reason to grow.

3. Continue learning.
Keep your business strategy fresh by continuing to discover new techniques and tricks. Reinvent the standard so that by the time your competition masters your old winning move, you have a new one.

TODAY'S ACTION ITEM

JANUARY 30

{ DO YOU HAVE AN ACCOUNTABILITY PARTNER? }

We all agree that taking care of ourselves is essential, but unfortunately, we don't always practice what we preach. Over the past several years, I noticed these patterns in myself and began taking the necessary steps for improvement.

Now I set a goal, make a plan and measure and monitor my progress. Sometimes it works, sometimes it doesn't. That is, until I added what I believe is the missing link to achieving my goals: an accountability partner.

I'm not talking about picking up the phone and asking your best friend to be your accountability partner. Find the right person who will support AND push you to be your best. If it's your best friend, then great! All the better. Just make sure it's someone you trust and will hold you to your word.

Having an accountability partner isn't easy because they are aware of your goals, tasks, priorities and deadlines that need to be met to accomplish your goals. And they expect you to achieve them. So, print your "to do" list and tape it at eye-level in your closet. And include the name of your accountability partner next to it. That way you will be reminded every day about the important steps to take.

Make sure you meet with your accountability partner regularly to talk through challenges, celebrate successes and discuss upcoming plans. Every quarter, review your list with that person and share updates, struggles and victories.

You are much more likely to succeed when you have someone watching your progress and helping you cross the finish line.

TODAY'S ACTION ITEM

JANUARY 31

{ FOCUS ON STRENGTHS, NOT WEAKNESSES }

Motivational speaker, business consultant and friend of mine, David Rendall, tours around the country sharing his methodology called "The Freak Factor."

In his talk, which is also detailed in his best-selling book of the same title, he takes the idea of weakness and essentially turns it on its head. He says, "What makes us weird makes us wonderful. What makes us weak makes us strong."

He posits that overcoming a weakness is about changing the framework for how you look at it. You should embrace your flaws as part of who you are and not let them detract from your perception of yourself and others' perceptions of you.

Rendall says we're all plagued by a negativity bias – a tendency to see what's wrong in a situation instead of what's right – and then we think negatively about the whole situation because of that one drawback.

His example is: If he did his whole presentation with a big, ugly stain on his shirt, the entire audience wouldn't be able to take their eyes off of it, and they would probably think less of him.

However, he says that rather than pointing out what's wrong with a situation, we need to learn to focus on what's right about it. Jokingly, he exclaims, "You should be thinking, 'Wow! His shirt is 98 percent clean. He's doing a pretty good job today.'"

When we focus on everyone's negatives, that's all we can focus on, and it becomes hard to see what their strengths are. As a business leader, that could prove detrimental. If you only think of the weaknesses of your team, then you may be less inclined to trust in their strengths – when, in fact, you need to think precisely the opposite.

TODAY'S ACTION ITEM

FEBRUARY

{ VITAMIN B-2 }

*You need vitamins to help change the chemicals
in food into energy. Spend the next month "breaking down"
the issues in your organization and converting them
into a new energy to keep innovating.*

FEBRUARY 1

{ STAY ON TASK, BUT DON'T MULTITASK }

I have three words to share about multitasking: It's a myth. It's impossible to do. Even when you think you're multitasking, all you're doing is switching between tasks quickly. This kind of split focus will make your work suffer and you could make costly mistakes.

It's not just me that thinks this. Psychologists have found that people who attempt to perform more than one task at a time become overwhelmed and less productive over time. If you believe you are the exception, think again.

When I work with new clients or hold seminars, I conduct a simple multitasking exercise – and every person fails. So the next time someone tells you during a job interview they're great at multitasking, do not hire that person.

To avoid multitasking overload, don't start a texting conversation right before you go into a big meeting or have the football game on while you're reading important papers. Turn your email off (or at least don't look at it) while you're writing an important article, and most importantly, don't check your phone while someone is talking to you. It's not only rude, but you're guaranteed to miss something important, and the person talking to you is bound to feel unimportant.

Make time and plan to do individual tasks on their own. You'll find you retain more, and you'll work more efficiently.

TODAY'S ACTION ITEM

FEBRUARY 2

{ HOW DO YOU BUILD A HEALTHY TEAM? }

Building healthy teams requires business leaders to take an interest in the professional, emotional and physical health of their team members. Those three components must be ingrained in the company culture if you want to grow your business, retain talent and keep your organization on the cutting edge.

The best way to know how your team members are doing is by having open communication, which also keeps your team engaged. When your team members are interested and committed, they look forward to coming to work; they are on board and enthusiastic about your company's core purpose and values; and they are actively working to achieve the goals of your organization.

As a business leader, it's your responsibility to create a work environment that embraces open communication. To do that you have to really get to know your team members. Have personal, authentic conversations with each of them regularly – or as often as you can. Sure, that can be difficult when you've got a busy schedule, and it can be stressful, as you may get emotional or feel vulnerable, but that's okay. Showing vulnerability allows your team to see more of the real you and will pay dividends when it comes to strengthening your relationship with them.

Take time to understand why you respect your team members. Learn what they want to hear from you and how they want to hear it.

High-performing, healthy teams are built around mutual trust and respect, and that can only be accomplished by knowing the members of your organization on a personal level.

TODAY'S ACTION ITEM

FEBRUARY 3

{ THE IMPORTANCE OF LAGGING INDICATORS }

Most businesses fall into one of two categories: They either measure everything and lose focus on what matters the most, or they measure nothing – and I mean nothing. I once walked into a $10 million business that had no financial statements; the company literally paid invoices based on the bank balance.

Businesses that measure everything usually have a good handle on **where they have been.** They are using lagging indicators to tell how they performed over a given time period and identify trends. Sales, cash flow and labor and materials costs are examples of lagging indicators.

It's true, producing these numbers is part of running a good business – business school will tell you so – but they're not the whole story. Using *only* this approach is the equivalent to only looking in the rearview mirror while driving your car!

As a business leader, you want to understand the reasons behind trends so you can course correct, but you don't want to spend too much time looking at past performance.

Narrow it down to two lagging indicators. Ask yourself, "If I was stuck on an island and could only get two numbers, which two would allow me to understand the health of the business?" Once you've chosen these, find a way to gather the right data so that you can update them as often and accurately as possible. It will help you transform from being a backward-looking company to one that looks to the future.

TODAY'S ACTION ITEM

FEBRUARY 4

{ 3 STEPS TO BUILDING A BUSINESS YOU ACTUALLY LIKE }

Many have dreams of entrepreneurial grandeur that go something like this: You stomp into your mundane 9-to-5 job and hand your out-of-touch boss an effective-immediately resignation letter. You puff up your chest, hold your shoulders back and declare you're sick of working grueling hours and taking on endless work just to benefit his pocket. You express that your boss can shove it because you're going into business for yourself.

But once you actually take the plunge, you realize building a business you like might be harder than you think. Follow these three steps to create a business you actually will like to run:

Step 1: Develop a strong company culture. You achieve this by defining your company's core purpose, believing in that purpose and finding others who believe in it as well. If some team members don't believe in it, find others who do. Having a strong company culture begins with having the right people in the company.

Step 2: Develop systems and processes that allow your business to run without you. Many times a company has one or two knowledge-keepers who everyone turns to for answers. That knowledge-keeper is most often the business owner.

Step 3: Create a strategic plan and use it. Most strategic plans are great doorstops and nothing else because they are never put to use.

We make business more complicated than it needs to be. We expect things to fall into place without putting them there. So remember, the keys to a successful business model are people, planning and process, which leads to profit. Your company cannot be great unless it's great without you.

TODAY'S ACTION ITEM

FEBRUARY 5

{ BECOME MORE EFFECTIVE IN 10 MINUTES }

We live and work in a time of rapid change. One of the ways I teach my team to stay ahead of the curve is by continually evaluating our efficiencies. It's all about finding the systems in which you can perform at top quality in the shortest amount of time.

Creating efficiencies, for some, feels as though they're stripping the amount, and consequently, the value of their work. You have to shut this attitude down. The value created by a team member who improves a business process is far greater than the benefit of one who shows up, puts their widgets in the widget box and goes home.

Rally your team by making it a contest. Collect ideas and reward the most effective ones. When it comes to brainstorming, forget cost or time constraints. Feel free to think entirely out of the scope of reality. In doing so, you might actually land on something doable that brings exponential improvements.

Make no mistake, creating a culture that supports constant and proactive reflection is a big undertaking. You have to inspire your team to take on this high-level thinking and support members that are willing to ask hard questions and create sound solutions.

To truly open up the company for improvement, you have to be willing to be questioned as a leader. This process isn't easy, and it's not fun. But, if you want to have an innovative culture, you have to know when to check your ego at the door. I guarantee it's the lesser of two evils compared to irrelevance.

TODAY'S ACTION ITEM

FEBRUARY 6

{ THE EFFECTS OF DEPARTMENTAL SILOS }

Guest contribution from Petra Coach Jennifer Faught

Team. Departments. Divisions. Silos.

Wait, what?

If you're not familiar with the business jargon, "silo" is a mindset present in some companies in which certain departments or sectors do not wish to share information with others in the same company.

This silo mentality can lead to lack of alignment, frustration among employees, duplicate work and poor customer experiences – to name just a few of the consequences.

When teams are separated from one another, a weird competitive atmosphere develops, promoting power struggles, job protection and politics. Communication becomes slow and disjointed throughout the organization.

Everyone may be marching in the same general direction, but the plans are different for each team, and no one is discussing what the outcomes should be.

As a result, the company functions awkwardly instead of nimbly, which ultimately prevents growth. The key is to connect your silos and ensure the departments are communicating effectively with each other. This isn't done with bean bag chairs or a ping pong table, but with a clear vision and shared culture. Employees are fulfilled when they know what outcomes they are working toward and when the teams have transparency on everyone's progress toward those goals.

TODAY'S ACTION ITEM

FEBRUARY 7

{ PREVENTING DEPARTMENTAL SILOS }

Guest contribution from Petra Coach Jennifer Faught

As discussed yesterday, "silo" is a common business term referring to a department that sections itself off from others in the company. It's okay to have clear-cut departments, but you need to make sure they are healthy and thriving with regular cross-departmental communication.

Get clarity from the top.
Company executives and leaders must get on the same page and meet regularly about strategic goals and company priorities. And they must communicate these plans often throughout the entire organization.

Different departments may have their own goals, but, when working to accomplish whole-company initiatives, all the units need to come together as one. It takes everyone cooperating – and offering their unique expertise and insight – to achieve big organizational goals.

Create shared culture, purpose and values.
Maintaining healthy divisions also requires developing a shared culture, purpose and values, which creates an environment of trust and fosters increased sharing of information and knowledge. Don't let the idea of trust falls and awkward team-building exercises hinder you from taking the leap. Team huddles, notes of kudos and quarterly outings are stress-free ways to build a culture of collaboration.

Additionally, streamline your project workflow. Create teams that are agile and collaborative. Your business will benefit from the diversity of thought, and your employees will thank you for distributing the workload more thoroughly.

Many CEOs and executive teams are afraid to break down silos because they worry they will lose control. However, when you connect your departments through a shared vision and culture, communication, efficient workflows and goals, you actually gain control through transparency, alignment and accountability.

TODAY'S ACTION ITEM

FEBRUARY 8

{ GIVE YOURSELF PERMISSION TO SAY "NO" }

Leaders are always being pulled in seven different directions. I understand entirely because my coaching schedule has me busy almost every day of the year.

That means I simply cannot say "yes" to every single opportunity that comes my way. No one should feel obligated to, even if your schedule isn't as tight as mine.

If you're the kind of person who gives time and energy to others at the cost of your own needs, now's your opportunity to turn that around.

Saying "yes" to everything doesn't help if you can't say yes to yourself. With constantly busy and stressful days, you need to be able to take some time to take care of yourself and accomplish your own goals.

Otherwise, you'll feel like you're putting in everything you have, but accomplishing nothing – the surefire sign of burnout.

Nobody will fault you for being honest and saying you just can't take something else on. Allowing yourself to say "no" to others doesn't mean you're neglecting them. Odds are for every "no" you dole out, you've said "yes" dozens of times.

It's essential to set limits for yourself with others to free up time for self-care and reduce the likelihood that you'll run out of time to attend to your own priorities. In other words, don't burn yourself out on others' accounts. Just say "no" sometimes.

TODAY'S ACTION ITEM

FEBRUARY 9

{ EMPOWER YOUR PEOPLE }

Accountability. What do you envision when you hear the word? Standing before a stern judge, being held accountable for crimes and misdemeanors? Being called to the carpet in the boardroom for less-than-stellar earnings? If so, you're not alone. "Accountability" has gotten a bad rap in recent years, but it shouldn't be that way.

The best business leaders foster a company culture where accountability is celebrated and plays a crucial role in moving the team – and the enterprise as a whole – forward in positive ways. After all, if you're going to set individual and company goals and expect full participation in achieving them, then everyone from the top down must be accountable for completing specific tasks.

The essence of accountability isn't about punishing mistakes. It's about allowing everyone to set goals and find success in a transparent way and with the support (and motivation) of your entire team. When done right, it fosters a culture where individuals help each other perform better, while building trust and loyalty.

Since accountability and expectations go hand-in-hand, be careful the system doesn't turn into micromanagement. It monopolizes precious time that you should spend developing your business and stirs up resentment from your team. When you're in the weeds with day-to-day operations, you become reactive rather than proactive, and you will never move your business forward.

Trust your team. You hired great people, so step back and let them do their jobs. Empower them to step up and take the initiative. Then, your team members will hold themselves accountable for their results, and who knows, they may even do the job better than you.

TODAY'S ACTION ITEM

FEBRUARY 10

{ THE ART OF PRAISE AND CRITICISM }

Many of us have challenges with praise and criticism – both giving it and receiving it.

For example, think about the last time someone paid you a compliment. If you're like the average person, you probably shrugged it off with a dismissive comment.

"You like my shirt? Oh, this old thing?"

A response like this makes the person who complimented you feel less than great, and they are less likely to compliment you again. The correct answer to a compliment is always a simple, "Thank you."

But don't compliment someone's shirt just for the sake of praising them. Appreciation should not be contrived, and mediocrity should never be rewarded. Doing so will devalue the recognition and gratitude you want to convey.

On the flip side, don't berate anyone who needs to hear constructive criticism. Instead, have a conversation where you begin with a positive, and then express the issue in a positive way that shows you want to help. A straightforward way to do that is not to use the word "but."

For instance, "Sam, you're always great about communicating with your client, but…" You see, when you use that word, you diminish the initial compliment. To fix this, replace "but" with "and." This allows Sam to keep the positive feeling and not feel crushed with what follows.

Giving and receiving appropriate appreciation or criticism is a skill that needs to be learned, like riding a bike, so make sure you're practicing it every day.

TODAY'S ACTION ITEM

FEBRUARY 11

{ WHY YOU SHOULD MEDITATE }

As a business owner, husband, father, co-worker and friend who is on the road almost every week of the year, I know what it's like to look burnout straight in the face. I came to a point where I desperately needed a reset – one that a weekend, vacation or even sabbatical couldn't provide.

Meditation isn't just for mountain retreats and yoga studios. In fact, business leaders have used meditation for years because it can be done at any time, anywhere and the only equipment needed is your brain. Still on the fence?

The time I've dedicated to meditation has made a profound impact on my life. Before founding my current business, I spent an entire year clearing my mind. With a combination of paddleboarding, which gave my brain a rest while I focused on the physical activity, and using tools like Breatheaware and the app Headspace, I got in the habit of a daily meditation routine.

I encourage you to find resources and activities that will work best for you, so you too can regularly take the time to meditate. You'll soon find, like I did, that on the days you do, you're not as grouchy, more productive and more creative than on the days you don't. Trust me, your family, your team and your company will thank you.

TODAY'S ACTION ITEM

FEBRUARY 12

{ HUDDLE UP, IT'S MEETING TIME! }

From 8:33 to about 8:48 every weekday morning you can find my team and me jammin' out to AC/DC while we talk business. It's our team "huddle" or daily meeting, and it's a vital ritual that's structured to create company accountability and alignment.

"Come on, Andy, I don't have time for another meeting. Is it really that important?"

That's the response most busy business owners give me as they cross their arms and raise an eyebrow when I tell them that routine daily huddles are essential to their company's growth.

Yes, it's that important. Make the time. Think about it, would you put money on a football team that didn't meet for a quick huddle? No, not unless you wanted to lose your money.

So emulate your favorite sports team during your daily huddle. Gather your team, stand in a circle, talk fast, keep the energy high, play some "Eye of the Tiger" and close with a cheer. Not only will this create team alignment, but it will also add some fun – something we could all use a little more of in the workplace.

The most efficient and effective huddle includes the entire team. Don't create separate huddles for each department if you can avoid it. Separate huddles deter alignment and communication, and they reinforce the default barriers that already exist between departments, which is precisely the opposite of what you want to achieve.

Huddles should also follow a set dialogue, or defined discussion topics, which will speed up the process. Team members will know what they're expected to contribute to the conversation and will be less likely to go off on tangents or digressions.

TODAY'S ACTION ITEM

FEBRUARY 13

{ KEEPING AND GROWING YOUR TEAM }

People join companies, but they leave managers. As a business leader, it's your job to keep your people happy at work.

Here are my top three tips to ensure your team members are satisfied:

1. Play to their strengths.
People generally enjoy doing what they are good at. However, strength is more than something you're skilled in – it's something that gives you energy. A weakness, then, is something that drains you. Take the time and effort to make sure your A-players are doing more of what energizes them and less of what drains them to keep them thriving.

2. Provide a line of sight.
Once team members understand their work responsibilities and how they contribute to the greater mission of the company, make sure you are setting consistent expectations about desired results. Focus on defining the "what" instead of the "how." Give them the freedom to chart their path toward success. Set up individual priorities and metrics in a regularly scheduled one-on-one meeting (what we call a "Rocks" meeting) with a supervisor, when employees can receive clear guidelines about the direction they should go.

3. Put out potential fires.
One of the most frustrating and demotivating experiences is working with C-players. They slow down productivity by making mistakes, asking stupid questions and producing average work (that often will have to be fixed). Deal with a consistently troublesome employee or client before they have the chance to fatally impact your team.

TODAY'S ACTION ITEM

FEBRUARY 14

{ BREAK THESE 3 BAD HABITS - NOW! }

Every business leader has bad habits. Whether we admit it or not, we all do things that hinder the growth of our company and the development of our team members.

In my work as a coach, here are the three bad habits I consistently see hold leaders back:

They feel like they have to have a hand in every decision.
When leaders believe they have to be involved in all decisions, they stifle the growth of their teams. You surrounded yourself with talented people, so ask for help, listen to what they have to say and give more responsibility. Your company will grow faster if you work together.

They rush to the urgent at the expense of the important.
There are essential things that must be done to grow any business. There's also noise that slows us down and gets in our way. Usually, that "noise" is not important, though it can seem urgent. If you find yourself stuck doing urgent or non-urgent work that's not important, then it's time to dig into (or revisit) the Urgent Important Matrix by Stephen Covey (author of the best-seller *The 7 Habits of Highly Effective People*). It's a powerful tool to help you manage your time more effectively.

They don't have clearly defined core values and a core purpose.
If you don't know why you are doing what you do – and it is never only to make money – then you'll never get it done. Make sure that what you are doing on a daily basis dovetails with what's most important to you and your company.

TODAY'S ACTION ITEM

FEBRUARY 15

{ 'TIS THE SEASON FOR A BUSINESS SLUMP }

Guest contribution from Petra Coach JT Terrell

While all business is driven by demand, specific industries – such as the hospitality industry – can be harshly impacted by seasonality and lean economic times. It affects clients, employees and, ultimately, the financial health of the company.

While it's difficult to foresee the ebb and flow of the overall economy, here are three tips for surviving lean times, preventing layoffs and keeping your clients happy.

1. Obtain financial planning advice.
To help team members cope with working fewer hours and the corresponding smaller paychecks during lean times, provide basic financial planning sessions to help them manage their money.

2. Offer rebates or discounts during lean seasons.
Offer modest rebates for professional clients who want to pay invoices early. It will provide a much-needed cash infusion to meet payroll and other obligations during lean months. Clients will love it because they get a discount. Win-win.

3. Renegotiate financial commitments.
If you have any bank debt, negotiate the terms to defer payments during slow sales periods. It will be a complex undertaking, but it will preserve cash when you need it most.

TODAY'S ACTION ITEM

FEBRUARY 16

{ THERE ARE TWO SIDES TO EVERY COIN }

In the book *The Freak Factor* by motivational speaker, business consultant and friend of mine David Rendall, there is an exercise to identify your top strengths and then your top weaknesses.

Once you have your top five of each, he asks you to put the lists side-by-side to compare. Many find that a lot of their positive characteristics line up with their negative traits. The weakness is just rephrasing the strength with words that have a more negative connotation.

As Rendall explains, "Each strength has its equivalent weakness. They are two sides of the same coin." What matters is your perception and how you act on it.

For example, someone who is easy-going could also be perceived as irresponsible. Someone adventurous might seem dangerous to others. Spontaneity can be viewed as impulsiveness.

Rendall adds, "Just like you can't have medicine without side effects, you can't have people without side effects."

Every single person you hire has specific character traits that you may seek out and admire. But those characteristics have their opposites, and you need to be able to accept them too.

Employees you see as stubborn or obstinate could see themselves as dedicated and persistent. Recognize that they may have the best of intentions, and treat them with the benefit of the doubt. In other words, rather than chastise for that weakness, praise the subsequent strength.

You will find that when you validate your teams' strengths, they'll feel respected and valued for what they bring to the table. And that's how you cultivate a hard-working, motivated team.

TODAY'S ACTION ITEM

FEBRUARY 17

{ LEADERS: KNOW WHEN TO HIT "SEND" ON YOUR EMAILS }

We all rely on email. It speeds communication and improves productivity by cutting down on the number of phone calls and face-to-face meetings. But there's a flip side to email that, if not used properly, can cause more work, stress and miscommunication.

Leaders should remember that most emails involve issues that are best left to others to handle, such as an update about a deadline set by another team member. It's also important to be mindful about sending or replying to emails outside of work hours – especially late at night, before the crack of dawn or on weekends on holidays. If you do, team members may feel the need to respond, causing bitterness and frustration. Additionally, leaders must pay close attention to the tone of their emails so that the receiver correctly interprets the message.

If you've done your job as a leader, members of your team can handle the majority of emails. Delegate responsibility and don't get caught up in the details. Set clear expectations of who needs to respond. Create a culture of disciplined use of email so it doesn't suck valuable time and energy from running the business.

TODAY'S ACTION ITEM

FEBRUARY 18

{ WHY YOU NEED AN EXECUTABLE BUSINESS PLAN }

Typically, when I ask leaders if they have a business plan for their company or division, they either point to a stack of papers that's doubling as a doorstop, or shrug their shoulders and say, "Ah, we never got around to doing that," or, "We just got started."

Unfortunately, most leaders view business plans as a secondary concern, or worse, entirely unnecessary. Here's what I have found to be true: In every case, both in business and in life, having a plan will generate better results than simply winging it.

At a minimum, a business plan sets in motion the thought process required to complete your project in less time. I'm not saying to never be spontaneous, but when you leave things to chance, you leave room for error.

There are 60 workdays in a quarter. If your team members work eight hours per day, 40 hours per week, that's 480 hours per person per quarter. That's a lot of time to waste on chance.

Write out a purposeful business plan that considers who you are as a business – meaning who you serve, what you do and why you do it – and chart a course for your team to align and work toward common goals.

TODAY'S ACTION ITEM

FEBRUARY 19

{ GROW YOUR WORKERS, GROW YOUR BUSINESS }

YOU cannot grow your business. You must grow your people and your people will grow your business. According to a study from *Harvard Business Review*, people have four core needs to feel energized, appreciated, focused and purposeful:

1. Renewal (physical).
Don't burn out your employees. Encourage them to rest and renew their energy during the workday. They will return to their desks more productive. Start a time-out program where everyone stops and goes outside for five minutes.

2. Value (emotional).
Show your team that their hard work and commitment to the company is valued. "Feeling valued creates a deeper level of trust and security at work, which frees us to spend less energy seeking and defending our value and more time creating it," the study claims.

3. Focus (mental).
From web surfing to open floor plans, distractions can take away from employees' productivity in the workplace. Make sure that your office environment allows employees to concentrate so that quality tasks are completed efficiently. Create quiet time where everyone stops interaction for 30 minutes daily and focuses on important tasks.

4. Purpose (spiritual).
Employees thrive when they feel that what they do matters. Share why the business exists and why employees should care. Make sure they can see how their work contributes to that higher purpose.

The study shows that if your company meets even one of these needs, it will have a "dramatic impact" on every performance variable studied, including engagement, likelihood of retention, stress reduction, focus, life satisfaction and positive energy at work.

TODAY'S ACTION ITEM

FEBRUARY 20

{ DO YOU NEED A BUSINESS COACH? }

Business coaches are a lot like personal trainers. People turn to them when they need help in reaching their goals.

Compare this logic to your health and fitness goals. Yeah, you're cutting the fats and carbohydrates from your diet and you're hitting the gym three times a week, but you can't seem to lose those last five pounds. Most often, it's the final small step toward success that is the hardest. A coach can help you get there.

A personal trainer will work with you to make sure you maximize your gym time and perfect your diet. Success – you reach your ultimate fitness goal.

Just like gym visits, business-coaching sessions aren't always easy, and they can be a little painful. And just like a personal trainer, a business coach can only help your business if you're ready for change and willing to admit fault.

The coach's job is to show you the mirror. People often know when something isn't right, but they choose to look past it. Business coaches can help you identify your problem and push you to succeed because they bring a professional, outside perspective, honest feedback and tested strategy to move you to the next level of success.

TODAY'S ACTION ITEM

FEBRUARY 21

{ ONBOARDING SHOULDN'T FEEL LIKE WATERBOARDING }

This play on words from Verne Harnish's *Scaling Up* describes how unfortunate the onboarding and training programs can be at many companies.

When employees just starting, it's a valuable time to connect and assimilate them into your culture and processes. However, many companies don't take advantage of it.

Instead, many will scramble at the last minute and stick the person on someone in the office who's unprepared, or frankly unenthused, about showing the newbie the ropes. But be careful about that. You want to impress your new hire and show you are happy he or she has chosen your company. It usually takes three months or less for a new hire to either settle in to the company or decide it's not the right fit.

Make the most of this time. When the new hire comes in for that first day on the job, he or she should be welcomed with positive attitudes and handed an itinerary for training. Some companies have a formal training process, and others onboard through shadowing and mentoring. Either way, have a plan and people designated to carry it out.

Include time on the itinerary for lunch with the whole team so that everyone can meet on an informal level. Some companies will also sign a welcome card or deck out the new hire's desk with fun decorations.

Just do *something* to communicate that you're excited for the person to be there. Make his or her start at the company feel like the beginning of something special because it is. You've just gained another A-player, don't lose them!

TODAY'S ACTION ITEM

FEBRUARY 22

{ ARE YOU READY TO BE A BOSS? }

The idea of being an entrepreneur or leading a company – being the boss – is glamorous. That is until it's time to put in the hard work and long hours.

Starting a business, growing a company division, hiring and firing, working late hours – it's all incredibly stressful.

But it doesn't have to be that way. You need to start taking well-thought-out steps and implement time-tested methodologies until they become habits – for you and your team members. I learned that the hard way when I was building my wireless company, NationLink. I thought I knew it all and didn't need help. Bad idea!

Many would argue that the difficult challenge for most business leaders is to create a solid plan that identifies what steps to take. But I think it's something else.

In my experience – both personally and in my work with other companies – the most difficult challenge is to set aside the need for control. Allow the strengths of your team members – and your faith in their decision-making capabilities – to keep the ship sailing powerfully and in the right direction.

If you can do that, you're ready to be a boss.

TODAY'S ACTION ITEM

FEBRUARY 23

{ YOU MUST WANT CHANGE FOR IT TO OCCUR }

The first day I began implementing the Rockefeller Habits at NationLink (the wireless company I had founded and was running) taught me a lot, especially one crucial fact: You must want change for change to occur.

For business leaders, one of two conditions must exist to exact real change: You either need to be so frustrated with your business that you don't want to be around it anymore, or you're fearful of missing an opportunity.

My inspiration happened in 2005 when I attended the Birthing of Giants program at the Massachusetts Institute of Technology. It was then I realized I was holding my company back because I was a dictator. That's when I knew I had to change – I had to get out of my own way and let my team members help me build the business.

At Petra Coach, we ask our clients, "Are you frustrated or scared about where your business is going?" And we let them know that if they aren't scared and frustrated, then they are not sufficiently inspired.

Change won't happen unless you want it to.

TODAY'S ACTION ITEM

FEBRUARY 24

{ HANDLING CRITICISM LIKE A CHAMP }

No one is immune to criticism, though many people avoid it like the plague. But I say: Embrace it. Criticism can be a powerful tool for change and growth if you let it.

Here are my three tips for taking on criticism:

1. Listen.
Truly listen to what the person is saying. Don't spend that time telling yourself all of the reasons they're wrong or brainstorming how you'll improve next time. The ability to listen is a rare skill today, and this is an excellent opportunity to practice. After all, there is always at least a little bit of truth in the critique. Listen to where and how you went wrong so that you can analyze and execute better next time.

2. Pause.
We've all said something we regret in the heat of the moment at one time or another. Receiving criticism leaves us vulnerable and defensive, which can spur extreme emotions. After receiving criticism, always take a deep breath and count to ten to allow yourself to decompress and think rationally. Once you have a chance to let your emotions subside and consider the situation logically, you will be better able to formulate a respectful response.

3. Learn.
While no one likes to be told they've messed up, no one has ever been successful without first failing. Even greats such as Albert Einstein, Walt Disney or J.K. Rowling failed before they achieved success. What if you actually thanked the person who took the time and effort to point out your mistakes, rather than dismissed them? Receiving feedback is an invaluable gift. Treat it that way.

TODAY'S ACTION ITEM

FEBRUARY 25

{ THE SMELL OF YOUR CULTURE }

Guest contribution from Petra Coach David Pierce

We've all experienced it: walking into a place of business and, within a few seconds, having that "feeling."

It's the feeling of discomfort that resonates from the employees – the scowling, unfriendly, "why are you here?" feeling. You can see it in their eyes, in their body language, and hear it in their tone of voice. The place actually feels like there's a storm cloud in the room.

And then there are the times you walk into a business and feel so welcomed that you have to look twice to see if it's mom and dad behind the counter. Every employee has a smile and is eager to help in any way possible, offering suggestions and pleasantries along the way. The surroundings are immaculate and you could swear the sun is shining inside.

These impressions are what I refer to as the "smell of the culture." The first one "smells" like a pigsty and the other a rose garden, metaphorically speaking.

But a fragrant culture must be cultivated or it will likely revert to something that stinks. And a stinky culture makes for a bad experience for everyone – employees and customers alike.

As a leader, make sure you are constantly aware of how your culture is smelling, and if starts to smell rotten, that's your moment to step in with gloves and Lysol and make some changes.

You want your office smelling daisy-fresh, right?

TODAY'S ACTION ITEM

FEBRUARY 26

{ AVOID THE COMFORT ZONE }

Many business owners fall into the comfort zone – a place where you feel like you can finally sit back and relax. But just because business is booming now, it doesn't mean it will continue to do so in the future. So don't get comfortable. When you think you are the best, you're not, and competitors are always next in line.

I don't mean to scare you but to keep you focused on success at all times. Here are ways to keep moving forward:

1. Request feedback.
As the top dog, you tend to receive far more compliments than criticisms. That's great, and you deserve it, but it's often more valuable to learn about your shortcomings. To improve, request honest feedback from your employees, mentors and customers. Address it directly and have something to show for it.

2. Stick with your system.
Have you heard stories about people who have won the lottery? An overwhelming number of them lose their newfound fortune almost as soon as they gain it. Why? They changed their systems. Often this means spending money like they never have before, doing things they've never done and working less. Instead, stick to your budget. Make extra sales calls. Hold quarterly planning sessions with your team. While enjoying the fruits of your labor isn't a bad thing (see below), do things that will ensure long-term growth instead of a short-term reward.

3. Celebrate.
The best part of success is the celebration. If you did something well last quarter, pinpoint it, celebrate and keep doing it. As you go from the best to even better, reward and recognize your team's achievements. It will provide additional motivation to your employees to keep pushing and doing their best work.

TODAY'S ACTION ITEM

FEBRUARY 27

{ START AT THE START }

At the beginning of this year, you were probably energized and ready to take on all the projects you had procrastinated about for the past year. A fresh start and a new calendar were just what you needed, right? Well, now it's the end of February, and you may have gotten stuck on the hardest part: starting.

Here's how to (finally) get past the start.

1. Determine your top priority for the day.
Before your morning becomes a rush of urgent emails, choose one important item (or at least less than three items) to accomplish right as you begin your day. Work on it until it's done – or else your top priority could quickly become your last priority. In each moment, stay focused on what's most important.

2. Limit interruptions.
Once you know your top priority and schedule for the morning, turn off your phone, disconnect your email and close your door. Don't let distractions derail your most essential tasks.

3. Just start.
Goals can be intimidating. It's easy to think about all the ways that you might not achieve them. Don't overthink it. Just get started. The first step is the hardest to complete. Don't get discouraged if your goal feels too big. We tend to think that if we get all the small tasks finished first, then we can attack our biggest priority. But this rarely happens.

Whether it's the beginning of the year, the end of the year or just a random month in between, there's no perfect time to get started achieving your loftiest goals. But with a little preparation, and a solid "start," you'll cross those big goals off your list in no time.

TODAY'S ACTION ITEM

FEBRUARY 28

{ ARE YOU FULFILLED? }

In the hustle and bustle of daily life, it's important to take a moment and think about what you're thankful for – and to perform an honest self-evaluation of what you value, in both your personal and professional life. This check-up should include assessing how fulfilled you are in your career.

So, how can you tell if you're actually fulfilled in your job? Start by asking yourself these two simple questions:

Do you have a desire to succeed?
To be fulfilled in your role, you must have a certain level of ambition – it's the drive that gets you up in the morning and the push for that last part of the workday when even the most dedicated team members start to slump. Are you dragging your feet, or do you feel the challenge to push yourself toward new successes?

If you are continually pushing yourself to do more and reach higher, it means your job is sufficiently challenging and motivating.

Are you in it only for the perks?
Let's get real for a second – a job is about money, but to be truly fulfilled, you need something more than a paycheck or free lunches. Identify the benefits of your position. They could be personal successes or friendly team members. If money has become your only motivator at work, it may be time to look for another position.

Take time to consider your career and where you're headed. If you've asked yourself these questions and are struggling to find fulfillment in your role, it's time to move on. Life is too short to spin your wheels in a dead-end job.

TODAY'S ACTION ITEM

MARCH

{ VITAMIN B-3 }

*This vitamin helps you reduce
the inefficiencies that are
clogging the arteries of your organization
and keep the workflow pumping.*

MARCH 1

{ STOP MICROMANAGING TO GROW YOUR BUSINESS }

"If you want it done right, you have to do it yourself."

That mantra may have gotten you where you are, but hard work without *smart* work will inevitably cause your business to plateau and maybe even crumble.

Here are three good reasons why you should stop micromanaging to grow your business and focus on working smarter:

1. Your business will thrive.
Micromanaging monopolizes time that could be spent working *on* your business rather than *in* it. When you're always *in* your business, your day-to-day operations are reactive instead of proactive. Stop micromanaging and get in the driver's seat.

2. Your employees will be happier.
Ninety percent of employees included in *Entrepreneur Magazine*'s Great Places to Work survey in the small-to-middle-market category say management trusts them without constantly looking over their shoulders. Happy employees produce better work and will stay with your company longer.

3. Your employees will improve.
When you fail to empower your team members to use their brains, you handicap them. They'll never learn to do anything themselves. You must delegate. Yes, it's tough in the beginning as your team goes through inevitable growing pains, but it's a short-term sacrifice for a long-term investment. In fact, your team members may even prove to do the job better than you did – and that's a good thing.

TODAY'S ACTION ITEM

MARCH 2

{ SIMPLE STEPS TO IMPROVE YOUR FOCUS }

Picture this: You're in your office reviewing your company's quarterly financials. You've got a smartphone buzzing on your desk. Your office phone is ringing, and team members keep popping their heads in to ask questions. Not to mention, your stomach is growling because it's almost lunchtime. You can't finish anything because you're doing too many things at once.

Sound familiar? I see leaders and teams struggle with this all the time. Why? They aren't getting focused and giving each priority their full attention.

In my planning sessions, I'll often play team-building games that require an element of focus. I make these exercises competitions with a prize at the end. It becomes a whole "production," and 10 times out of 10, people take it very seriously. Individuals will focus on the task at hand, excluding distractions, and come together with a shared vision. It's a great reminder that when you make focus an activity and raise the stakes of the game, human beings will automatically be more invested in the process and do what it takes to focus.

Distractions are everywhere. While some can't be controlled (like firetrucks blaring their sirens outside your window), some are self-imposed (like having your smartphone next to you at your desk at all times).

To improve focus, you must remove unnecessary distractions. Set your phone to silent, and put it in your desk drawer. Close your office door, and let your team know that you need an hour to complete an important task. Even if it means setting aside time daily to remove yourself from the outside world, find ways to eliminate distractions.

TODAY'S ACTION ITEM

MARCH 3

{ REMEMBER THE "WHY" TO SURVIVE THE ROLLER COASTER RIDE }

The process of starting your own business or leading your own team can feel a lot like a roller coaster ride.

Full of excitement, you step onto the ride. The feeling of anticipation grows as you buckle up and get ready to go. Your adrenaline is pumping and your stomach ties in knots. As you head slowly up the hill towards the first big drop, you find yourself a little unsure of why you decided to jump on the ride in the first place.

Like this carnival ride, the first step in starting your own business is uphill. You have a great plan, and you're passionate about the idea, yet wagering your life savings on it feels a little insane. Suddenly the people with their feet on the ground – the ones with a 9-to-5 job and benefits – seem like the levelheaded ones.

That's why it's always important to remember why you want to be an entrepreneur.

If you've decided to start the journey of entrepreneurship, it means that you have an idea you believe in firmly. However, when you're working late hours and pulling triple shifts as your company's only employee, you may have to remind yourself why you started.

And don't keep it to yourself. Post your new company's purpose where you can see it often. Keeping this mantra top-of-mind will motivate you during the low points when you're tired and your social media channels seem to be flooded with pictures of the fun that everyone else is having. Let's be honest, their lives aren't as exciting as they appear to be on Instagram anyway.

TODAY'S ACTION ITEM

MARCH 4

{ MAKE ROOM FOR FAILURE }

Being held accountable is a gift – an opportunity to shine as an individual while contributing to a larger effort. Unfortunately, as a business coach, I've seen too many leaders who make accountability a negative proposition. That can result in team members who are tentative, are afraid to fail and don't bring their best ideas and energy to their work.

Henry Ford, one of America's greatest entrepreneurs, said, "Failure is simply the opportunity to begin again, this time more intelligently." The bottom line: Failure is inevitable in business. If you're not failing, you're not taking enough risk in growing your company. You can only discover your true potential by entering the discomfort zone, taking a risk and accepting responsibility for the outcome – which includes the occasional failure.

Business leaders should encourage the same attitude and action from team members. Acknowledge mistakes, but celebrate risk and encourage your employees to keep giving their all. When you have a positive attitude toward failing, everyone on the team will feel the freedom to take more chances.

Learning from your failures also provides valuable feedback, so your team will be better prepared to handle future challenges. Position failures in a way that helps your team discover more about their true talents and where the company's focus should be.

Michael Jordan summed it up: "I've failed over and over and over again in my life. And that is why I succeed."

TODAY'S ACTION ITEM

MARCH 5

{ BEING A "HEART-SMART" LEADER }

Book smarts and street smarts aren't the only types of intelligence that make effective leaders. Emotional intelligence – how you connect with people and understand human emotions – is also essential.

Daniel Goleman, author of *Leadership: The Power of Emotional Intelligence,* explains that there are four capabilities of emotionally intelligent leaders, or as I like to call them, "heart-smart" leaders:

1. Self-awareness.
Recognize your strengths and your weaknesses, and depend on other team members to fill gaps. It's also important to understand your feelings and how you work, so you don't put yourself in stressful situations.

2. Self-management.
Keep your feelings in check. Don't blow up at team members if they make a mistake but calmly help them solve it. It's also about adapting to change. Be resilient. If you lose a client or face a crisis, your team members will look to you – their leader – to reassure them.

3. Empathy.
Great leaders listen to their team members. Take the time to understand what they are saying and consider their feelings when making decisions. With empathy, you will build positive connections and trust with your team members.

4. Relationship skills.
As the head of the company, you must continuously inspire and motivate your team members. Make sure that the full team is knowledgeable and aligned with the goals of the company, as this will help them understand how their work is positively impacting the business. On the other side of the spectrum, leaders must also use these relationship skills to manage conflict.

So don't just focus on decision-making, problem-solving and the company vision. Make emotional intelligence part of your tool belt too.

TODAY'S ACTION ITEM

MARCH 6

{ THE HARDEST PART OF THE WORKOUT IS GETTING TO THE GYM }

If you're like me, good health is something I take seriously, and it's most certainly one of my top priorities in life. I make it a goal to hit the gym on a regular basis. On the days I make it, my workouts make me feel great. I spend my time wisely. I exert the energy needed to maximize my time. I find myself accomplishing what I set out to achieve.

Of course, that's only when I actually make it to the gym. Some days life just gets in the way – and my priority of getting some healthy exercise moves to the back burner.

To make sure I get my workout in, I had to learn how to control my schedule and set aside personal time. Between work and home, we get pulled in a thousand different directions and end up neglecting the most important things. It's easy to promise to do something for your boss, colleague, friend or family member and push other priorities aside.

Best-selling author Stephen Covey said, "Time management is essentially a set of competencies. The idea is that if you can develop certain competencies, you'll be able to create quality-of-life results." I firmly believe being healthy falls into the "quality-of-life results."

From now on, promise that you will drive your schedule and that you will not let it drive you. Block time for exercise and staying healthy; and although it might sound drastic, protect it with your life. Don't let other people sway you to take time away from something you deem important.

TODAY'S ACTION ITEM

MARCH 7

{ THE ILLOGIC OF WORK-LIFE BALANCE }

Work-life balance. Many people complain about not having it, and most are searching for it. But here's the thing: You won't truly find work-life balance because the phrase is illogical and doesn't consider all options.

When you say "work-life balance," you're implying work and life are mutually exclusive. They're not. Work is a part of life.

The phrase also suggests work and life are opponents – work being the antagonistic nemesis. That's a bleak outlook. Your professional life and personal life should be allies, not enemies.

When people search for balance in this equation, they often measure it in equal time segments. Meaning, if I spent eight hours at work, I should enjoy eight hours of life, or play. This equation doesn't account for purposeful or quality time. We should stop measuring balance in time increments.

Soapbox aside, I understand what people mean when they suggest they're searching for work-life balance. They are looking for fulfillment, professionally and personally.

In life, we feel satiated when we feel purposeful. If your job sucks your energy and drowns your passion, change it.

We've all heard the saying, "If you love what you do, you'll never work a day in your life." Live that. Seek out meaningful opportunities that drive your enthusiasm.

TODAY'S ACTION ITEM

MARCH 8

{ ACTUALLY ACHIEVING YOUR GOALS }

It's that time of year – the time when the "new" wears off and people with good intentions start to flake on their New Year's resolutions. Business leaders are not immune – we can also get caught up in the hustle of day-to-day operations and lose sight of our end goals.

Resolutions encourage self-reflection, goal setting, priority planning and self-improvement – and I'm a big fan of all of them. Don't let them slip away because of a simple lack of focus or motivation. Here are two tricks I use to get my goals back on track:

1. Stay accountable.
It is crucial to surround yourself with honest and encouraging colleagues who know your goals and will push you to be your best. Count on your team to call you out, make you better, teach you and help you. If you make accountability a priority this year, I promise it will make all the difference.

2. Hit "refresh."
I love the quote from Maria Robinson, "Nobody can go back and start a new beginning, but anyone can start today and make a new ending." This statement is an important reminder that you can't just rewind the tape and start over. However, you can prepare yourself for the next task – and with the year already underway, there's no time to waste. Commit now to take the goal-achieving process seriously.

Set yourself up for success by sticking to realistic goals and surrounding yourself with motivated supporters. When you're focused, you can attain all the things you've set out for this year.

TODAY'S ACTION ITEM

MARCH 9

{ KNOW YOUR FINANCIAL KPIS }

Understanding financial metrics is essential for all leaders, and that means having timely data at your fingertips. A financial dashboard with the right key performance indicators (KPIs) will help you evaluate the financial health and performance of the business on a daily, weekly and monthly basis. It will also serve as an early-warning system to identify potential challenges. Here are a few important metrics to include in your dashboard:

- **Operating cash flow:** shows an adjusted net income that factors in non-cash expenses (depreciation and amortization) and other items, such as changes to inventory, accounts receivable and accounts payable.

- **Gross profit margin:** measures the percentage of revenue that exceeds the cost of goods sold; it gauges your company's ability to pay for other operating costs.

- **Days sales outstanding:** shows the average number of days it takes your clients to pay their invoices.

- **Accounts receivable aging:** lists invoices that need to be paid by your customers and how effective your accounts receivable team is in collecting that cash.

- **Inventory turnover:** calculates the average number of times in a year your business sells and replaces its inventory.

- **Budget variance:** compares actual results to budget totals; this evaluates how your company is performing financially compared to forecasted results.

Every business has different critical numbers. As the company leader, it's your job to make sure you're watching the right ones like a hawk so you can keep your company moving forward.

TODAY'S ACTION ITEM

MARCH 10

{ CROWDSOURCE IDEAS FROM FELLOW BUSINESS LEADERS }

Finding new solutions to business challenges is a never-ending and often exhaustive task for entrepreneurs and business leaders. One source that I've used to help me problem-solve has been a business advisory group (BAG) comprised of professionals in businesses operating in non-competitive markets.

I found that members in a BAG can relate to the daily challenges I face running my company, managing teams and growing the business. BAG members can provide you with invaluable insight into how they run their companies and how business solutions they have implemented may apply to your business.

David Kord Murray wrote a best-selling book, *Borrowing Brilliance,* that explores how you can capitalize on the wisdom, experience and expertise of others to grow your business. That's precisely why you want to form a BAG.

I'm not talking about a BAG comprised of peers or friends you know in your networking groups (personal or professional). This is about bringing in people who will truly serve as advisors to you and your company.

Many of our clients have had great success by learning from BAG peers who have "walked a mile in their shoes." They can work collaboratively to come up with actionable solutions to business challenges. A BAG can be a goldmine to identify and apply innovative ideas to your business and help you stay ahead of the competition.

TODAY'S ACTION ITEM

MARCH 11

{ 3 HACKS TO IMPROVE TEAM MEETINGS }

You've implemented your SLED (Suck Less Every Day) philosophy for all meetings *(see January 4)*, but you're still not 100 percent satisfied with the result. That's OK. I've been there, done that.

Here are three incredibly useful hacks to make your meetings faster, more productive and more enjoyable (yes, it's possible!) for your team.

1. Make every meeting a stand-up meeting.
Stand-up meetings are exactly what they sound like: All attendees are required to stand throughout the duration. This not only saves time and allows employees to get back to work sooner, but it also boosts attentiveness and engagement among attendees. Standing is not comfortable and creates "speed" to finish.

2. Ban electronics.
"Electronic pacifiers" are my biggest pet peeve, especially in meetings. Mobile devices are a distraction, threatening productivity. When you unplug, you are present and focused on the matters at hand. Pass around a bucket and have everyone put their phones in it or stack them up in a central location.

3. Bring a timer.
Want to make sure everyone sticks to a time limit during a meeting? Bring a timer and set it up where everyone can see it. Some experts have estimated that 50 percent of every meeting is wasted time. A timer is a powerful tool that can help your team see if precious meeting time is being wasted on non-productive discussions.

TODAY'S ACTION ITEM

{ YOUR BUSINESS IS NOT ABOUT YOU }

A conversation that has replayed continually in my head is when my daughter asked me at 14 years old, "Dad, how do you know when someone is a grown-up?"

I thought for a while before answering. "Well, you're an adult when your life becomes more about others than yourself."

Thinking about it further, I realized that this perfectly describes a mature business. If you want to grow your business, recognize that business is not about you.

Yes, I know…you own or run the business. It's your time, your money and your risk. But trust me, this attitude won't get you or your business anywhere except all alone on the playground. Think you can grow your business alone? It won't happen.

Leadership expert and author of *The 5 Levels of Leadership*, John Maxwell, says only one percent of leaders reach the fifth and highest level of leadership: respect. Respect is not given; it is earned. And the way you earn it is by leading the business selflessly.

Use words like "us," "we" and "our," instead of "me," "I" or "my." Give team members credit when things go right, and take the blame when things go wrong. Show team members how they have contributed to the company's success, so they feel valued.

Don't make your team members do what you are not willing to do yourself. Remain consistent in your actions, expectations and procedures. Make the office a comfortable place for everyone, not just "how you like it."

Take the focus off of you in your business and see for yourself how fast your business matures.

TODAY'S ACTION ITEM

MARCH 13

{ TRUST YOUR TEAM }

Many CEOs and business leaders have something in common: They believe they are the only ones who can do everything. As a result, they lose trust in their employees and start micromanaging.

But here's how to stop:

Hire rock stars.
Your people are the only factors that truly separate you from your competition. Your competition can have the same equipment, the same rates and the same business plan, but they cannot have your people. Further, if you don't have the right team, you can't entrust them with important tasks. Hire slow and fire fast. It's the most important thing you can do to distinguish your business and stop micromanaging.

Give thorough directions.
When you delegate, make sure they are S.M.A.R.T. goals *(see January 22)*. This criteria gives the goal an exponentially greater chance of being accomplished. Additionally, when a goal is accomplished, inner-team trust is emboldened, and the need for micromanaging diminishes. Unfortunately, the converse is also true. If a task is delegated and not completed, team trust is jeopardized, and the need for micromanaging increases.

Share financials.
If you want your team to care as much about your business as you do, give them the inside scoop. If your team knows what factors contribute to their salaries or raises, they'll make sure to tend to those aspects. That frees you to focus more on growing your business.

As a business owner, you can influence lives, meaning you have the opportunity to empower, encourage and strengthen people. Stop micromanaging, start delegating and trust in your team.

TODAY'S ACTION ITEM

MARCH 14

{ BOOST YOUR ENERGY FOR EVERYDAY SUCCESS }

Guest contribution from Petra Coach Marshall Martin

Are you feeling burned out, as if you're exhausted emotionally but not tired physically? The problem could be stemming from an issue with your energy levels.

In the increasingly busy day-to-day of modern lifestyles, our packed schedules mean there is less time to fit in everything. In fact, many people sacrifice a lot of energy coordinating the plethora of activities and tasks.

As an Ironman athlete of 27 years, I know that a comment about working out could receive an "easy for you to say" response, and I recognize it can be tough for some. Indeed, I am coming from a unique comfort level because I start each day with some sort of physical activity. But a wellness regimen isn't only about working out; it's also about taking care of yourself to maximize energy levels.

Trust me – any dividends paid through health and fitness carry over to all facets of life – physically, spiritually, professionally and personally.

How do I know it works?

When I reflect on some of my most demanding jobs in leadership positions, I realize that my best work performances were during the years in which I delivered my best race results.

Coincidence? Hardly. By maintaining a high level of fitness, I was able to leverage that sustained energy, endurance, commitment and drive in my contributions at the office.

TODAY'S ACTION ITEM

MARCH 15

{ PUTTING TOGETHER A WELLNESS REGIMEN }

Guest contribution from Petra Coach Marshall Martin

As discussed yesterday, one of the first things stressed leaders drop is a wellness regimen.

When I recommend one, the first response is invariably, "I don't have time," but I say you can't afford *not* to do it. Otherwise, you'll end up mentally burned out, and one thing we know from psychology is that how we feel mentally influences how we feel physically.

More than just exercise, a wellness regimen includes all the ways we need to take care of our bodies every day.

The most important part of a wellness regimen is sleep because a rejuvenated mind and body are the foundation for success in your personal and professional life. I can assure you from personal experience: There's nothing attractive or heroic about working at all hours and lacking the energy to get things done. Get your doctor's recommended amount of shut-eye.

Your wellness regimen should also include maintaining the mental capacity to do great work. We all have moments that get our blood boiling, but a positive mind is a productive mind.

Finally, set fitness goals. Yes, fitness is a part of this, too. Even if you don't work out regularly, or if you've never done any sort of physical activity at all, you can start by setting a weekly goal to get your blood flowing. Once you've met your first goal, you'll notice a significant change in your attitude and energy levels. (It will also make it easier to keep up the fitness regimen.)

Focus on a wellness regimen that takes care of personal you, and watch professional you follow suit. You might also raise the bar for your friends, family and team members.

TODAY'S ACTION ITEM

MARCH 16

{ NEVER FORGET TO SHOW YOUR APPRECIATION }

The most effective leaders are the first to admit they don't have all the answers. They know their strengths and weaknesses, and they don't let ego or pride get in the way of building their companies.

One of the biggest mistakes I see business leaders make is thinking they can't learn anything from people around them. Everyone has limits, and the best leaders seek others' help and opinions. They build teams of amazing people, empower them to share their ideas and make decisions, and groom them for future leadership positions.

In my experience growing my first company, NationLink Wireless, I learned the value of surrounding myself with passionate, dedicated and smart people. It was the totality of our team effort that helped us reposition the company for growth by capitalizing on the cellular revolution and exiting the pager industry. Otherwise, we would have quickly gone out of business.

A survey conducted by OfficeTeam in 2017 found that 66 percent of employees said they would likely leave their jobs if they didn't feel appreciated, up from 51 percent in 2012. Savvy leaders also know it's vital to give credit where credit is due and publicly celebrate team member contributions with the entire company. In addition to being the right thing to do, it just makes business sense. Showing gratitude will keep your team motivated and ready for the next challenge.

TODAY'S ACTION ITEM

MARCH 17

{ DON'T WAIT FOR GROWTH – PLAN FOR IT }

I feel very fortunate to live in Nashville. Great city, great people, great business environment. Plus, our city has received some incredible publicity over the past several years. It has been a steady stream of positive news, and the growth and national attention is something that our company leaders have been working on for a long time.

That got me thinking about how companies manage growth. Rather than waiting for demand from customers to force growth, why not chart your course ahead of time so you're prepared when opportunity comes knocking?

When prospects for growth appear, leaders and business owners often consider adding team members, inventory and infrastructure. Although those additions may be necessary, this approach to dealing with growth risks creating a bigger business that generates less profit. More work. Less money. What's the point of that?

A better approach is to project your business's growth rate and increase the efficiency of your people and processes to match, or better yet, exceed that rate. For instance, if you expect your business to grow by 20% over the next 12 months, your team members and your systems need to get 20% better over the next year.

With growth comes change. It's inevitable. Planning for long-term growth can help keep you ahead of the competition and position the company for success.

TODAY'S ACTION ITEM

{ LEAVE THE PETTINESS AT THE OFFICE DOOR }

It seems natural to assume that an adult with a steady office job will have a certain level of maturity – unfortunately, that's not always the case. And immaturity is especially on display when conflict arises. Most people learn from a young age that not everyone is going to agree with you all the time, and we figure out how to deal with that and move forward. But for a few, that unmet expectation of agreement is a surprise that brings out negative and petty childish behavior.

And that immature pettiness, if left untamed and unresolved, can spread pretty quickly in a workplace, crushing productivity and camaraderie.

Before I begin any coaching session with a company, I sit everyone down and tell them my number one rule: *Always leave the pettiness at the door.*

I make sure it's clear that we are all adults who are getting together to solve issues and make effective change. Once everyone makes the promise to act their age, our sessions are much more productive.

When you go into the office every day with a mature mindset, you'll find that others will do the same. Leading by example is the best way to demonstrate the behavior that you would like to see – a principle that harkens back to early childhood education. It's crucial that team members act like team members and support each other in the effort to succeed. You're all in it together after all, so there's no reason to be immature and compete with each other when instead everyone can be a winner.

TODAY'S ACTION ITEM

MARCH 19

{ WHEN PHONE CALLS SUPERSEDE EMAILS }

Effective communication is essential. Period. Whether it's talking with coworkers in the break room, calling an out-of-state relative or even receiving a touching email from a forgotten friend, the need to convey emotion and information is fundamental to the way we interact.

In our ever-connected world, we've now become entirely reliant on digital communications. Brusque emails and texts and terse voicemails have become the highways we use to communicate with others.

Don't get me wrong. I rely on digital communications to keep my business and my family life moving efficiently. But when communications start to get sideways, it's important to stop, pick up the phone and make a phone call.

And I'm not talking about trading voicemails. Voicemail can be a crutch to avoid a conversation. And besides, it's inefficient. Think about the number of times you listened to the voicemails that were agonizingly long or insanely short.

I follow a three-email rule, and I include it in my email signature: "After three, we talk."

Conversations carry more weight than emails and texts. The personal, two-way nature of the conversation helps keep both parties on the same page and avoid misinterpreting what the other person is saying.

So before you send that next email or text, ask yourself this question: "Will I achieve the results I want faster by calling?" If it's yes, then go old school and make the call.

TODAY'S ACTION ITEM

MARCH 20

{ ATTITUDE IS EVERYTHING }

You've heard it a thousand times in hundreds of different ways: Attitude is everything. Seems simple, doesn't it? Well, it is. At least, it should be.

So, why do so many of us go about our lives expecting the worst? Maybe your job isn't everything you want it to be. Maybe it's been a tough year for your family. Whatever the case, success and happiness are always in your grasp. The key is changing your perspective, and that starts with attitude.

There's a story I've heard repeated dozens of times in the last few months. It goes something like this: "If you're having a bad day, remember that in 1976, Apple co-founder Ronald Wayne sold his 10 percent stake in Apple for $800. Now it's worth over $58,000,000,000." Makes you wonder if you're really having such a bad day, doesn't it?

It's all too easy to get lost in negative feelings and lose sight of what's right in front of us. Whether you made a wrong turn or just woke up on the wrong side of the bed, there is a way out.

Attitude is a choice. And it can be the difference between success and failure. Each day, take a moment before you walk out the door to put yourself in a positive frame of mind.

TODAY'S ACTION ITEM

MARCH 21

{ ELEVATE ENGAGEMENT }

Keeping your team engaged is vital to retaining talent, growing your business and keeping your organization on the cutting edge.

Engaged team members look forward to coming to work, are on board and enthusiastic about your company's core purpose and values, and are actively working to achieve the goals of your organization.

To maintain employee engagement:

1. Give individual attention.
No matter the size of your organization, employees should get one-on-one time with a supervisor or leader in your organization at least once per month, but I recommend bi-weekly. Implement a system that allows supervisors to track the progress of employees' work. Supervisors should also provide a listening ear for any concerns and help employees set goals that both interest them and benefit the company.

2. Show trust.
I'm assuming that you are an adult who also works with adults, so treat them as such. If your hiring process is thorough, you shouldn't have to micromanage your team. Implement a remote work policy, even if it's just one day per month, or allow some flexibility with working hours. Trust that your employees work hard for your company and that they are responsible enough to manage their time inside and outside of work.

3. Get social.
You've heard it said before: Working with those you like makes a difference in how much you enjoy your job. Make this easy in your workplace by holding company culture events as often as possible: happy hours, a group baseball game outing or even a quarterly donuts-and-coffee celebration in the breakroom during a morning huddle can go a long way in strengthening the camaraderie among your team.

TODAY'S ACTION ITEM

MARCH 22

{ YOU CAN'T STEER A PARKED CAR }

As a business coach, I have encountered so many individuals who are "stuck" somewhere – in their careers, their personal goals and even their relationships.

The word "stuck" implies that there's a power beyond your control preventing you from moving forward, like steering a parked car. But, "stuck" is an illusion. It's actually inertia – and there is a cure: move. Shift your gears into drive and go.

1. Set goals and define success.
Name what you want to accomplish and then ask yourself, "What does that look like?" Avoid using words like "more" (e.g., "I want to exercise more"). Say, "I will go to the gym three days a week for one hour." The more specific you are, the more tangible the goal becomes, and the more likely you are to achieve it.

2. Make a plan.
How are you going to achieve your goal and ensure success? Identify steps that will lead you to your final goal and set dates by which you plan to achieve those milestones. When you're at the base of a mountain, it can seem impossible that you'd ever reach the summit. But if you execute your plan one baby step at a time, it'll feel more doable.

3. Identify your obstacles.
You've got to know what might get in the way of accomplishing your goal so you can mitigate any bumps along the way. If you don't, they can breed excuses ("I didn't have enough time") or resignation ("I guess it just wasn't meant to be"). Decide what you want to achieve, consider your obstacles and get them out of your way.

TODAY'S ACTION ITEM

MARCH 23

{ 4 LEADERSHIP LESSONS FROM CLIMBING MOUNT KILIMANJARO }

Guest contribution from Petra Coach David Pierce

My wife and I climbed Mount Kilimanjaro in Tanzania, which is the tallest mountain in Africa and the highest free-standing mountain in the world. The trail we took reaches a height of 19,340 feet. Climbing that mountain was the most physically and mentally challenging adventure of my life, and I learned a lot on that trip, such as:

1. It's a team effort.
Just as no one can climb Kilimanjaro without the assistance of an experienced guide, no great achievement is possible without the support of a qualified team. A great business leader finds the best team, gives them clear goals and expectations and lets them perform.

2. Great leaders put the team first.
Early into our climb, the support team leader assessed each trekker's experience, conditioning, goals and expectations. He made it a point to get to know each of us. A great leader takes a sincere interest in his or her team and helps them achieve their goals.

3. Great leaders unite teams.
Our group of trekkers had varied life experiences, but we all had one goal in common: to get to the top. Companies must gain this shared sense of purpose and 100 percent buy-in from employees to be able to work together toward company goals.

4. Effective leaders prepare their teams.
We scheduled our trip during a season when the weather was expected to be mostly dry and sunny. We were cautioned, however, to prepare for anything. Great business leaders consider all the possible outcomes and help the team prepare in advance for the worst-case scenario.

Takeaway: Learn from your experiences but also take time to enjoy the present. Go climb your mountains!

TODAY'S ACTION ITEM

MARCH 24

{ TIPS FOR STEPPING INTO A LEADERSHIP ROLE }

The "tone" of a company – how the business works, how people communicate, the culture of the organization – is typically established from the behavior of the top executive. When that champion leaves, there are always changes.

As the incoming leader, you've got a big job ahead of you. The first steps you take will be critical to employees' engagement and the company's continued success.

Remember: You're the new kid on the block. Don't just "take over" without any consideration for the folks who've been there for years.

Take time to figure out how things worked before you got there. What's going well that you need to continue? What needs to be changed right away, and what can wait? Listen to long-time employees and learn about the history of the company. You'll gain their trust and loyalty, which is imperative if you want to succeed.

Most importantly, be yourself. You've got some big shoes to fill, but don't feel like you have to pick up where someone else left off. Instead, bring your genuine and best self to every situation. Being authentic and transparent will help increase the organization's trust in your abilities.

The members of your team are the ones who'll be doing the work and helping you execute the vision of the company. Even if you've got all the numbers worked out and have a solid "plan," if your team isn't behind you, you've got no chance at all.

TODAY'S ACTION ITEM

MARCH 25

{ BREAKING THE BAD NEWS }

Every company has its good and bad days. How an organization deals with challenges is just as important as how it celebrates its victories.

To avoid stoking the rumor mill, you want to relay bad news to your team quickly and in a way that doesn't have any additional repercussions. But how do you do that?

Talk about it.
Open communication does not come naturally to all leaders, so you've got to be intentional about it. If you know something bad is going to happen (or has already happened), gather your team in a room as soon as possible to talk about the news. Having the conversation is only step one, but it's the most critical step.

Be transparent and don't sugarcoat it.
It's no use gathering your team to share the news if you're going to hold back information. When times are tough, trust can be the first thing to erode if people feel like they're not being told the whole truth. Ensure that everything is on the table and there are no secrets. Remember: Bad news is bad news, and you can't always spin it positively. You've got to be genuine.

Hear from everybody.
The opinion of a senior vice president should have no more weight than that of your front-desk receptionist. If you want to have a team, you've got to be willing to hear from each one of them and address any questions or concerns. That will reinforce that everyone (yourself included) is in this together and that you're open to differing opinions. You may not be able to answer every question or address every issue, but listening to each person is crucial.

TODAY'S ACTION ITEM

MARCH 26

{ DON'T MAKE PROMISES YOU CAN'T KEEP }

You may have heard about brand promises before, and asked yourself, "Does my company really need one?" The answer is: definitely yes.

A brand promise does more than just commit something to your potential customers; it is the glue that holds your company together. A brand promise is what unites your employees and builds loyalty in your customer base. Plus, a great brand promise will spread like wildfire, giving you more fans than you could ever pay for.

Here are three ways to get started creating yours:

1. Keep it simple.
Your company or brand is sophisticated, which is why many leaders hesitate to narrow a brand promise down into just a few sentences, but you need to. Don't confuse a brand promise with a mission statement, which can be longer, or with a slogan, which should be even shorter.

2. Make it different.
I would argue that you are not the only company in the world that provides the services that your company offers. If your brand promise sounds similar to others, how will you distinguish yourself? Take a minute (or several) to ponder what gap your company is filling in the market. What makes you unique from your competitors? What does your company value that others don't?

3. Intend to inspire.
It's no secret that people often can feel an emotional connection to a person, company or product. Craft your brand promise to inspire connection with your target audiences and anyone that comes across your brand. Why does your company matter to the world?

TODAY'S ACTION ITEM

MARCH 27

{ YOU MAY ALREADY HAVE ALL THE TALENT YOU NEED }

I've uncovered a lot of truths for leaders in just about every business I've coached over the years. For example, regardless of company size or industry, honesty, gratitude and transparency are critical to a team's success. But one of the most important (and most overlooked) truths for leaders is this:

Every business has valuable, hidden assets that may be underutilized.

I was reminded of this vital lesson recently through a Timehop photo on Facebook of a notecard on which I had jotted that timeless insight. That's right – while most people reminisce about old photos of friends, I'm excited to see old business lessons from years ago.

Many businesses look outside their organizations to inject "fresh blood" into their teams. Executives who think their organizations are missing some secret ingredient to success will go on the hunt for shiny new talent.

But I have found that the external searches should not be the default first step. I suggest that, instead, businesses look inward for these hidden assets.

In the book, *Free the Idea Monkey*, G. Michael Maddock says that innovative and creative individuals with big ideas (the idea monkeys) should be allowed to thrive within an organization. However, all too often, these individuals are constrained and kept in roles for which they're ill-suited. You probably have innovative people in your company right now, but in positions that don't allow their creativity to shine.

You may not be able to uncover existing creatives in your teams for every role or responsibility. However, you can find new and interesting details about existing team members that broaden your possibilities and expand future capabilities.

TODAY'S ACTION ITEM

{ THE SELF-MADE MYTH – ALL BUSINESS LEADERS HAD HELP ALONG THE WAY }

I'm about to share an unpopular opinion: The self-made person is a myth.

No successful entrepreneur or business leader is a self-made man or woman. If you think you are, then you need to take a long, hard look in the mirror. Your success is made up of contributions from family, friends, teachers, mentors and coaches. If you don't see it, then you're not looking hard enough.

As a business coach, I've seen companies grow from kitchen tables to $100 million enterprises and then collapse because the owners thought they knew everything. As they say, pride comes before the fall.

The world's most effective business leaders know they didn't get to where they are by themselves. They recognize that ideas can come from anywhere, and they actively seek out people who can help them on their journey.

Business is a team sport. No great company has been built solely by the efforts of one person. The entrepreneurial spirit can take you far, but when you're running a business, you will need to rely on people who may have better ideas than you. When that happens, you'll not only become an improved leader; you'll see your business and company culture grow exponentially.

TODAY'S ACTION ITEM

MARCH 29

{ LISTEN MORE, TALK LESS }

In my sessions with leaders, I preach the importance of listening – and I'm not talking about holding eye contact and waiting for a space to interject. Real listening means letting team members steer conversations. Leaders who listen actively will absorb feedback and take in details that help them craft mindful responses. Any true self-assessment isn't complete if it's missing a listening skills check-up.

Research by Zenger Folkman found that leaders who listen well are "significantly more effective" than those who don't. Listening also allows you to form a stronger bond and build genuine trust with team members, which, in turn, inspires them to do more and greater work.

When a leader listens, team members learn they can talk about any issues they might have. Those concerns may be about the team itself, larger company matters or even personal matters, which may be affecting their performance.

When team members trust you and believe that there will not be any negative repercussions, there can be real communication in the workplace. That, in turn, will improve morale, company culture and productivity. So make sure to encourage input early and often – and listen.

TODAY'S ACTION ITEM

{ YOU WORK FOR NO ONE, AND NO ONE WORKS FOR YOU }

This may seem like a weird idea: As a business leader, you need to understand that people do not work for you. I hear it all the time. "He works for me" or "I work for (fill in the blank)."

I think differently: You do not work for anyone or anything; you work for a *purpose.*

If you are lucky, it is a purpose that you share with the business in which you spend your time. Most companies have never taken the time to clarify their purpose and ensure that all team members clearly understand it and align with it. But before we go any further, promise me that you will stop saying, "work for" and begin saying, "work with" when talking about your profession. Promise? Good. Now on to defining your purpose.

Both professionally and personally, we need to understand our purpose clearly. It is the "why you exist" of your business, not "what you do" or even "how you do it," so be careful not to confuse that. Similarly, on a personal level, it's essential to know what it is that drives you, that fulfills you. Then you can make sure your personal and professional "whys" coexist in harmony.

Generally, a purpose falls into one of four categories: service to others, the search for knowledge and truth, the pursuit of beauty and excellence, or a desire to change the world. Ask yourself why you do what you do, then ask why that matters, and then ask why *that* matters. Note the answers that give you energy and excitement. You'll know when you have it right.

Now stop saying "work for" and begin saying who you "work with," unless you're talking about your business's purpose.

TODAY'S ACTION ITEM

MARCH 31

{ JUST SAY IT }

Guest contribution from Petra Coach JT Terrell

No matter a company's size, the roadblock that I see most often is when team members wait for their colleagues to behave how they want, rather than asking for the change that they'd like to see.

We can all fall into the habit of assuming people can read minds, expecting them to anticipate exact wants and needs. That always leads to frustration on both sides.

Wouldn't it be easier to tell people exactly what you want from them? Then they'll know what you're expecting without any of the guesswork.

For example, a client told me one of his most significant issues was not getting referrals from his existing client base. As we began to talk through his organization's proposed referral program, I then asked what would happen if they asked for a referral right now. Everyone looked at me like I had two heads. They – incorrectly – saw it as taboo to ask straight out for the referral.

Another CEO I coached was concerned about one of the members of his leadership team. He said that the leader "knows his role very well and, overall, he does a very good job. It's just that I'd like to see him work with more of a sense of urgency, and I don't know if he has it in him." Yet, the CEO had not voiced that to the employee.

Bottom line: People need to know what the expectation is before they can begin to deliver it to you.

TODAY'S ACTION ITEM

APRIL
{ VITAMIN B-4 }

*B-4 brings to mind the idea of dwelling on the past.
Don't waste too much time this month focusing
on what happened "before," but instead use what
you've learned to keep moving forward.*

APRIL 1

{ UNPLUG AND ENGAGE IN REAL LIFE }

I'm sure you know the value of technology in your daily process. But how often do you take a step back to consider the impact that today's non-stop technology has on your personal life?

Our constant connection to our smartphones and tablets can directly impact our most important relationships. Unfortunately, too many of us still keep our heads buried in technology and end up missing out on what's going on around us.

That's why learning to unplug from the daily battle for our attention has never been more critical.

Put a "device detox" on your calendar and prioritize that time to focus on the things happening around you. Engage your senses and change the constant habit of looking at your phone or laptop. Not sure if you can do it? Then you most definitely need it.

Intentionally spend face-to-face time with other people around you, and you'll find that it's easier to become more attentive and absorbent of information. Genuine interpersonal interaction can do wonders in terms of communication. It's something emails, texts or emojis will never be able to accomplish.

Some people may find it more challenging to unplug than others. For instance, the younger generation is accustomed to being on their devices constantly, while an older crowd may find unplugging more natural. To help influence those around you, be purposeful about how you focus time and how you spend your time with technology.

If you set aside moments with the people you care about, you'll set an example for those in your business and in your personal life to do the same.

TODAY'S ACTION ITEM

APRIL 2

{ HUDDLE UP: THE COACH HAS SOMETHING TO SAY }

I love to be inspired. I get inspiration from a lot of places, including my family, my team and the entrepreneurs and executives I work with every day. And I love to inspire others to be better leaders and better people.

But there's one group of people who've turned inspiring teams into an art form: great sports coaches.

Can you watch the movie "Rudy" and not get a tear in your eye and a surge of motivation to be your best? Similarly, can you listen to Jim Valvano's 1993 ESPYs speech and not be inspired to take on the world? (If you haven't seen it, I suggest you take a moment to Google it and watch it.)

Great coaches have been a stable source for speakers of corporate leader training sessions for years. And I often see famous quotes from coaches plastered on motivational office posters.

A good locker room speech – real or fictionalized – has the power to inspire. Great coaches seize those moments to share who they are with their teams and demonstrate authentic leadership. They have passion and impart it to their team through personal connections.

However, in my experience coaching companies across the U.S., I've found that many leaders who take cues from their favorite coaches consistently miss the same key piece: the personal connection.

It takes vulnerability and honesty with your team to make those connections. Once you get over that fear, I promise that your reputation as a leader will soar, and your business results will follow suit.

TODAY'S ACTION ITEM

APRIL 3

{ YOU CAN'T "FIX" WEAKNESSES }

David Rendall's book *The Freak Factor* gives an interesting framework in which we should think about weaknesses.

It's been drilled into our heads our whole lives that weaknesses are something we should "fix." He uses the example of coming home from school with a report card that had all As except for one C in Math. Your parents would most likely sign you up immediately for a math tutor, rather than praise you for all your hard work in your other subjects.

We are conditioned to pinpoint weaknesses and do everything in our power to get rid of them.

But Rendall's book lets us in on the biggest secret of them all: You cannot fix weaknesses.

He explains that when you focus on fixing weaknesses, you lose a little bit of the corresponding strength because they are in a delicate balance with each other. For example, when you work on being less blunt or rude, you may lose some of the direct honesty that your colleagues find useful in a brainstorm session.

So you have to be diplomatic with yourself. Be willing to give and take to find the right balance between that strength and its weakness.

Studies show that when you build on your strengths, you'll see massive and exponential improvements. But when you work on your weaknesses, the pay off is not nearly the same.

In other words, spend the time making your strengths strong enough that your weaknesses become less relevant and detracting.

TODAY'S ACTION ITEM

APRIL 4

{ MAKING THE MOST OF YOUR MORNING MEETING }

When handled the right way, morning meetings can build team spirit, foster accountability and provide quick solutions. The system I use for our "huddles" is:

What's up?: This is where each team member quickly shares their meeting schedules and anything of relevance to the team. For example, "I met with Steve Smith yesterday, and his company is relocating across town, so his logistical needs may change."

Key performance indicator (KPI) updates: Have team members report their progress towards individual and company quarterly goals. This creates an environment of accountability because standing in front of teammates and reporting on incomplete goals is never fun.

Stucks or needs: This is when team members can bring up a project or task they can't move forward without someone else's collaboration or assistance. They must tell the other team member directly and specifically, in front of the entire group, what they need and by when.

Top priority: Team members announce one item on their to-do lists they WILL complete TODAY. It's important to emphasize the use of "I will" versus "I'll try" or "I'm supposed to."

Now you know the recipe for daily huddle success, let's conclude just like we'd end a huddle…

On the count of three say, "I will implement a daily huddle!"

One-two-three… Break!

TODAY'S ACTION ITEM

APRIL 5

{ 3 WAYS MEDITATION WILL HELP YOU BECOME A BETTER LEADER }

When you read the word "meditation," what's the first thing that pops into your head? Yoga? Monks? Another thing to add to your to-do list?

Meditation shouldn't be intimidating or time-consuming. In fact, it may be the easiest and most effective way to spend 10 minutes of your day. Meditation can help you:

1. Stress less.
Meditation is scientifically proven to decrease your blood pressure. Find a quiet space, close your eyes and focus on your breathing for three to five minutes. Identify what you hear, smell and feel around you. Measured breathing and being still will reduce your heart rate, allowing you to return to your day mentally and physically healthier.

2. Gain perspective.
The time spent in meditation can help you think more clearly about your current concerns and figure out why you're experiencing them. When you carve out a few minutes to calm your brain and rationally think things through, it's easier to feel gratitude for challenges and to find new ways to approach any problems.

3. Master motivations.
When was the last time you made time in your day to encourage and inspire yourself to achieve your next best thing? For many of us, we know where we want to be, but we rarely reward ourselves the time to think through our personal goals and outline a plan to make them happen.

Without all of the buzzing and nonsense in your head, you'll be able to see clearly the road ahead and identify specific steps to get started.

TODAY'S ACTION ITEM

APRIL 6

{ BE THE ADULT IN THE ROOM }

Office politics can be petty. It's amazing how small disagreements can quickly balloon into big misunderstandings. There's a reason people refer to the office as a "sandbox," because some folks refuse to act like adults. And, if the level of childish behavior rises to tantrum pitch and the culture becomes toxic, there's no chance for communication or growth.

The office is not a playground, and we're not children. So, every day we must enter into an "adult agreement" as we walk through the doors and begin our day.

When I work with companies looking to improve their business – whether it be culture, revenue, employee engagement or all of the above – I begin by explaining our joint agreements for the day. One of those is an "adult agreement." It informs the work we do for the entire day, and hopefully beyond.

It says that we all agree to act like adults:

1. Adults don't shoot each other down

2. Adults own up to mistakes and bring them to the table

3. Adults don't hide problems

4. Adults don't argue with reality

5. Adults don't shy away from sharing ideas

We've got to support each other in our efforts to be truthful and vulnerable. A team is only as strong as its weakest link, so we must lift each other up. When we act like adults – especially in the sandbox – we all win.

TODAY'S ACTION ITEM

APRIL 7

{ 3 TIPS TO FIND SALES PROSPECTS FASTER }

Every industry has a sales cycle – the step-by-step process to identify and guide potential buyers from initial contact to final purchase. And every sales cycle starts with one of the most challenging parts: prospecting for new clients.

In a perfect world, your marketing team identifies prospects as warm leads, companies that are ready to buy now. But that's rare – it generally takes longer to close on deals than you may expect.

Too many businesses have sales processes that go something like this: Reps are handed a random list of prospects and told to go out and sell. In their quest to meet a quota, the sales team doesn't vet the leads, so they end up bringing in too many less-than-desirable clients.

Instead:

1. Examine your current client list, and identify common reasons as to why they chose you and not your competitors.

2. Confirm those reasons are what you want to be known for, and use that to create a list of ideal attributes for your next clients.

3. Build a "Dream List" of prospects whose needs best match your product or service. Sales reps will close faster when they have a clear profile of their "dream client." And prospects will buy sooner when their needs best match the seller's profile.

Know the decision-makers, which is generally more than one person at a company – an average of 6.8 people, according to *Harvard Business Review*. Sales reps must understand the roles and motivations of all key individuals involved, anticipate their needs and provide meaningful information that will facilitate the prospect's purchase.

TODAY'S ACTION ITEM

APRIL 8

{ CELEBRATE WELL AND OFTEN }

My responsibility as a coach is to help company leaders define what motivates them and ensure those reasons are consistent with their business's goals and objectives. Similarly, I encourage leaders to inspire their team members to seek out their own motivation.

One of the best mantras that many companies use to encourage their employees is simple but effective: Expect results and celebrate victories.

Before you give your team their marching orders, let them know you have confidence in their abilities. Take time to explain why a successful outcome is important to you personally and for the business.

Not every goal, task or objective will foster the same amount of excitement and teamwork. If what you want is challenging or risky, let your team know. They'll respect your transparency and be more likely to trust you and your leadership.

And they'll be much more likely to meet your expectations – not because they're doing it for you, but because they're working hard for the benefit of the whole team. It's also crucial to celebrate wins and to express your appreciation. I can't stress that enough. An individual reward can be a great motivational tool, but it's just as vital that you celebrate as a team.

All leaders have days where they're more inspirational than others. Nonetheless, when you've got a team to lead, you have to step it up and show them how it's done.

Positive energy is infectious. When you live by example and spread it around, it will become embedded in your company culture. You'll see the results every day and, as an added benefit, you'll create your next group of leaders.

TODAY'S ACTION ITEM

APRIL 9

{ THERE IS MORE TO CUSTOMER SERVICE THAN A SMILING FACE }

Recently I went to dinner with my family at a chain restaurant. Nothing too fancy, just a sit-down place you probably know. Our server was a tall, young man named Marshall, who was new to the job and excited to wait on us.

Marshall, bless his heart, did as well as he could. He got one of the drinks wrong and made a mistake on the salad dressing, but he replaced both quickly without much fuss. He joked about how dumb he felt and hoped his smiling face, not his flubs, would be what we remember. Marshall had the enthusiasm, but not the institutional knowledge that comes with working at the same company for an extended time.

Here's the takeaway from this story: *It's okay to be new, but it isn't okay to be a neophyte.*

Before your team members interact with customers, make sure they understand their job. If you're selling products, have them walk the floor every day and familiarize themselves with not only what you're selling, but also where to find it. If you're selling services, have them review case studies and client files so they can answer customer questions accurately and quickly. Identify common mistakes that new employees make and drill your people on them.

In the grand scheme of things, a mixed-up drink order or the wrong dressing on a salad isn't going to ruin anyone's dinner. But any of those things could sully the dining experience enough that I might choose a different place next time, and the manager would never know why.

TODAY'S ACTION ITEM

{ BREAK OUT OF THE PRISONS CALLED 'WORRY' AND 'FEAR' }

Guest contribution from Petra Coach David Pierce

Out of all the obstacles that come our way in life, worry and fear may be the two biggest killers of success. These self-made "prisons" prevent business leaders from taking risks, making them think they don't deserve opportunities or won't succeed. Leaders that give in to these struggles enough times often question their self-worth.

The first step to breaking out of these prisons is to realize that most of the things we fear, when looked upon in hindsight, never actually happen. In his article "The Fog of Worry (Only 8 percent of Worries Are Worth It)," author Earl Nightingale wrote this describing the things we worry about:

1. Things that never happen: 40 percent. That is, 40 percent of the things you worry about will never occur anyway.

2. Things over and past that can't be changed by all the worry in the world: 30 percent.

3. Needless worries about our health: 12 percent.

4. Petty, miscellaneous worries: 10 percent.

5. Real, legitimate worries: 8 percent. Only 8 percent of your worries are worth concerning yourself about. Ninety-two percent are pure fog with no substance at all.

Only 8 percent of worries are actually worth concern? I like those percentages.

So, start eliminating 92 percent of your worries. For the remaining 8 percent, create an action plan on how to deal with them.

TODAY'S ACTION ITEM

APRIL 11

{ HOW TO MOVE FROM STRATEGY TO TACTICS }

Strategy is easy. Tactics are hard. Taking care of the daily, weekly and monthly activities to grow a business is what separates the wheat from the chaff. Far too many business people delude themselves into believing they will succeed because they have a great idea and strategy. The necessary tactics, they rationalize, can be addressed later. It's a huge mistake.

Think about it. We've all made noble goals and had a strategy to achieve them. New Year's resolutions, anyone? But, without outlining the specific work needed to achieve the goal, initiative falls flat. Strategy without tactics – the nitty-gritty steps that must happen to achieve the objectives – puts your business at risk.

For example, if a sales / business development objective for the quarter is to obtain 20 percent more referrals, you might need to reach out to your customers to do that. And that may start with a survey or poll that allows you to gauge your current customers' satisfaction and willingness to refer others. Or, other tactics might include creating marketing collateral for your customers to share with friends or offering incentives for these individuals to refer other people. Tactics are the building blocks that will ultimately help your organization reach its goal.

Without these fundamental steps, your company will likely never gain traction on goals for the future. The next time you sit down at the whiteboard for a company planning meeting or executive discussion, remember to move beyond dreaming and organize your thoughts into goals with measurable objectives, a winning strategy and detailed tactics.

TODAY'S ACTION ITEM

{ DISCOVER AND DEVELOP FUTURE LEADERS }

You may have all the talent, drive and big ideas in the world, but understand this: You can't go it alone. You have to surround yourself with people who have passion and skills outside of your comfort zone. If you let people do what they do well, you'll have more time to do what YOU do best.

Business leaders should do everything possible to help team members excel. Your support and their effort sets the stage, so when team members are ready to move into a leadership role, they are well prepared to lead and engage colleagues and clients.

Are you holding a bi-weekly meeting with them? Before you roll your eyes at me for asking you to schedule yet another meeting into your day, consider that these meetings with your employees might be your most valuable. Your team members aren't just your results-makers; they are your brand ambassadors. They can sell for you, or they can scathe you. They can go the extra mile, or they can do the minimum to get by until the clock strikes 5:00. Most of these decisions will be impacted by how much they think you care about them.

Are you offering ways for your team to grow and develop? When your team members are learning, everyone benefits. Offer a personal development budget or encourage them to take online classes to learn about something that your company might need to know in the future. Give employees freedom and responsibility to learn and grow. It will stimulate them mentally and encourage improvement in all aspects of your company.

TODAY'S ACTION ITEM

APRIL 13

{ SOLVING YOUR PEST PROBLEM }

Problems at work can be like pests in your home. If you squash a bug in your kitchen, I guarantee that there are hundreds more behind the walls. You may have solved the problem for the moment, but you've hardly eliminated it. Pretty soon that problem will become even bigger and more difficult to handle.

Can you identify a problem in your workplace? If so, you need to take the first step now to eliminate any more of them crawling out from inside of your walls.

The first and most difficult part is to set aside the time you need.

There are roughly 500 working hours in any quarter. Set aside 2 percent of that time (10 hours) and get in a room with your team to talk about the problems your business is facing. Which ones occur over and over? What's taking up the most time? It will quickly become clear which issues should be addressed in the near-term.

The next step is to pick one to work on. You might think, "One problem at a time? That's not very efficient." But, you're wrong. You're going to need to stay focused, so starting with one will allow you to talk through your problem at a granular level and determine what steps you need to take to make it go away forever. Once you've solved one problem, you can move on to the next.

Now, where can you fit in 30 minutes into your day today to start making an effort to squash your problems?

TODAY'S ACTION ITEM

APRIL 14

{ ARE YOU MAKING THE MOST OF YOUR FEAR? }

Fear. We've all felt it. Sometimes it energizes us to make quick decisions or sometimes it paralyzes us and limits us from reaching our full potential.

Even if you're a seasoned entrepreneur and CEO, you're still going to feel fear, and so are all the members of your team. It's the human condition, and it's unavoidable. But far too often, I see business leaders making decisions based on their fears, rather than the facts on the ground and their aspirations. Don't let that happen to you.

My daughter Madison is an actor, and she gets the proverbial butterflies in her stomach before any performance. In many ways, it's the fuel that drives her onstage. Those nerves remind her to be on her game, and they help her focus before giving (what is always) an excellent performance.

As a leader, don't let the butterflies in your stomach stop you from moving forward with a decision or from considering a new idea. A bit of nerves can be a good thing, but if we turn them into fear, they'll do nothing but hold us back from our potential. Instead, harness that energy, focus it and turn it into an excellent performance.

TODAY'S ACTION ITEM

APRIL 15

{ JUST SAY YES }

Guest contribution from Petra Coach Marshall Martin

Through my experience coaching, I've seen an increasing trend in business leaders saying "no" – not in the right way, such as to guard their time. They use the word to vote against launching new products or investing in their workforce. It seems that saying "no" is easier than saying "yes" (and identifying and achieving the follow-up tasks that a "yes" requires). I hear things like, "Everything seems okay, right? So why push?"

If you're not sure how to start saying "yes" in your business, commit now to make the effort and stay mindful of new opportunities by taking the following steps:

1. Identify high payoff activities that move the business forward.
Have a plan in place that identifies potential opportunities or activities that have a high return on investment. Once secured, sit down with your entire team to evaluate these opportunities. Encourage everyone to keep their minds open and be willing to say "yes," even if some ideas seem out of the box or a little risky.

2. Learn to say "no" to things that waste time or don't add value.
Just as it's important to be open to a "yes," it's important to know when saying "no" is powerful and crucial. You should be able to identify things that waste time or lack value for your business. Once identified, don't be afraid to shut those things down.

3. Have a peer network for bouncing ideas.
Go to your peer network for advice on whether you should or should not say "yes." If you don't have a peer network, get out there and start building one. Your peers can provide you with insights into how they would approach the opportunities – and in a no-nonsense way.

TODAY'S ACTION ITEM

APRIL 16
{ KEEP IT SIMPLE }

There's no doubt that starting and growing a business is no easy task. Often, you find yourself working past midnight and starting again early the next day. Being an entrepreneur takes sweat, grit, determination and strong will to succeed. Some folks make it look easy, but it never is.

Here are two tips to help you avoid some of the mistakes that can make being an entrepreneur harder than it needs to be:

1. Set aside the need for control.
You're in charge. You make the decisions. And, if you want it done right, you usually have to do it yourself. Sound familiar? If it does (especially if it's what you currently believe), you need to release control.

You hired the A-players around you to do a job – now let them do it. Get your ego out of the way and have faith in their decision-making capabilities. That will afford you time to focus on other things. Plus, the trust you show will breed loyalty in your team.

2. Adopt good habits and practice them.
When I discovered the Rockefeller Habits, they not only changed how I manage my business, but they changed my life. Once I had a system in place whereby I could set goals and achieve them, I began to experience a new level of success both in my work and my personal life – but it wasn't overnight.

Like anything new, it took practice for me to fully integrate better habits into my daily routine. Practice enough, and you'll build muscle memory for your habits. Neglect them, and you'll fall back into your old routine.

TODAY'S ACTION ITEM

APRIL 17

{ MAINTAIN (OR IMPROVE) COMPANY CULTURE }

Change is inevitable. And change within a company can be a good thing if it's done correctly. However, if you don't make the right preparations, a change could be bad news for both your business and your culture.

Company culture can be stated through core values and core purpose, but the way a company lives out those values is what matters most on a day-to-day basis. Maybe the company holds a happy hour every Friday afternoon. Or, perhaps employees have been encouraged to seek a better balance with the ability to work remotely.

Those things might seem trivial, but I assure you they're not. Those traditions should be maintained even as other changes happen within the company, including leadership changes. And perhaps new customs should be added. The key is to focus on small things that have a significant impact on supporting or boosting your company culture and the morale of your team.

If company change creates a volatile situation, and members of the team are vying for power or hashing old disagreements, don't engage, and don't take sides. Be careful not to be dragged into any power struggles – it will undermine your message and lower your status among the team.

As I like to say, "Be the adult in the room." Take the lead and encourage the team to move forward in a positive way.

Change is rarely easy, but you can set yourself and your company up for success if you focus on your people first. Your company's best days might be just around the corner.

TODAY'S ACTION ITEM

APRIL 18

{ CELEBRATING "REJUVENATION DAY" }

Are you the type of person who thinks of everyone else before yourself? If you are, you probably don't even realize it. Business leaders are particularly prone to this trait. We have a responsibility to our team and our customers, and that can become a singular focus.

But when your weekly date night with your partner or spouse starts to become monthly, and your evening workouts are replaced with late-night office hours, you might be putting yourself on the back burner. And that doesn't help anyone.

If you're too tired or stressed, the people who are most important to you, whether it's your employees or your family, won't benefit from all you have to offer. So, as your to-do list grows, remember your personal priorities.

One practice I embraced a long time ago is to take one "Rejuvenation Day" each month. It's a full day dedicated to me. I exercise, read and reflect. Sometimes I even indulge.

The first step to taking care of you is recognizing that it needs to be done. Don't discount your value – make a point of maintaining your well-being. You'll find that caring for others is much easier when you've taken care of yourself.

TODAY'S ACTION ITEM

APRIL 19

{ DELEGATE OR DIE }

As a leader in any capacity – in your business, job, family, etc. – your primary responsibility is to grow other leaders. That means you must delegate leadership responsibilities.

Most leaders become paralyzed at the thought of delegating. Why? It's usually one of three reasons:

1. They've done it before unsuccessfully, so they've convinced themselves it's not worth their time.

2. They've never attempted it because they're afraid that they will give away their information, and they will lose their edge and their elevated position with it.

3. They're shortsighted. Many who shy away from delegating will say something like, "It will take me three hours to teach them when I can do it in 20 minutes. I don't have the extra time right now, so I'll take care of it."

Delegating is harder than it seems like it ought to be. But, no matter how good a person is, no one can do everything. Leaders have to learn how to hand things off. Eventually, it becomes easier. Plus, as information is transferred, processes can be documented, making it easier for others to take over in the future.

Remember, as a business leader, time is one of your most valuable resources. Effective delegation is often the difference between success and failure, for yourself and your team. If you rank yourself low on your delegation skills, today's the day to start changing.

TODAY'S ACTION ITEM

APRIL 20
{ DO YOU HAVE A DISC? }

One of the first things I do when I start working with a new team or company is have every member take the DiSC assessment. There are a lot of personality tests out there, but this one is unique in that it is specifically designed to uncover the communication and productivity style of yourself and your colleagues, making it ideal for the workplace. Let's break down the basics of the test and why it matters:

What do the letters mean?

- **D=Dominance** – focused on results, sees the big picture, gets straight to the point

- **i=Influence** – focused on relationships, likes to collaborate, can persuade others

- **S=Steadiness** – focused on dependability, cooperates well with others, shows sincerity

- **C=Conscientiousness** – focused on quality, ensures accuracy, good with details

Every person is a combination of all four traits, but each person displays a trait or two more prominently than others. The results of the test show what a person places the most emphasis on in the workplace and in turn how that impacts their behavior, communication, emotions and actions.

Understanding your team's DiSC profiles is as close as you can get to taking a peek inside of their minds. What are they motivated by? Discouraged by? Encouraged by? No one result is better than another. But each result is customized to the person. Each team member will better understand themselves and how they work, and the results help you better understand and motivate your team.

What are you waiting for? Take your DiSC test today!

TODAY'S ACTION ITEM

APRIL 21

{ IMPROVE YOUR OFFICE SPACE TO IMPROVE YOUR BUSINESS }

It pays to focus on your team members' happiness. The "100 best companies to work for in America" earn shareholders 3.5 percent higher annual returns than typical industry averages, according to a University of Pennsylvania study.

I coach hundreds of companies around the globe. I can tell you from experience that those with pleasing office environments have happier, engaged team members and earn higher revenues. The good news, you can reinvigorate your workplace with these two simple tips:

Let the light in.
If you have blinds covering your windows, open them. People who spend more time in natural light than in artificial lighting have increased productivity and alertness, according to a study by the Swiss Institute of Technology. If window seating isn't an option in your existing office space, urge your team members to spend some time outdoors during their lunch breaks to soak up some vitamin D.

Reduce noise.
If a handful of your team members like listening to music while they work, make sure they wear headphones. Background noise is more than annoying to other team members – it's a health risk. The National Institute for Occupational Safety and Health has found that ambient noise increases general stress levels and aggravates stress-related conditions like high blood pressure, coronary disease, peptic ulcers and migraine headaches. Monitor your workplace noise to enable focus and better health.

Chances are your team members spend more time at the office than at home. Let your work family know you value them by giving them a positive home away from home.

TODAY'S ACTION ITEM

APRIL 22

{ DEVELOPING EMOTIONALLY INTELLIGENT TEAMS }

If you're a good listener, a great conflict-resolver and an emotionally mature person, then you are probably a heart-smart (a.k.a. emotionally intelligent) leader. Someone like that will rise to the top of any organization.

But it may not have occurred to you that one of the best ways to help your business is to recognize these traits in others.

Use your talents to develop other heart-smart leaders and mentor them. The more emotionally intelligent people you can place in management positions within your company, the better your overall picture and company health will become.

Why does it matter?

Because emotionally intelligent people are very receptive to others' feelings, so they can help take the temperature of their colleagues and those they supervise. They can read between the lines (or hear between the words) and recognize signs that you're not seeing.

Also, an emotionally intelligent leadership team will push you to keep developing your heart-smart skills, just as you are helping to develop theirs.

Heart-smart business leaders look out for the next generation to ensure the stability and longevity of the business.

TODAY'S ACTION ITEM

APRIL 23

{ THE ONE THING YOU'RE DOING THAT NOBODY LIKES }

Guest contribution from Petra Coach Jennifer Faught

"You shouldn't eat that."
"Your kids should be going to bed earlier."
"If I were you, I would speak up more in meetings."

What emotions do those statements spark in you? Defensiveness? Insecurity? Doubt?

Even when advice is well-intentioned, if the person receiving it doesn't feel like it's relevant or helpful, it can create tension. We've all received advice at some point that actually feels like criticism.

On the flip side – have you ever had someone, instead of criticizing, tell you a story about a personal, relevant experience and what they learned from it? If so, how did you feel? Reassured? Relaxed? Understood?

When we share our experiences with someone, versus telling them our opinions, there is less debate on what's right or wrong, less blame administered, less hurt caused.

That doesn't mean that you can never share advice or tell someone what they "should" do. Just proceed with caution. Many times people who are giving advice want to share something that they genuinely think is helpful and with good intentions.

Before giving advice, ask if the person would like to receive it by simply saying, "Would you like some advice on this?" Even better, share an experience with them so that they can come to their own conclusion with the newly acquired information.

This simple change is a powerful tool for leaders to motivate and support, instead of control and frustrate.

TODAY'S ACTION ITEM

APRIL 24
{ GOALS VS. STRATEGY }

Most likely, your organization created an annual "strategic plan" at the beginning of the year. You probably spent hours in a conference room with other leaders and employees to brainstorm goals for the year ahead, and you ended up with a list that includes things like: become the leader in our market; grow the business; expand our team.

However, these statements are not strategies nor plans. They are goals – vague statements of intent.

Here are three items that must accompany each organizational goal to achieve long-term success:

1. Strategy.
A strategy is the path you take to achieve the defined goal. You cannot merely write down a goal and cross your fingers, hoping it happens. You must outline a plan that you and your team can execute.

2. Objective.
An objective is a measurable step you take to achieve a strategy. Say you choose to expand your company into different markets. Your objective may look something like this: Launch three store openings in different cities throughout the state and start earning profits by the fourth quarter. That is a specific and measurable action that will lead you to accomplish your strategy.

3. Tactics.
Tactics are tools used in pursuing an objective connected with a strategy. There are several tactics involved in expanding into three different markets. They could include conducting an extensive competitive analysis in those target markets, outlining your marketing plan and determining who will oversee the work.

Together, your strategy, objective and tactics provide a detailed plan that will allow you to achieve your loftiest goals.

TODAY'S ACTION ITEM

APRIL 25

{ DON'T VENT. COMMUNICATE. }

I talk to business leaders every day about how healthy communication within a company can mean the difference between a successful business and one that's poised to die on the vine. But what is healthy communication? Well, one thing it isn't is venting about problems or criticizing others, without offering solutions.

Communicating a problem means sharing what the issue is in an open setting where all parties can be heard and then talking through possible solutions. Venting, on the other hand, is often behind closed doors, between two or three colleagues and most often, not constructive. Sure, it can help get a metaphorical weight off of someone's chest. However, venting typically hurts more than it helps, and it can start rumors that spread like wildfire. People talk about "healthy venting," but there's nothing healthy about it if issues are not resolved.

As a leader, emphasize that the only way to find a solution is to share openly. Then provide an example on how to do that. Share a personal story of communication gone wrong and the effect it had on you.

Make healthy communication a standard in your business. The more you reinforce that standard by living it yourself and requiring that your team all follow suit, the more successful you'll be. You'll retain and attract the people who can live that vision and repel the people who can't. It might take some time to change old habits, but it will be worth it, and your company will be a more open and honest place to be for everyone.

TODAY'S ACTION ITEM

APRIL 26

{ LEARN FROM YOUR PAST VULNERABILITIES }

As a leader, you're probably accustomed to doing things your way. My guess is that you've also experienced your fair share of disappointments and struggles. Trust me: This is not only normal for leaders; it's expected.

Anyone who refuses to acknowledge past struggles or failures will never learn from them.

The first step to overcoming a fear of vulnerability is to look your wins and, especially, your losses square in the eye and see them for what they are: learning experiences.

Why did [insert situation here] happen? What is the lesson from that experience? How can telling this story help my current team?

Begin your journey to overcoming the fear of vulnerability by making a list of the learning experiences of your past. Then, prepare to share.

Having a personal conversation with team members can be stressful, even panic-inducing, for many leaders, especially the ones who tell me they "focus on the future, not the past."

It's true that forward-looking initiatives are crucial to business success, but understanding your past mistakes may be just as important, if not more.

TODAY'S ACTION ITEM

APRIL 27

{ HOW TO CHOOSE A BUSINESS COACH }

The process of hiring a business coach can be daunting. Will the coach understand my business? Will it be worth my time and money? How do I measure results?

Before hiring a business coach, here are five crucial questions to ask:

1. Can this coach do what he says he can do?
Talk with the business coach about his abilities, and ask for a track record of success.

2. Will this coach do what she says she will do?
Ask to talk with her clients. Their feedback will give you a greater sense of the coach's abilities.

3. Is this person someone I want to work with?
Plan an in-person meeting with your prospective coach to make sure you jive. If you hire him or her, you'll have to work together through challenging discussions and situations to build your team and your business.

4. Does this coach serve my genre?
Find a coach who has experience in your industry, but even more important, with your company size. Some coaches, like me, focus on entrepreneurial businesses while others work with large corporations. What works for a small $5-20 million business may not apply to a multi-billion dollar corporation.

5. Can I afford the time and money required for a coach?
Prepare to invest in your company's success. Coach costs can range from $300 an hour to $60,000 for a year's retainer, depending on the amount of contact you receive. Some sessions may be an hour while others last all day. Figure out what works for you before you price it out.

Overall, look for coaches who put the client first. And make sure you're willing and ready to grow.

TODAY'S ACTION ITEM

APRIL 28

{ DON'T HIRE JUST TO FIT A TITLE }

When job applications come in that match all the characteristics you're looking for, it can be cause for celebration. However, if you delve deeper, you may find that the candidate simply mirrored the qualifications that were detailed in the job ad.

I tell the leaders I coach time and time again: Qualifications on paper don't tell the whole story. Even if the information is all true, it is only half of a candidate's overall fitness. Looking only for specific experience and skills may be the way business has been done for half a century, but that doesn't mean it's right.

You also need to look at each candidate's personal and emotional strengths to determine if he or she is right for your company and its culture.

Consider holding a group interview with the candidate's potential team – the people that the hired person will work with every day. It's a great way for the team to get to know the prospect and gauge, then and there, if he or she is a fit before any contracts are signed. You'd be surprised how quickly the person will click if they really are a fit, or how quickly things will get awkward if not.

Let the whole team have a chance to weigh in on how the person performed in the interview. They may even point out things you didn't catch, like excessive nervousness or a particular personality trait that is off-putting.

Once you have identified the right candidate, you can then build a position that will enable your new team member – and your company – to succeed.

The right candidates will not only blow your socks off in the short term, but they'll shape the role for years to come.

TODAY'S ACTION ITEM

APRIL 29

{ EMERGENCY LANDING OFFERS LESSONS IN BUSINESS & LIFE }

When a woman in the airplane seat in front of me had a medical issue, several passengers, myself included, stepped in to help. Our group, who had never met before and including the crew and a nurse who was on board, were able to provide her the care she needed – and we saved her life.

Here are four key lessons I learned from that flight:

1. Sometimes you have to stop and think.
Even without knowing all of the details about the woman's condition, we gathered all the information we could, so that we could decide on how to proceed. Sometimes we should take a step back and think about how to ensure, as best we can, the greatest positive outcome.

2. It's okay to change your path.
Once we decided the woman needed professional care, the next step became clear: Land as soon as possible. It's never easy to change plans. Many businesses end up being something much different than originally intended because they found success in Plan B.

3. Grab a friend.
On our flight, the small team of caregivers and the woman became friends. In life, either professionally or personally, you will need a friend or two. Find yourself a few true friends that will be there when times get tough.

4. You are not alone – ever.
This was something that surprised me on that flight. No matter where you are in life. No matter how tough it gets. No matter the circumstances. We are never completely alone. There will always be someone that will help us. We just need to ask and be open to it.

TODAY'S ACTION ITEM

{ VISUALIZE SUCCESS TO SUCCEED }

Visualization is one of the essential tools in every leadership toolkit. To gain maximum benefit, you must make your visualization as realistic as possible. Athletes have been successfully using visualization for years in their training. A golfer may visualize the perfect chip shot or a basketball player the ideal process for making a free throw.

Great leaders harness the power of visualization to paint a picture of what success will look like in the future and inspire others to join them in the journey. As noted author Stephen Covey wrote, "In effective personal leadership, visualization and affirmation techniques emerge naturally out of a foundation of well thought-through purposes and principles that become the center of a person's life."

Visualization can be as simple as closing your eyes and imagining – in as much detail as possible – the upcoming steps you must take to achieve success. It can be as brief as a few minutes or as long as necessary to complete the mental picture of what you want to accomplish. Mornings and evenings are the best visualization times because that's when we tend to be the most relaxed.

Visualization allows you to envision how you will successfully navigate business challenges and opportunities. It can also help you paint a picture of how you will inspire your team members to achieve their goals.

TODAY'S ACTION ITEM

MAY

{ VITAMIN B-5 }

*Just as your body needs healthy red blood cells
to carry oxygen throughout it, your organization
needs the right people to keep it running,
so focus this month on your team.*

MAY 1

{ LET IT GO }

Most entrepreneurs are Type A personalities. They want things done now and they want them done right. Thus, long hours are put in at the office with little reprieve from the stress of running your own venture.

While this style of (micro) management may help you feel in control, it will inevitably cause your business to plateau and maybe even crumble. It is time to learn the joy of delegation and how working smarter, not harder, can help your company thrive.

Work on your business, not in it.
Micromanaging monopolizes time that could be spent working on your business rather than simply working in your business. When you are focused on the day-to-day operations of your company, you become reactive rather than proactive and will never move your business forward.

Hire smart, direct well.
Learning to delegate starts with hiring a great team to move the company forward. Then, it's all about the way you lead them. Provide thorough training and direction so that your team has a baseline for understanding how your business functions. Discover together S.M.A.R.T. goals – specific, measurable, attainable, relevant and time-bound. This gives your delegated tasks a greater chance of getting accomplished.

Improve your employees, and they will improve your company: You must empower your team to step up in the company or you will never see employees take initiative with their work. Encourage leadership skills and foster new ideas by delegating work to the up-and-comers in the company – who knows, they may even do it better than you.

TODAY'S ACTION ITEM

MAY 2
{ BEING THE "COOL BOSS" }
Guest contribution from Petra Coach JT Terrell

You hear all about the "cool boss" who hosts happy hours, buys a beer fridge for the break room or hosts ping pong tournaments, but the little gimmicks can only win you so many points as a leader.

How can leaders really become cool? What is being a cool boss about, and how can these special skills apply in the workplace?

It's as simple as looking for ways to engage your team. Ask questions to find out who needs help or feedback, and then do something with that information. Write a note. Schedule a lunch. Give a damn. Your team wants to follow a leader worth following.

You can also decide to be a mentor to more junior employees. A popular image features a CFO asking a CEO, "What happens if we invest in developing our people and then they leave us?" The CEO responds, "What happens if we don't and they stay?"

There's a lesson to be learned there. Trust that your investment will breed loyalty, and know that it will ignite your recruiting. Once the word gets out that you are changing the lives of team members, your bench will fill up quickly.

As a coach, I intentionally look for ways that leaders can be vulnerable and let their employees see behind the curtain. Invariably, it lets the team know that behind that C-level title, there is an actual person who is subject to the same pressures and stresses that they feel, only magnified 10 times.

If you engage with your team, you will boost morale, increase productivity and yield higher profits.

TODAY'S ACTION ITEM

MAY 3

{ WHY YOU SHOULD STOP EMAILING AND WRITE A LETTER INSTEAD }

Our society's instant communication has transformed the way we interact and lessened the impact of the messages we want to convey. Yet one of the most important and meaningful means of correspondence has taken a lowly priority: the handwritten letter.

Here's why you should go old school and write a letter:

It's meaningful: Think about the letters you've received in the past. Remember those that affected you so profoundly you still keep them today? We don't send as many letters these days because we've forgotten about the power of the handwritten word.

It's distinctive: If you type up a note and email it to any CEO, chances are it's going to find its way into their inboxes alongside the hundreds of other emails they get every day. If the subject line doesn't grab them, your note will most likely move down the list into digital oblivion. A handwritten letter is a thoughtful follow-up that'll keep you fresh on someone's mind.

It's tangible: You can hold a letter or postcard in your hand. You can pin it to your wall and reflect on it. It's more permanent than a phone call and more personal than clicking a 'Like' button or thumb-typing a text message. Postcards, journals and letters are reminders of places we've been, memories we've made and relationships we've built.

In an age where handwritten letters are almost obsolete, your colleagues, friends, family and business connections will relish the feeling of receiving a personalized letter. Nothing says care, concern, congratulations or contentedness like a letter, and that is something you can write home about.

TODAY'S ACTION ITEM

MAY 4

{ ARE YOU USING 'BAD WORDS' AT THE OFFICE? }

Do you remember learning about "bad words"? Just the thought of the term, which usually refers to language that parents classify as strictly off-limits, can conjure up negativity and memories of harsh reactions.

Word choice can often make a difference in business too – how or if decisions are made, if a sale is closed or not, or if someone chooses to take a job. If you're unsure about whether or not you're using "bad words," or even why they matter, here are some specific examples and slight changes in language that can have a more positive outcome:

Price vs. Investment: The term "price" seems harmless – and it is, most of the time. However, "price" can correlate to "cost," which is not always the most effective association. Replace it with "investment," which connotes trust and mutual benefit.

Contract vs. Agreement: The word "contract" implies there will be a lot of complicated verbiage and might involve attorneys. Use "agreement," which better reflects the attitudes of both parties and has more positive associations.

Objections vs. Areas of Concern: This example is simple: If you "object" to something, you're stating a direct opposition. Most conversations in business don't require such a staunch stance and would be better suited by expressing "areas of concern."

Cheap vs. Inexpensive: The common use of "cheap" in the workplace can have many subliminal connotations, ranging from "lemon" to "bargain" – none of which help in a conversation. The term "inexpensive" better bridges the cost gap and contrasts the term "expensive," which itself has ties with negative emotions.

TODAY'S ACTION ITEM

MAY 5

{ PEOPLE DON'T HAVE TO BE PERFECT }

Asking for help as a human being is hard. Asking for help as a business leader is even harder.

Why is that?

As leaders, we often have to bear the weight of perfection. However, the path towards ultimate perfection only leads to burnout because it's unachievable. The closest you will come to perfection is when everyone on your team is doing their very best, including you.

One of the easiest ways to start moving the needle on your goals is to delegate ancillary tasks that are preventing you from getting into deep, focused work. That said, delegating tasks is no easy feat. We feel tied to our work and gratified by our accomplishments. *How can anyone do it as well as I can? What if they make mistakes?* Surprise: they will! But training those around you to do more will ultimately benefit you and your company.

Be okay with less-than perfect. Perfection is rarely reached. The good news, it's rarely necessary and often subjective. Your team will never do it exactly as you would. That's okay. Your team members may even do it better than you did. That's great!

TODAY'S ACTION ITEM

{ 3 TIPS TO IMPROVE CASH FLOW MANAGEMENT }

Cash flow management. It's a safe bet those three words don't fuel your passion every day.

Take my advice: Start paying attention to how your company manages its precious cash.

As a business leader, it's virtually a given that you will encounter challenges managing cash. Here are three tips to help you manage your company's cash flow:

1. Create a cash flow forecast.
This is an indispensable tool for monitoring and predicting the flow of money moving in and out of your company's bank account. Build a week-by-week forecast to get a granular view of the cash needs of the business. The shorter the time horizon, the more accurate your forecast should be – and the better you will be able to identify potential obstacles that may impede the growth of your business.

2. Encourage honesty and accountability.
The most accurate cash flow forecasts are created when team members do not hold back information and freely share their predictions about how the company will perform in the future. Then hold everyone accountable, yourself included, to review the accuracy of the data used to create the forecast.

3. Include cash flow discussions during your daily huddle.
Include short updates and conversations about cash flow during your team's morning huddle. It's an efficient and effective way to cover an issue that affects the whole company.

Following these tips will ensure you have a better system in place to manage the financial needs of your company, which is always a key factor in growing a business.

TODAY'S ACTION ITEM

MAY 7

{ DECIDE TO BE DECISIVE }

Your business becomes the result of the decisions you as a manager or owner make. That being said, the best leaders must be equipped with one common strength – decisiveness.

Napoleon said, "Nothing is more difficult, and therefore more precious, than to be able to decide." I couldn't agree more. Decision-making is difficult and risky for a reason. You're responsible for not only the positive potential outcomes of the decision, but also the negative. You could potentially damage your or someone else's career, business or even life. With all that on the line, no wonder so many are trapped by indecision.

When you find yourself similarly stuck, remind yourself that there is something worse than making a poor decision – not making a decision at all. Theodore Roosevelt said it best: "In any moment of decision, the best thing you can do is the right thing, the next best thing is the wrong thing, and the worst thing you can do is nothing."

The most important thing is to keep the company moving forward and not obsess about making the perfect decision. Don't let paralysis by analysis take hold. Remember, when your team is in alignment, they will provide the necessary insight to keep the company on track.

TODAY'S ACTION ITEM

MAY 8

{ FINDING SO-CALLED "WORK-LIFE BALANCE" }

I've noted before that I believe the phrase "work-life balance" is illogical, since work is a part of life – but I do think it's important to have balance. Here are a few tactics that have helped me achieve better balance.

Chase purpose.
We feel satiated when we feel purposeful. If your job sucks your energy and drowns your passion, change it. We've all heard the saying, "If you love what you do, you'll never work a day in your life." Live that. Seek out meaningful opportunities that drive your enthusiasm.

Unplug.
Instead of constantly plugging into electronics, seek out experiences and activities. Strive to be ever-present while you engage in memory-making activities with your friends and family. No one has ever looked back and remembered the time they sat on the couch eating potato chips watching a CSI re-run.

Control your time.
If you don't, someone else will. You are the only one responsible for what you do with your time. If you don't believe this, you will continue to fall victim to others' demands. If it's essential, you will find the time, but if not, you'll find an excuse.

Plan your day ahead of time.
When interference comes knocking, ask yourself, is this going to matter a year from now? Chances are, probably not. Don't let the urgent get in the way of the important.

I guarantee you have enough time to accomplish way more than you think. The key is in maximizing that time. Always keep in mind that time is a non-renewable resource. We must spend it with purpose, plan and control.

TODAY'S ACTION ITEM

MAY 9

{ HOW TO HAND-PICK YOUR CLIENTS }

If you know exactly what you want, you increase the likelihood of getting exactly what you want.

The converse is also true.

If you don't know what you want, or what you're doing, you're likely to cast a wide net, cross your fingers and wait. When you're fishing, for example, this results in catching littered coke cans, old shoes and a few miscellaneous sea creatures, if you're lucky. If, instead, you know exactly what you want, you're likely to cast your net at dusk during low tide and skim the bottom near the shoreline. This preparedness drastically increases your odds in catching what you want – lots of good-sized shrimp.

The lesson: When you're fishing for clients, know what you want, or you could end up with a less-than-desirable catch.

Unfortunately, most businesses set themselves up to catch less-than-desirable clients. For instance, most businesses hand their sales reps a random list of prospects pulled from the phone book and send them out to sell. The goal is simply to catch something rather than catch the right thing, resulting in a mismatched and sparse client list and a frustrated team.

The solution: Prepare first. Build a "Dream List," which outlines the best clients for the company, so you know what you want to catch before you go fishing.

TODAY'S ACTION ITEM

{ PEOPLE CAN'T BE MOTIVATED, BUT THEY CAN BE INSPIRED }

Motivation is an interesting animal.

Business leaders rarely lack self-motivation, likely because of an innate entrepreneurial drive or "leadership mentality."

But because it comes so naturally to them, there can be a disconnect between leaders and their teams when they don't seem to have the same drive. In fact, one of the most common questions I receive from leaders is, "How do I motivate my team members?"

Imagine their surprise when they hear my answer, which is the same time and time again: "You can't."

As a business leader and coach, I help company leaders understand the reasons behind their personal motivation and how it aligns with the objectives of their businesses. An important realization for leaders is this: Your team members do not and will not share the same outlook or motivators that you do. So don't attempt to force a "why you should" statement or reasoning with your team.

Instead, inspire your team members to find their own motivation.

TODAY'S ACTION ITEM

MAY 11

{ LEADING WITH A GROWTH MINDSET}

As a leader, it's critical to adopt a growth mindset so you can give appropriate feedback to your team. That means believing you can rise to a challenge – and having the inner motivation to do so.

In other words, the first step is that you, as the leader, are not afraid to screw up.

If you are always worried about making mistakes, you will stay where you are comfortable instead of taking on new responsibilities and challenges. You will stop learning, and your productivity will decline. The negative attitude will spread to your team members. Eventually, everyone will feel anxiety and even burnout.

Instead, view new opportunities and risks with a desire to grow. Give yourself permission to learn, to take on new challenges and, yes, to fail. You will realize that, with effort and persistence, you can accomplish big goals. That, in turn, will give you more confidence and inspire enthusiasm in your team.

With a growth mindset, challenges are opportunities to tackle new things and develop new skills. There is energy and excitement as everyone works together to overcome difficulties. The team will be more confident because they will have a track record of taking on obstacles and succeeding.

This way of thinking can pervade your company's culture and influence the way everyone feels about the work they do. You will find that you have created a healthy environment of smart risk-takers who are more innovative, creative and productive.

TODAY'S ACTION ITEM

MAY 12

{ COMPLAIN UP }

"Gripes go up, not down."

In "Saving Private Ryan," Capt. Miller, played by Tom Hanks, explains this important lesson in leadership to Pvt. Reiben. Leaders can complain up to their superiors but not down to their followers.

Why?

Complaining to those around you or underneath you only accomplishes two things:

1. It undermines leadership efforts.
One of the main goals of leadership is gaining buy-in from colleagues. Constantly complaining about company issues or difficult clients only erodes your reputation as a leader who effectively handles and leads through challenges.

2. It makes you a gossip.
Authenticity is one of the most underrated traits of a leader and one that can be practiced in any situation, including conflict. When you come across an interpersonal challenge, deal with it tactfully in person, instead of waiting to gossip about it when they leave the room.

Complain to someone who can resolve the problem. Start setting this example now, and your peers will follow suit.

TODAY'S ACTION ITEM

MAY 13

{ 4 STEPS TO DELEGATING LIKE A PRO }

Being a great delegator takes time, commitment and consistency. Through the journey, remember: Your business cannot be great unless it can be great without you.

I learned how to excel at delegation through trial and error, counsel from fellow successful entrepreneurs and devouring dozens of books on the subject. Here are four steps I live by to delegate like a pro:

1. Make a list.
Jot down the responsibilities that someone else could do. If you're struggling, start by asking yourself, "What is the best and most effective use of my time in my business?" Once you've pinpointed this important activity, make a list of everything else on your to-do list that's not your primary task. Find a way to transfer these other tasks to team members.

2. Ask for help.
Let your team know why you need help, and then ask for volunteers rather than assigning the task. When you explain your reasoning, the team will better understand why their contribution is necessary, and they'll be able to select where they'd like to contribute, enabling them to perform better.

3. Communicate the task.
Once your task has an owner, make sure that person is set up for success by clearly defining the task, the expected end result and a deadline. Let your team members know you're there for any questions they may have along the way, but then remove yourself from the process.

4. Accept mistakes.
Your rock star team members will succeed most of the time, but understand that they will make mistakes and even fail sometimes. When they do fail, your goal is to help them move past it quickly. Don't allow the failure to crush the process.

TODAY'S ACTION ITEM

MAY 14

{ CREATING A BUSINESS STRATEGY }

A business plan is similar to a battle plan. With that in mind, a quote from Sun Tzu's *The Art of War* says it best: "Victorious warriors win first and then go to war, while defeated warriors go to war first and then seek to win." In other words, make sure your business has a plan before battle. If you need to spend an entire day preparing, do it. It could mean survival.

First, state your business strategy in one sentence. It's intimidating but essential. There are two ways you could come up with this sentence.

1. Think of your existing "big hairy audacious goal" (or BHAG) and core purpose. You created these by combining your top business goal and the "why" behind what you do. Including your "why" in your business strategy is how you make it matter to you.

2. Think of what you do that your competitors don't do, and base your one-sentence strategy on enhancing this unique quality.

You want it to be specific and succinct. Six to ten words is all you need. This is your battle doctrine. Are you ready for the fight?

TODAY'S ACTION ITEM

MAY 15

{ GETTING THE MOST
OUT OF IN-PERSON INTERVIEWS }

One of the most important parts of the hiring process is the in-person interview, so make sure you:

Start slow.
We've all been in the hot seat at one time or another and can appreciate some friendly small talk before the actual interview begins. Nervous applicants will relax and feel more comfortable opening up.

Bring a partner.
When two people conduct the interview, there are two sets of notes to reference and two different perspectives on the potential employee. This will help in the deliberation stage when one person is indecisive. Also, if there are two people listening, you're more likely to catch an applicant's inconsistencies or realize when things aren't adding up.

Ask for stories.
Questions that demand stories reveal context and show you how applicants approach problems. You'll also get a clearer picture of what exactly they did at their previous jobs.

Answer thoroughly and follow up.
An in-person interview is a two-way street and top talent will use this time to assess your company. Be honest about company struggles, issues previous employees may have faced and your company culture. If applicants know exactly what they are signing up for, they're less likely to be surprised or overwhelmed when they start the day-to-day work in their role.

Turnover is tough on the morale of your loyal employees. It's also a huge waste of time and resources, so make sure you make the most of the time spent hiring.

TODAY'S ACTION ITEM

MAY 16

{ BECOMING A "GREAT LEADER" }

I put it in quotes because it has become a cliche in the business world. However, I do believe that great leaders exist and that anyone can become one.

All it takes is a change of thinking and some focus.

If you're a blossoming leader striving to become one of the greats, the first thing you must do is check your humility and self-awareness. Set aside time to get honest with yourself and map out your strengths and weaknesses. Then establish ways to course correct. Accept that you won't always have the right answers, and welcome honest feedback.

Continue to ask yourself tough questions, such as "Is there anything I could be doing better?" or "Who can take these execution tasks off my plate, so I can focus on the big picture?" By continually making adjustments and checking improvement, you'll not only pay better attention to the road ahead but form a habit of honing your abilities to become a great leader.

Don't get sidetracked because of distractions or fear of the unknown. Defy the odds and become a truly great leader by planning ahead and tracking your progress along the way. One day, you'll be a source of inspiration for another leader heading out on the journey.

TODAY'S ACTION ITEM

MAY 17

{ MY SECRET TO NETWORKING EVENTS }

With social media networking literally at our fingertips, many of us don't get as much practice with traditional networking. Engaging with colleagues, business prospects and friends face-to-face requires different skills than online interactions.

For instance, you must think on your feet in a real-time networking scenario, while social media networking allows for some delay in between interactions. For example, someone may post on your Facebook wall, and you can respond hours later with a crafted response. But to have any amount of non-response or quiet time in a face-to-face networking session? Awkward.

Further, traditional networking requires you to translate social cues and control your own simultaneously. In social media networking, all you have is words. The complexities of tone and body language can't be fulfilled with emoticons.

With digital interactions now occurring more regularly than in-person exchanges, many of us need to brush up on our traditional networking skills, but that can be an overwhelming task.

To calm your nerves at your next networking event, **lend a helping hand.**

Instead of focusing on how connections can help you, discover ways you can help your new acquaintances. In a world where many are focused on self-glorification, finding ways to bolster others is refreshing and appreciated. Ask, "What can I do for you?" If people are talking passionately about an industry hot topic, tell them about a blog post you recently read on the subject and offer to email the link. Once you follow through in the coming days, you'll show that you're reliable and thoughtful. Plus, by extending the conversation past the networking event, you've deepened your connection.

TODAY'S ACTION ITEM

MAY 18

{ IMPROVE YOUR TRUTH-TELLING SKILLS }

Guest contribution from Petra Coach Greg Eisen

We've all heard the expressions. "The truth shall set you free" (John 8:32). "The truth is rarely pure and never simple" (Oscar Wilde). "The truth hurts" (everyone).

Unfortunately, accepting the truth is easier said than done. People tend to prefer justifying daily mistruths rather than challenging them. Many simply avoid confrontation out of fear of making others uncomfortable or feeling uncomfortable themselves.

However, the truth doesn't have to hurt. In fact, the truth may just be the competitive advantage your organization needs. Instead of simply accepting existing behavior, you can realize major gains by directly addressing the truth and building an organizational culture that does the same.

Don't be afraid to put it all out there, but maybe do it tactfully.

When sharing something difficult, put the positive before the negative. Studies show that although you may feel better when you get good news last, you are more motivated to do something about the bad news when you get the bad news last.

Improved development and long-term results almost always trump instant gratification.

As a coach, many of my business communications revolve around the tough and sometimes awkward task of telling the truth, but that's the only way that the teams I coach can improve.

If you can muster up enough courage to tell your employees, colleagues, family and friends the truth, you'll have taken the first big step toward improving your relationships for the better.

TODAY'S ACTION ITEM

MAY 19

{ STOP DISAPPOINTING YOURSELF }

For many, it's become too easy to give up on a goal halfway through – or worse, never even get started.

Why? The answer is simple, yet troubling: As humans, we've become okay with disappointing ourselves.

If you want to take your life or your business to the next level, you've got to end the cycle of self-disappointment, make yourself a priority and follow through on your goals.

You made a choice to change something. Great, but why did you make that choice? If you're going to put in the effort to reach a goal, you've got to know why it's important to you and what the consequences will be if you don't achieve it.

As a leader, think about what you're modeling for your employees. Like the "put on your mask before assisting others" principle on an airplane, be the example for your team members by planning and following through on your own goals first. If your team sees you doing it, they'll be more likely to imitate that behavior and adopt it as part of the company culture.

This is also a way to set up a system of accountability, a crucial element of the Rockefeller Habits and something I discuss regularly with my member companies. If you've gotten in the habit of making plans and setting goals in private – and then not achieving them – it's time to go public.

You deserve better than to disappoint yourself. It's the worst kind of failure really, because you're letting down the person who should be most central to your life: you.

TODAY'S ACTION ITEM

MAY 20
{ FACING THE FEAR }

"Will my business survive an economic downturn?"
"Will my customers abandon me if I change course?"

These are common questions every entrepreneur asks themselves. However, it's how you react to that question that is the difference. Some of us will work through those initial fears, but others will be overcome by and surrender to those fears – and that's no way to run a business.

Here are three ways to move through it and make the best decisions for your business:

1. Do a cost/benefit analysis.
It's the oldest trick in the book, and you probably did it growing up: Make a list with two columns – one that includes your fears (the costs and everything you think could go wrong) and the other with benefits (everything you could gain and think could go right). This exercise will help you avoid surrendering to fear at the outset and make a decision based on facts, rather than fear.

2. Find your Spock and McCoy.
Any classic Star Trek fan will remember that whenever Captain Kirk had to make a decision, he always gathered his two most trusted advisors, Dr. McCoy and Mr. Spock. Find the members of your team who will help you see the full spectrum of any situation. Listen to them, and make decisions accordingly.

3. Trust but verify.
When Ronald Reagan spoke about his decision-making process around the nuclear arms policy and the United States' relationship with the then Soviet Union, he took a balanced approach. He said he would "trust" that the Soviets would abide by any agreement, "but verify" that they were indeed complying and were holding up their side of the bargain.

TODAY'S ACTION ITEM

MAY 21

{ GOALS ANYTIME OF YEAR }

There is nothing special about January 1st. There, I said it. Now we can get past it.

Setting good goals depends on you, not the date of the year. Now that we're a little ways into the year, ask yourself: Did I set quality professional and personal goals that, if I work at them, I can achieve this year? If you didn't, consider these steps below to help you set new, quality goals no matter how many weeks we are into the new year.

1. Ask yourself, "why?"
The process should have started at the end of last year with self-reflection, but there is no better method for jumpstarting reflection in a moment's notice than by asking "why?" Think about any unmet goals from last year (i.e. lost revenue, hiring processes, effectiveness of leadership, etc.), and then identify why those problem areas fell short of success. Don't stop at the easy answers either. Dig deep and unearth the real factors behind issues, even (and especially) if they are hard.

2. Make sure your goals are S.M.A.R.T.
Even if you've already created New Year's resolutions, for yourself or your business, you need to make sure there is a plan for achieving them. In other words, your goals should be S.M.A.R.T. – specific, measurable, attainable, relevant and time-bound.

TODAY'S ACTION ITEM

MAY 22

{ HEALTHY COMMUNICATION = HEALTHY TEAM }

Most business leaders have seen their fair share of healthy teams and unhealthy teams. As a business leader, it's your responsibility to create a healthy work environment that retains and attracts talented team members and maximizes their productivity. The cost of having an unhealthy work environment is astonishing.

Building a healthy team requires a deep commitment. But if you follow these three steps, you'll find your team members will become emotionally and physically stronger and will be in the right shape to help you achieve your company's goals.

1. Communication is vital.
Get into a regular meeting rhythm and keep the lines of communication open to ensure everyone is engaged, informed, and aligned.

2. A daily huddle increases engagement and alignment.
In his breakthrough book *Mastering the Rockefeller Habits,* Verne Harnish describes how John D. Rockefeller held team meetings every day for 19 years while he built Standard Oil into an energy colossus. Daily huddles allow team members to share what's going on in their lives, personally and professionally.

3. Have weekly, monthly and quarterly meetings with your team.
In addition to helping everyone stay on track to meet the business's goals and objectives, there's another important benefit: The rhythm of regular meetings benefits team members by reinforcing the need to stay engaged collectively and, just as importantly, support each other when challenges arise.

TODAY'S ACTION ITEM

MAY 23

{ COMMUNICATE POSITIVELY, NOT PASSIVELY }

Business leaders should use language that affirms positive outcomes. Think about the subtle difference between the words "I am" and "I will be." The former puts you in the mindset of already achieving what you want, while the latter implies something you will do in the future. Be mindful of how you express yourself.

Boxing legend Muhammad Ali is famous for saying, among other phrases, "I am the greatest!" I'm confident that you'll agree: "I will be the greatest" just doesn't pack the same punch.

The same goes when you are talking to your team members about your company. "We will be a great team" falls flat compared to "We are a great team."

When you're talking to team members, clients or even prospective clients, have a clear vision of what you want to accomplish and what you want the result to be.

Using language that affirms positive outcomes will also benefit those around you. It helps motivate, inspire and create a positive energy.

TODAY'S ACTION ITEM

MAY 24

{ WHAT UGANDA TAUGHT ME }

After learning about significant technology shortcomings affecting some business owners in Uganda, my company embarked on an initiative to address the issue.

We felt compelled to assist these Ugandan business owners because helping businesses succeed is what we do. From a big-picture view, we know that helping small businesses succeed in a developing economy has ramifications that extend far beyond the success of individual companies.

See, this big picture inspired us to act – but actually making something happen required thinking on a smaller, more tactical scale. It required us to think about who, specifically, we could enlist to help us make this happen and how exactly we were going to do it. That is, we had to map out the incremental steps toward attaining our goal.

First, we enlisted the support of friends and colleagues, which is a relatively easy pitch because we were relying on personal relationships.

The next step was to ask our network of companies we coach to donate small amounts of money. In this case, though a personal relationship was involved, the importance of the cause also played a role. The results were astounding. Many of our member companies pitched in, and together we raised enough money to purchase 20 computers for Ugandan businesses.

There's a business lesson here. Can you spot it?

Incremental steps bring about big results over time. Same in business: Success is often a culmination of small accomplishments over an extended period, and it requires an unrelenting commitment to reaching a goal and the patience to be satisfied with incremental change instead of dramatic, overnight results.

TODAY'S ACTION ITEM

MAY 25

{ HIRE SMART BY PROMOTING WITHIN }

A strong hiring culture sets your company up with top talent and engaged team members. Before you post the next job opening on LinkedIn, though, take a look at your roster of current team members.

One of the main reasons to consider promoting from within is a healthier bottom line.

In a 2012 study published in Administrative Sciences Quarterly, Wharton Assistant Professor Matthew Bidwell found that external hires were paid 18 percent more than internal team members in the same job position. Why? Because they have nothing to lose by "naming their price" for a new opportunity.

For money-conscious employers, this is a problem. Plus, hiring an external applicant has a lower success rate than hiring someone already working at your company, as detailed in Development Dimensions International's white paper, "The Case for Internal Promotions." Bottom line: the gamble doesn't pay off.

Outside hires also can be a drain on the time and energy of a team. They must be trained on everything from how to make copies to how to follow existing workflows and protocols correctly. Once trained, they must do it enough times to get comfortable (and make their superiors feel comfortable). It takes time.

Promoting a person who is already familiar with the feel of the office and company procedures will make the transition considerably smoother.

TODAY'S ACTION ITEM

MAY 26

{ LEADING LIKE A BUSINESS COACH }

When I meet with a team for a coaching session, I often find that everyone looks to me for all the answers. While I am there to help them get their priorities together and align their business and company culture, I'm NOT there to hold their hand through every decision that needs to be made. That's where the team leaders come in.

I look at my job as the "teach a man to fish" principle: I teach them how to think like I do, so they can continue to have insightful and productive conversations when I'm not there.

Here are two key characteristics of a business coach that all leaders can and should adopt.

Listening: A big part of my job is listening to my member companies – the good stuff and the bad. The only way I can help people improve is by knowing what works well and what their pain points are. Don't immediately start problem-solving your way out of the conversation or you'll miss what's truly important.

Looking for weaknesses: Once I've heard about the issues a company is having, I can start to figure out where they are stemming from. As leaders, we sometimes want to ignore weaknesses and problems because, frankly, it can be tough to admit they exist and that you may hold some or all responsibility for them. But that's how a leader can push his or her company forward – by taking a high-level view and objectively finding the areas that need to be improved.

TODAY'S ACTION ITEM

MAY 27

{ APPLYING THE LAW OF ATTRACTION IN BUSINESS: WHAT DO I WANT? }

The Law of Attraction – the belief that positive thoughts attract positive outcomes and negativity begets negative outcomes – has gotten a lot of attention in recent years. Some people don't believe it exists, while others swear by its effectiveness. Whichever camp you're in, there are lessons business leaders can apply to both their personal and professional lives.

Some of the biggest successes in business, politics, sports and entertainment credit the Law of Attraction for their success. As legendary basketball player Michael Jordan once put it when he described his view on thinking positively, "You must expect great things of yourself before you can do them." As a business leader, you have to envision yourself in the place you want to be before you can get there.

There are a lot of different ways to put the Law of Attraction to work for you, your company, employees and clients, but it starts with the one question every business leader must answer: *What do I truly want?*

You need to be specific about what you want so you can figure out how to get there. Do you want to find your next great hire? Do you want to grow your business 20 percent by year's end?

Hyper-focusing your mind on the answer to that question will set you on a course, consciously and subconsciously, to making things happen, and it'll allow you to tap into a new way of thinking that will benefit you both professionally and personally.

TODAY'S ACTION ITEM

MAY 28

{ LEADING TYPE-A PERSONALITIES }

When my business coaching team gets together for our annual planning session it's an opportunity for us to practice what we preach, taking the time to tell each other the truth, get all our issues out on the table and set goals for the quarter and coming year.

To do this, I've had to learn how to cut through the egos and the expectations to run an efficient and effective planning day.

The most important advice I can give is to listen. That's all.

It sounds so simple, but it can be very difficult for people who are used to running things to begin by listening.

As a leader, the best thing you can do is listen and not respond until the other person is finished. Coaches and CEOs alike have a tendency to want to "get in there" and problem-solve. There's a time for that, but if we don't start by really hearing the other person and thinking about what we're being told, we won't get very far.

Then it's time to tear things down and build them back up.

That means stepping back and looking at what was done in the past and asking, "Is this really the best way?" Find all the things that are not working or could go wrong, and shine a light on them.

Once there is a new plan in place that feels right, it's time to solidify it and put in the work to make it happen. Systems and people can always improve.

TODAY'S ACTION ITEM

MAY 29

{ WHY YOU NEED A BAG }

How cool would it be to be able to call your competitor and ask them what level of inventory they keep in a certain product area, or how much they expect a salesperson to produce in a given period, or if they were looking at any new solutions to add to their offerings next year? How cool would it be if you could do this with multiple competitors?

You can, and you should. But likely not how you may think.

If you are making strategic decisions of any kind in a business, you need to get input beyond just your four walls. Some of the best input can be from a business advisory group or BAG. There are three main kinds:

Industry-specific: This type of BAG allows you to take a very broad view on an organization, yet dig deep where it's needed. The key is to ensure non-competing markets so everyone is comfortable with sharing genuinely.

Role-specific: If you sit in a certain seat in an organization, like CFO or marketing director, there are hundreds of other people right in your town who have the same role, albeit at different businesses. Gathering a group of six to 10 like-minded professionals who have similar challenges can be a powerful tool for you in your role.

Leadership-specific: Much like the role-specific BAG, the leadership BAG should consist of similar leaders from a variety of businesses. If you operate a $10 million business with 75 team members and are in your 50s, build a group of people in similar situations so that they understand where you are in life.

TODAY'S ACTION ITEM

MAY 30

{ BALANCE HOME & WORK LIFE BY HITTING THE RESET BUTTON }

The end of the school year is often a big deal if you have children. But I remember one year vividly: The time when my youngest daughter would be heading to high school and my oldest would be starting her senior year.

In our family, summer is a time to slow down and reset. This summer, stop and examine your life and yourself, both personally and professionally, on a regular basis. It's hard to pour your energy into both sides because if you're just simply going through the motions for either, you're likely to accomplish nothing.

At my company, we have programs in place that help the entire team reset. Every two weeks, team members meet one-on-one with their adviser to talk about personal and professional highs and lows, ways they can improve, how the company can help them and the most important tasks to complete over the next two weeks.

You might be thinking, "I don't have time," or "We can't schedule another meeting." Stop making excuses. Your team members are too important. One powwow every other week helps you share wins, troubleshoot challenges, build trust and provide a safe and consistent space for your team members to be heard.

It's all about finding purpose and being intentional at home and at work, which can be hard. Balancing both at the same time can feel impossible. But your success and, more importantly, your fulfillment in both depend on it.

TODAY'S ACTION ITEM

MAY 31

{ CHOOSING A QUARTERLY THEME }

One part of any company's planning session is determining the organization's "quarterly theme." After a long day of discussing the upcoming quarter, talking business and setting personal and professional goals, team members come together to agree on one overarching theme that will carry them through the quarter and help them achieve their chosen goals.

Here are three steps for a successful quarterly theme:

1. Compete for your theme.
What's better than a friendly competition? Divide the members of your team into two groups – or more, if needed. Taking one of the main company objectives, each team will develop a fun way to track progress toward the goal. Then, come together as a company and have each team present its idea to the group as a whole and have everyone vote on it.

2. Make clear goals with measurable results.
As you develop your theme or challenge, make decisions about how you'll measure success. What does a "win" look like, and what are the steps you need to take to get there? Make sure it's clear to everyone how they can succeed and that expectations are realistic.

3. Reward yourself!
Any good challenge – when achieved – deserves a reward! Sure, bragging rights are fun, but people like to celebrate success. Decide what might be a fun prize to motivate team members through the tough times, and reward them at the finish line.

TODAY'S ACTION ITEM

JUNE

{ VITAMIN B-6 }

*Some vitamins, like B-6, have a variety of functions.
While your body needs this vitamin to wear many hats,
your company does not necessarily need the same from you.
Focus in on your biggest priorities this month,
and delegate the others.*

JUNE 1

{ WHAT ARE YOU READING RIGHT NOW? }

I like to start my business coaching sessions by asking a question to the group. The question varies from session to session, but lately, I've been getting great responses from "What are you reading right now?"

It's a simple question that can be answered quickly, and I can tell a lot about the individuals in the room from their responses: what topics interest them, whether they like fiction or nonfiction or if they even read at all.

Regardless of the specific question, the best responses open up a dialogue among team members that never would have happened otherwise. After about five minutes, every member of the organization knows something about their teammate that they didn't know when they arrived that day.

Open conversation is at the heart of healthy workplace communication. It's crucial for a team to work well together. After all, how can you really know what people are interested in or capable of unless you ask and give them the opportunity to show you?

One simple question is all you need to begin a conversation. Don't start out by asking questions so deep or probing that you catch your team members off guard, and definitely don't talk about work. Questions like, "What are you reading?" or "What music do you like?" are great places to start.

Small talk, if you do it right, can yield big results.

TODAY'S ACTION ITEM

JUNE 2

{ CAN YOU HANDLE THE TRUTH? }

If you're a CEO or business owner, it all starts with you. But, big egos and tunnel vision can cause leaders to think they've got all the answers. They dictate terms to their employees and expect them to fall in line – all the while in total denial of the bad example they're setting. As a result, many companies find that real honesty has left the workplace – to the detriment of the workforce at large.

Just to be clear, we're not talking about "brutal honesty" – which is really just an excuse to be insensitive due to lacking communication skills. I'm talking about being genuine, saying what you mean, meaning what you say and embracing the truth about yourself and other people.

We've all got blind spots. They are the things we ignore – either because we don't think they exist or because we choose to act like they don't.

Are you terrible at spreadsheets and yet still insist you handle the company's finances? Are you perpetually late, but insist on handling your own calendar? Guess what? You've got blind spots.

Other people have more insight into you than you realize, and they can see things that you might never see – both the good and the bad.

Surround yourself with truth-tellers. Make sure the people around you aren't just "yes" people.

"The truth" is we've all got room to grow. There are lessons we can learn from other people, and the seed of our next "big idea" might be planted by someone else.

TODAY'S ACTION ITEM

JUNE 3

{ IT'S OKAY TO FAIL }

I struggled with delegating for many years. When I started my first company, I was convinced I was the only person who could effectively accomplish any given task. In my defense, it wasn't because I thought I was smarter than everyone else, it was because I started the business, developed all of its processes and helped it grow. It was my baby. I knew all the ins and outs.

As my business grew, I started to hire smart, engaging, responsible, passionate employees who I knew could help me scale. But, as it became evident that I had too much on my plate, I still had a difficult time letting these brilliant people lend me a hand.

One of the things I've come to know to be true about delegating: It will make you and your team better, stronger and more efficient.

Isn't that what every team craves?

Don't let your fear of perfectionism hold you back today. I know how difficult it is to start, but I promise it's worth it.

Accept mistakes.

Your rock star team members will succeed most of the time. But, understand they will make mistakes and even fail sometimes. If they don't, you're not pushing them to grow. When they do fail, your goal is to help them move past it quickly. Don't allow the failure to crush the process.

TODAY'S ACTION ITEM

JUNE 4

{ 5 STEPS TO SOLID DECISION-MAKING }

As a business leader, the buck stops with you when it comes to making decisions. Becoming a better decision maker requires discipline and the wherewithal to form and stick to good habits. Here are five steps that I follow to become a more effective leader and decision maker:

Step one: Understand what you want to achieve.
Whether you're choosing where you want to eat lunch or how you want to grow your business, know what you want. Your underlying goals will guide your decisions.

Step two: Consider the paths.
Multiple roads can lead you to the same destination but will have different obstacles along the way. Contemplate the different paths, so you're well aware of your options. This process should include research, recalling past experiences and applying existing data.

Step three: Choose.
You've decided what you want, you know the different ways of getting it and you've done your research – so be confident and choose.

Step four: Rally the troops.
Present your ideas to your team and get them on board. Make it a conversation. If you had to make a decision without their input or because the team couldn't agree, fill them in on the circumstances, the options and your thought process.

Step five: Follow through and track your decision.
Jumpstart the decision by making a plan and gaining the agreement of your team members to take ownership of that plan. Once the plan is in action, you must monitor progress and effectiveness.

TODAY'S ACTION ITEM

JUNE 5

{ THE MYTH OF THE "JACK OF ALL TRADES" }

In the book *Uncommon Service,* authors Anne Morriss and Frances Frei assert, "Striving for all-around excellence leads directly to mediocrity."

There's just no way to be excellent in every single category without something breaking down. It's just a fact of life.

Morriss and Frei go on to say that true "excellence requires underperforming on your weaknesses, so you can over-perform on your strengths." It means using your talents, tools and energy to make a small number of specific things so awesome, that your weaknesses don't even matter.

In his talk "The Freak Factor," Dave Rendall uses the example of a hotel chain that has chosen to forego some of the common "luxury" hotel experiences and focus on its standard services that are used most often by guests.

For instance, rather than offering room service OR quick-service meals, and doing both well but not immaculately, it offers only "fresh, on-the-go" meals, putting a ton of energy and resources into making them the best. Most guests don't mind much that there's no room service available because the quick service food that's available is excellent and just as accessible.

Any business can take a note out of this company's book. Pinpoint your company's top strength and hit it out of the park with that aspect. You'll find that you can serve your clients better too.

After all, as Peter Drucker puts it, "Organizations exist to make people's strengths effective and their weaknesses irrelevant." How can you maximize your clients' strengths if you're not doing the same with your own?

TODAY'S ACTION ITEM

JUNE 6

{ PREPARING YOUR TEAM FOR BATTLE }

There are typically 60 workdays in a quarter. If your team members work eight hours a day, 40 a week (though, who works 40 hours anymore… more like 60+ isn't it?), that's 480 hours per person per quarter to get things done. It's important that your team members are using that time efficiently and doing things correctly. Here's how:

Start with making sure everyone knows the company's business strategy. Once you've established the strategic theme of your business plan, break out some tasks that team members can own.

When the tasks are outlined, follow these steps to make sure they are completed:

1. Each task should be stated in a way that makes sense to the whole company, and there should be a way to track the progress of completion. It should also have an owner – someone responsible for seeing it through, whether or not that same person actually does the task. These are essential benchmarks that will ensure you and your team are on the same page.

2. Assign due dates. No, it's not micromanaging; it's accountability. Your team will appreciate your clarity and feel extra pressure to complete their tasks.

3. Consider each team member's strengths, and use them to your advantage. I'm constantly shocked at how many businesses don't utilize this secret weapon. How do you feel when you are given an assignment that you have an interest in and know you are good at? Yeah, that's what I thought.

When your entire team is involved in and working on the business, everyone will have a stake in seeing it grow.

TODAY'S ACTION ITEM

JUNE 7

{ DO YOU NEED A 'DEVICE DETOX'? }

Like most business leaders, I have a tight schedule and need to stay connected to my gadgets (smartphones, laptops, tablets) to get work done. But what happens when those gadgets make their way into our personal lives? Is that call or email really so important that you miss out on what's right in front of you?

On one trip to New York I got a reminder of what's really important. During that trip – which I took with my two daughters – we stopped at a restaurant. Seated right next to us was another father and his daughter. For the entire meal (or at least until we finished up and paid the check), these two just scrolled through their phones as if the other was not even there. Now, I don't know who they were or what they might have been facing that morning, but it was a big reminder for me, nonetheless, to be present and take advantage of the time I have with the people I love.

If you're a parent, remember that we only have our kids for a little while. In every moment I get with my kids, I seriously do my best to focus on just them. It makes a difference – for them and for me. The same goes for our aging parents and our dearest friends.

I am not perfect by far, but I work very hard to create purposeful moments with the people I care about. Put away the cell phone. Shut down the email for a while. What may feel urgent at the time is not that important, and the people closest to you are watching.

TODAY'S ACTION ITEM

JUNE 8

{ THINK LIKE A BANKER }

Here's a new twist on how to view your business: Look at it through the lens of a banker. Yes, I realize that's an unusual way to look at your company, but bear with me.

As your business scales up, there will come a time when you need to borrow money to invest in new equipment or software or hire additional sales and marketing team members. In *Scaling Up*, Verne Harnish notes that thinking about your business like that will prepare you, so the bankers won't have the upper hand in negotiations.

There's another important benefit: You will gain a better understanding of the financial performance of your business. Banks are notoriously risk-averse and will not make a loan that they anticipate could default, regardless if it's guaranteed. Period. End of discussion.

Bankers will analyze your business's cash flow to make sure you can repay the loan. They will look at how future profits may be affected by potential risks inherent in your business, your industry and the overall economy. They will leave no stone unturned when reviewing the bankability of your business.

Building a profitable, thriving business requires knowing how to manage your company's finances. Thinking like a banker will provide you the knowledge (and experience) to know how to invest your cash where it will provide the highest return on investment.

TODAY'S ACTION ITEM

JUNE 9

{ LEADERSHIP DO'S AND DON'TS }

As a serial entrepreneur, I spend the majority of my time coaching other entrepreneurs and business leaders on how to grow dynamic businesses that focus on people, planning, processes and profit.

One of the topics I often speak about is leadership. Regardless of what you have been told, leaders are not born, they are made. Anyone can lead – you just need to know how and how not to lead.

Here are the two do's and don'ts that are most important for leading your business:

- **DO hire well.**
  Hire slow and fire fast. Understand what you are looking for in a new hire, including character, capability and involvement. If you don't have the right team members, you cannot entrust them with important tasks that are vital to growing your business.

- **DON'T micromanage your business.**
  This goes back to showing others how to lead. If you want your organization to thrive without your continuous personal involvement, you must develop leaders. Then, you need to have faith in them to get the job done.

TODAY'S ACTION ITEM

JUNE 10

{ 3 TIPS TO ACHIEVE PERSONAL GOALS AT HOME }

Ready to set personal goals and encourage family members to do the same? Because of the way I coach businesses every day, it's no mystery that my habits and methods have rubbed off on the people inside my home.

If the idea of having everyone in your family set – and meet – personal goals seems daunting, don't worry. With just a little effort, you can help your loved ones achieve great things. Here are three tips to adopt goalkeeping at home:

1. Dig deep.
Identify things you'd like to work on, hobbies that you'd like to take up or something you'd like to learn. If you don't have any emotional connection to your goal, you won't be motivated to achieve it. Ask yourself what it would look like if you could achieve it and how you would feel once you made that goal a reality.

2. Get real.
Once you've found out what you want, make sure that your timeframe to achieve it is realistic. Don't start with a "climbing Mt. Everest" goal, or you could be setting yourself up for failure. Smaller, measurable goals will always trump lofty, never-ending dream goals.

3. Plan it.
Break down the necessary steps to achieve each of your goals, and make a timeline specifying when you'll complete each step. Share your timeline with your family members to help keep you accountable and stick to it.

By taking the time to focus on you, and encouraging loved ones to focus on themselves, your personal time will be that much richer – and more productive.

TODAY'S ACTION ITEM

JUNE 11

{ COMPANY CULTURE IS ROOTED IN PURPOSE AND VALUES }

Guest contribution from Petra Coach David Pierce

Your company's culture is rooted in two things: your core purpose and core values.

Your core purpose speaks to why you exist as a business – why do you matter to the rest of the world? If your core purpose is understood and alive in your culture, it will motivate everyone in the company to be more engaged and willing to do whatever it takes to fulfill that purpose and reach beyond it.

Your core values are the set of rules by which you run your business. They are the principles on which your business stands and operates in order to fulfill the company purpose. Core values can come directly from the company's founder or can be created as a team.

Just like parents teach values to their children so they'll make the right decisions when they are on their own, a company's core values empower employees with a set of "rules" by which they can make decisions on behalf of the company.

Core values are used to hire and fire employees, and they attract the right kind of customers who share your company's values. When team members and partners believe in and live out your company's core purpose and core values, you can conquer the world.

TODAY'S ACTION ITEM

JUNE 12

{ THINK OUTSIDE OF YOUR WALLS TO GROW YOUR BUSINESS }

Leadership has its own set of challenges, and to be good at it you had better invest time and energy in personal improvement.

The best place to actively learn from the mistakes of others is in a BAG, or business advisory group. Never heard of it? Review May 28 for different types of these groups and which one may be the best fit for you.

Once you're ready to get started, here are my top tips for making the investment worth your time:

1. Create rules.
First, create your group "constitution," which will be your operating agreement. It sets up all the rules of how you will act, what you will do and what happens if someone doesn't follow these rules. Remember, you'll be sharing information that, if not held in confidence, could damage businesses and potentially lives, so get this right. Only allow people to participate who agree and will abide by these rules.

2. Create rhythms.
I suggest you set your meeting schedule as far in advance as possible and potentially schedule them to recur on the same day, like the third Thursday of each month or in person once a quarter and via Skype monthly. Do what you feel is needed to create the greatest benefit without making too heavy of a burden.

3. Create agendas.
In order to make the most of everyone's time, always have an agenda and strictly adhere to it. Distribute it prior to the meetings, so that everyone is prepared. Oh, and start and end on time – always!

TODAY'S ACTION ITEM

JUNE 13

{ DEFINING SUCCESS}

As you've probably noticed, I'm all in when it comes to personal and professional growth. I encourage everyone to create and stick to new habits that will improve your life.

That said, we all need reminders to keep us moving forward. Here's a simple checklist I keep handy to remind myself about the difference between successful and unsuccessful people:

Successful	Unsuccessful
Want others to succeed	Secretly hope others fail
Keep a journal	Say they keep a journal but don't
Accept responsibility for their failures	Blame others for their failures
Compliment	Criticize
Operate from a transformational perspective	Operate from a transactional perspective
Forgive others	Hold a grudge
Exude joy	Exude anger
Embrace change	Fear change
Read every day	Watch TV every day
Talk about ideas	Talk about people
Give other people credit for their victories	Take all the credit for their victories
Keep a "to-be" list	Don't know what they want to be
Set goals & develop life plans	Never set goals
Share info and data	Hoard info and data
Continuously learn	Fly by the seat of their pants

Which column are you in?

TODAY'S ACTION ITEM

JUNE 14
{ THINK BIG! }

What's the fundamental difference between an entrepreneur who is simply self-employed and one who wants to build a larger business? It's a question I get asked frequently. Here's my standard answer: Entrepreneurs think big. I mean really big.

Most business owners think in terms of, "How do I double my business?" Entrepreneurs think much bigger. It's what Jim Collins (author of *Good To Great* and *Built To Last*) calls "10X" thinking – or building a company to support 10X growth.

I know businesses that have grown from a card table to $100 million and then crumbled because the owners did not think big enough to build a structure to support growth. Then they restarted, focused on building the foundation to support the company when it's larger, and they were successful. This starting, stopping and restarting process is obviously much more painful than thinking big at the onset.

This concept applies to all business leaders at companies large and small, not just entrepreneurs. Think bigger than you are now, and create systems and processes to support bigger. You'll blaze new trails for yourself and your company!

TODAY'S ACTION ITEM

JUNE 15

{ MAKE IT A DATE }

Before you commit to a relationship, you date.

Dating allows for discovery. Is this person who he or she claims to be? Could I see myself with this person long-term? Are we a good pair?

The same commitment-free discovery process should be permissible in business. Woo your clientele by offering a money-back guarantee.

If a client comes to you and is completely dissatisfied, you'd give that client a refund, right? My suggestion is to use this to your advantage, and offer the guarantee upfront. This gets customers in the door.

Most clients are forced to marry their service provider before they date. Understandably, it's this front-end commitment that scares away prospective clients. When you offer a money-back guarantee, clients can date you and then decide if they want to seal the deal. With this commitment-free atmosphere, customers will be saying, "Why not? If nothing else, I'll get a free meal."

Test it out and see what you think. And let's face it – once they go on a date with you and see all you have to offer, they'll never leave your side.

TODAY'S ACTION ITEM

JUNE 16

{ PROMOTING = POSITIVITY }

I'm a big fan of promoting from within the company because it tends to help maintain a positive team.

In a company known for promoting from within, team members will work harder and presumably more efficiently to earn a promotion.

Offer professional development opportunities and constructive feedback at annual reviews. Let them know where they are and where you see them headed. Providing career growth opportunities will give them a reason to stay engaged and have a purpose at work.

In his book *Drive*, Daniel Pink says, "One source of frustration in the workplace is the frequent mismatch between what people must do and what people can do. When what they must do exceeds their capabilities, the result is anxiety. When what they must do falls short of their capabilities, the result is boredom. But when the match is just right, the results can be glorious."

Keep a temperature reading on your team and adjust. It's possible someone is already gunning for the next step or a new promotion, and it's a great idea to encourage that enthusiasm and drive.

TODAY'S ACTION ITEM

JUNE 17

{ WE ALL NEED A SHORT MEMORY }

In his hit song "Red Ragtop," Tim McGraw sings, "I can't remember who I was back then." I heard it on the radio the other day and it made me realize – I have a very short memory.

Sure, I vividly remember the important parts of my life – starting my own business, getting married and having my children. But the things I can't remember very well? The not-so-good times.

Having the ability to forget allows me to move forward without being hung up on the mistakes and failures in my past. Here are four tips to do it successfully.

1. Learn from your mistakes and applaud them.
The best lessons usually take place at the worst times. Setbacks give you an opportunity to grow stronger and improve. It's fine to fail sometimes; just keep pushing forward with the new knowledge you acquired. Innovativeness should be commended, not shamed.

2. Remind yourself that your successes are far more notable than your failures.
Unless you veer off the rails and do something senseless, people will forgive your failures and only recall the positive work you do. Accept that mistakes will happen, and let go of the negative energy.

3. Don't worry about what other people think of you.
Don't be ashamed about failure, and don't worry about how other people will see you because of it. Instead of spending time agonizing over how you're being perceived, use that time to think about how you can do things differently next time.

4. Openly discuss your wins and losses.
You are not alone in this ride. Business leaders everywhere experience very similar degrees of pain and cheer. When you share and listen to others, you'll quickly discover that you're going to be just fine.

TODAY'S ACTION ITEM

JUNE 18

{ DON'T LET YOUR SWOT ANALYSIS BECOME STAGNANT }

A lot of business leaders do a SWOT (strengths, weaknesses, opportunities and threats) analysis for their company and then stick it in a drawer or file it away on their hard drive and never use it because they don't know – or they don't take the time – to figure out how to put it to work.

Your SWOT analysis and process should be ongoing. At our company, we have a set of strengths, and we look for potential priorities every quarter to protect them. We have a set of weaknesses and we look for potential priorities in the quarter that can help eliminate them.

We have opportunities – those things we want to achieve long-term – that need to be prioritized, monitored and measured, so we know when we're closing in on and taking advantage of them. The same thing goes for threats – we select one each quarter and work toward mitigating it.

Every quarter we revisit our company's SWOT and ask questions such as, "Is this still a strength or is something else more of a strength today? Is this still an opportunity or has another one taken its place?" SWOT becomes a living document we use to make effective, pragmatic decisions for our dynamic and growing company.

This approach helps our company avoid the two barriers that often prevent a business from growing: people and processes. By using the SWOT to plan ahead we are able to chart the right course, hire the right people and put in place the right processes to achieve our goals.

TODAY'S ACTION ITEM

JUNE 19

{ FROM BISCUITS TO THE BOARDROOM }

Twice a year, I gather with some of the greatest thought leaders in business strategy, leadership and improvement at the ScaleUp Summit. Great ideas abound, and I always come away from it feeling energized and ready to share what I've learned.

Recently, one speaker who resonated with me was Ari Weinzweig, co-founder of Zingerman's Deli in Ann Arbor, Michigan. He began by talking about making biscuits. Being from the South, I grew up around a kitchen where someone was always making handmade biscuits, so this is a metaphor I greatly appreciate.

If you've ever baked anything, then you're undoubtedly aware of an ingredient called "baking powder." And it's likely that at some point in your biscuit-making career, you found yourself unexpectedly out of baking powder while in the middle of your biscuit-making process.

Based on the small amount of this ingredient that's needed, you probably thought there would be no real impact if you left it out, right? Wrong. The lack of baking powder renders your biscuits flat, flavorless and pretty much inedible.

What does this have to do with business?

To hire those A-players, you have to stick to the recipe. I've coached hundreds of companies to create a process for interviewing potential employees that's practically foolproof and results in a near 90 percent A-player hire rate. But still, people tend to go "off recipe," using their own "voodoo method" and work off of gut feeling, rather than following a proven path. They skip a crucial ingredient and mess up the biscuits. The dilemma is that these "biscuits" are hard to get rid of once they are yours.

In other words, don't mess up the biscuits because it's a costly mistake.

TODAY'S ACTION ITEM

{ THE DIFFERENCE BETWEEN "CAN DO" AND "WILL DO" }

You're probably looking at this and shrugging your shoulders, unsure of where I'm going with this.

Of course there is a difference between the two. Let's go back to basic definitions for a minute.

"Can do" means you are capable of accomplishing something. On the other hand, "will do" means in the future you will actually accomplish something.

The difference is a matter of tentative versus prescriptive language.

Saying you "can do" something means you are capable, but that doesn't mean you'll actually do it. Saying you "will do" it pretty much signs you up for the task at hand.

With all that in mind, I urge you to shift your thinking in your business and your life. When you're setting goals, don't just believe that you "can" reach that goal (and hope you don't disappoint yourself in the end). Tell yourself that you "will" reach that goal – it's so much more compelling.

I've seen this proven time and time again with all the companies that I coach and with my own team. When they say they will do something, they almost always get it done because they feel, in a sense, obligated. And I can tell you, the few who don't get done what they said they would feel pretty damn ashamed of themselves.

Change your thinking in this small way, and you'd be surprised how much less frequently you disappoint yourself.

Now, go out there and tell yourself what you *will* accomplish today.

TODAY'S ACTION ITEM

JUNE 21

{ CREATE A "BOARD OF APPRECIATION" }

The No. 1 reason people leave their jobs is a lack of appreciation, according to a study by Accenture. If that's the case, then it would make sense for us all to increase the amount of gratitude we share with one another, right? It costs us nothing, and we can give it with very little effort. So, why don't we do it more often?

A Board of Appreciation is one simple program you can start in your organization to create this much-needed culture of recognition.

Here's how the Board of Appreciation works: Get a picture frame or white board and a dry erase marker. Someone writes a note of gratitude on the board to a fellow team member, and he or she keeps the board until he or she wipes it clean and writes a note to another person. Kick the program off yourself. Who do you want to thank today?

Begin with "I appreciate you for/because..." Then, be explicit in what or why you are giving them the board. Avoid general sayings, such as "… because you go the extra mile" or "… because you are such a team player." Instead, think in terms of telling a story.

Next, tell the recipient how his or her action impacted you and/or the business. For instance, "Because of the patience you showed the client, the entire team learned a valuable lesson about how we live out our commitments to our clients and how important they are to our success in this market."

Simple, huh? The most meaningful acts usually are.

Bonus: You can even bring the idea home, and do it with your spouse and kids.

TODAY'S ACTION ITEM

JUNE 22

{ DO YOU REALLY KNOW HOW TO NETWORK? }

Traditional networking helps pave the path to deeper relationships, which are essential to professional and personal well-being. However, many of us feel too intimidated to attend a mixer or social gathering to even get started. Here are my top tips on how to prepare to network like a pro:

1. Brush up on industry news.
Leading up to the event, I refresh myself on the industry best sellers and spend a bit more time than usual ingesting news. Familiarizing yourself with relevant news ensures you can contribute to conversations on multiple levels and that you appear knowledgeable.

2. Shut up and listen.
When you're engaging in conversation, let the other person do most of the talking and listen to what he or she is saying. Lending someone your ear is a fast way to make a friend. Why? I go by an 80/20 rule – the other person has the spotlight and talks 80 percent of the time.

3. Set a goal.
The overall point of business networking is to establish and develop business connections. There's no reason to be shy about that. Maybe your goal would be to set up three subsequent face-to-face visits with contacts you meet at the event. These goals will keep you focused on the primary reason you're there – to do business.

I challenge you to think in these terms at your next event: How do I make this new connection last 25 years? Then, follow through with your actions accordingly.

TODAY'S ACTION ITEM

JUNE 23

{ FINDING YOUR TRUTH }

When I talk about "the truth," I mean understanding what's real about ourselves and the people around us – moving beyond denial, and getting to the heart of who we are, what we do well (and what we don't), so we can set an example for others and truly lead.

It's a lesson we all need to learn, if we want to be our best.

So, how do you change? And, how do you encourage change in others?

Figure yourself out first. I say this a lot: "You are the longest relationship you've ever had." Nobody knows you better than you do.

But, along the way many of us make decisions about ourselves that might not be based in reality. We create our own truth, and it's easy to get lost in the truth we've defined for ourselves – even if others can see that it doesn't ring true. That keeps us from achieving our maximum potential.

You've got to take the time to step back and get real with yourself. Are you open to other opinions, or do you "have it all figured out?" Do you make it a priority to invite feedback – and even criticism – or are others usually "wrong?" Ask yourself the important questions, and be open to the answers.

More importantly, accept that you're not perfect – I'll say it again: You're not perfect.

Stay open, and recognize that at times you're going to need the help and input of other people to grow your business and make it better.

TODAY'S ACTION ITEM

JUNE 24

{ ADMIT YOUR MISTAKES }

Great leaders should never be afraid to apologize because mistakes are inevitable. If you make an error, own it, admit it to the people involved and apologize. Apologizing means more than saying, "I'm sorry." Be specific about what you regret, and explain what you will do to avoid the same mistake again in the future.

If you get emotional, that's fine – it can even be a good thing. When team members witness you being vulnerable and showing humility, they'll realize you're more than just a "boss" – you're a human being just like them.

Once you've admitted your mistake and apologized, it's time to discuss what to do next. You may be surprised at how your team responds.

Great leaders are humble and take responsibility for their actions. They let team members know they don't always have the right answers and acknowledge areas they need to improve. This combination of humility and self-awareness enables leaders to move past their fears and weaknesses and lead more effectively.

Is there something you need to apologize for? Take a minute to think about it. Perform regular self-assessments to see how you're doing. The time spent is worth it because you will discover areas to improve, build stronger relationships with your team members and grow as a leader.

TODAY'S ACTION ITEM

JUNE 25

{ HOW TO GET WHAT YOU WANT FROM PEOPLE }

Guest contribution from Petra Coach JT Terrell

Often, I find that leaders will just wait around to see if team members will behave how he or she wants, but it's so counterintuitive. If you want someone to do something, just ask them! Here's how to do it:

Be specific with them.
Talk about exactly what results you want, and share with that person what it takes to get that result. Being clear from the onset will ensure there won't be any confusion about your expectations.

Ask them in person.
Emails and text messages are too easily ignored and misconstrued. Go see someone in person or, at the very least, via a video call. That way, she can see that you're concerned about the results you want and that your intention was not to personally attack her or her character.

Don't be afraid to ask early and often.
This is the new mission of my upstart referral-based client. Don't wait until a problem gets out of hand or you're overdue on a project to share with others what you need from them. Include others in the process to make sure you can accomplish the task without any mishaps or surprises.

Finally, express gratitude.
Now that you have gotten much better at communicating in a direct and real way, make sure that you say "please" and "thank you" – and mean it. Positive reinforcement is an important step to have direct conversations, receive feedback and attain success with coaching.

Making this kind of communication the standard in your place of business, or in your home, can make your everyday life much less challenging and provide stability in your relationships.

TODAY'S ACTION ITEM

JUNE 26

{ ENSURE A POSITIVE EXPERIENCE }

A few weeks ago, I went to a routine checkup at the dermatologist. This time, the doctor ended up finding a spot on my arm and removed it for testing. After a week of waiting for my results, I was getting frustrated.

That was just the beginning of the poor experience I had with my dermatologist's office. Here are two reasons my frustration escalated and the lessons learned for how businesses can better serve their clients:

1. Be responsive.
When the doctor called with my results and to schedule a follow-up visit, I was on a plane so he got my voicemail. I returned his call promptly, only to get the office's machine, which stated that they were too busy to take my call. However, when I called five more times at different times, I got the same message.

> *Do whatever you can to answer the ringing phone. It's most likely your client, calling about spending money with you.*

2. Know what's up.
Once I was finally able to speak with someone at the doctor's office, I was asked (several times) why I needed to come in. By any means possible, please know what the client is looking for. If you have multiple departments, find a way to keep records so that everyone has access to them and knows what's going on with your client.

> *The client experience depends on good communication.*

Think about these the next time you interact with your clients. After all, your business thrives on their support (and money). Do everything you can to make sure they receive the best experience possible – because if not, they'll find someone else who will.

TODAY'S ACTION ITEM

JUNE 27

{ WANT TO CHANGE YOUR LIFE? CHANGE YOUR ATTITUDE. }

It's no secret that humans see more of what they don't have than what they do. But if you are intentional about putting a stop to that practice, you will unlock a happiness that you've never experienced before. Here are some tips to get you started:

1. Make friends with change.
No matter how many times we hear that change is inevitable, many of us have an instinct to resist it. Now is your chance to embrace it. Keep learning. Stay curious and remain open to new experiences.

2. Credit the people around you.
If you want to be surrounded by great people, make sure to acknowledge their greatness. Be generous and genuine with compliments. You may be surprised how people rise to a challenge when they feel empowered.

3. Encourage success.
A rising tide lifts all boats. By spreading your positive attitude to those around you, you're setting yourself up for success along with your colleagues. Positivity is contagious, so be the one to start the wave – it'll come back around to you just when you need it.

4. Gratitude is the key.
Gratitude is a crucial part of any path to success. And it's pretty hard to be negative if you're busy being grateful. Whether it's your family, your health, or quality time spent with an old friend, appreciating the things that are going well in your life will invite other good things and keep you on the path to success.

TODAY'S ACTION ITEM

JUNE 28

{ TAKE ADVANTAGE OF FREE MOBILE APPS TO IMPROVE PRODUCTIVITY }

Technology can't replace the foundation of good business practices, but it does enable companies to be more efficient. Best of all, efficiency-boosting technology is not expensive, cumbersome or difficult to access. Look no further than the app marketplace on your smartphone.

The mobile apps listed below didn't exist 10-15 years ago! Now they are considered mainstream. If you are not using these free apps – or ones that are unique to your business and industry – then you're missing out on ways to be more productive with your time.

Dropbox – This is the best way to share and store documents, photos and videos. It's cloud-based so you or your business contacts can access permissible files wherever, whenever. You'll never have to email yourself documents again and you can easily share multiple documents.

Evernote – This note-taking, cloud-syncing app is a favorite and for good reason. The days of illegible hand-written notes that sit on your desk waiting to be digitized are over thanks to this easy-to-use free app. The best part, since it's cloud-based, you can access your notes from all of your devices. Lifesaver.

Tripit – With baggage fees, long lines and minimal leg room, air traveling is difficult enough. Use this app to organize all your travel plans so that you have one less thing to worry about. Essentially, it compiles and categorizes all of your flight confirmation emails and numbers, so you have it all in one convenient place. No more fumbling with computer confirmation printouts before check-in.

TODAY'S ACTION ITEM

JUNE 29

{ 2 REASONS WHY CEOS SHOULD PLAN FOR FAILURE }

Every successful company leader will tell you that failure is a part of business, but far fewer will admit they plan for failure.

The company I founded and sold, NationLink Wireless, started out selling pagers to retail shops like RadioShack. When we recognized that cell phones would be the future of the business, we took a calculated gamble and reallocated significant resources (human and financial capital) to compete.

Initially, I didn't want to adapt and give up on the pager business because my success as a business leader was linked to the product. My hesitation resulted in our company losing a lot of money and nearly going out of business.

Planning for failure while on the road to success is an approach I embrace at Petra Coach and recommend to the member companies that we consult – but with two important caveats:

1. Know the risks.
When taking a risk, make sure it's a calculated one. Evaluate the upside and downside and what they mean to your business. Remember, a failure that is aligned with your business's goals is still a step in the right direction.

2. Learn from your mistakes.
Every failure will provide important lessons for the future. Roll up your sleeves, and find out what went wrong. Be brutally honest about the hows and whys, but don't dwell on it or point fingers. Get your team together to determine the necessary changes and move forward.

In today's world where business seems to move at the speed of sound, the biggest risk is not taking any risk at all.

TODAY'S ACTION ITEM

JUNE 30

{ SHOW, DON'T TELL }

In many businesses, it's sometimes hard to quantify whether you've had a "good day" or not. Have you sold enough? Is your client happy with your services?

You need to be able to *show* your success, not just *tell* about it. Having tangible metrics is helpful not only to show your employees that they are on track, but also to show your investors that you are working toward specific goals and going above and beyond to drive the business forward.

So if you don't have the "hard numbers" to measure success, make some metrics for yourself – something that allows you to check the boxes as you go, so you can look back and see what you've accomplished.

The Petra member companies all use the Rockefeller Habits and key performance indicators (KPIs) to set goals and take steps every day towards those goals. As the Habits demonstrate, small changes can yield big results over the long term, and tracking those results – our clients use an online platform called Align – allows each team member to see how he or she is progressing and succeeding. It's extremely helpful to make employees' achievements tangible to them, so they stay motivated and drive the company forward toward newer and bigger goals.

Sometimes you feel like you are just hitting roadblocks and getting nowhere, but using KPIs and stats are a powerful way to demonstrate success, even on the most challenging of days.

The proof is in the numbers, after all.

TODAY'S ACTION ITEM

JULY

{ VITAMIN B-7 }

*Some vitamins aid in energy production and
others help you use that energy effectively.
This month, find positive outlets for your energy,
whether it's a good book or exercise.*

JULY 1

{ TIME MANAGEMENT DOESN'T EXIST }

Time management is a waste of time because it's impossible. Hear me out. Time is going to pass regardless of what you or I do. Management implies the ability to control. Since we cannot control time, we cannot manage it.

What we can do, though, is focus on what we can control – our priorities. Here are four steps to manage your priorities successfully within the time constraints we're all stuck with.

Choose wisely: Make sure you give your time to what is important rather than urgent. Important items are aligned with your short- and long-term goals, whereas urgent matters are typically distractions that usurp your time and derail you from forward progress. If you want to reach your goals, don't be a victim of urgency.

Narrow your focus: We get so wrapped up in our current growing to-do lists and big ideas that we forget to chart, deconstruct and focus on attainable priorities that could lead us to something bigger in the long-term. Taper your focus to only a few priorities at a time – I suggest three per quarter.

Schedule: Once you have your priorities set, it's time to block off focused periods of time for each of them. I recommend 90-minute timeframes. (If you're not willing to dedicate 90 minutes, then your priority may not actually be a priority.) Block these chunks of time and protect them with your life.

Measure: Create a way to measure your progress along the path to priority completion. What gets measured gets done.

TODAY'S ACTION ITEM

JULY 2

{ THE ONE-PAGE PERSONAL PLAN }

I continually reference Verne Harnish's *Scaling Up*, which outlines how to take the Rockefeller Habits a step further to bring your company to the next level.

As he says, the four main focus areas of a business – People, Strategy, Execution and Cash – can be translated into the main focus areas for your life: Relationships, Achievements, Rituals and Wealth.

He asks leaders to assess themselves in these four areas – how well they think they are performing and how satisfied they are – and create a plan to improve his or her lowest scores.

To put my own spin on the idea, I expanded them to the Six F's: Friends, Family, Fun, Finance, Faith and Fitness.

However you spin it, a self-assessment is an important beginning exercise for personal goal setting. It enables you to identify where you think you are, so you can start to think about where you want to be. Some people don't even know how they're stacking up in these areas, so the exercise tends to be a good eye-opener.

Once you create your personal plan, align it with your business goals. How will you balance these key areas with all the work that goes into your ambitious business goals?

That's what we want you to think about as you complete the exercise, in the hopes that you'll feel fulfilled in all parts of your life.

(You can download a copy of Harnish's One-Page Personal Plan at scalingup. com or my Six F's Wheel of Life at petracoach.com)

TODAY'S ACTION ITEM

JULY 3

{ FOLLOWING YOUR ROADMAP }

Your business journey is bound to have peaks and valleys – and you've got to be ready for both. The business leaders who understand this are the ones who survive and thrive. Here are four steps to plan your way to success when the going gets tough:

1. Accept the truth – you're lost.
Maybe you made a mistake or you were incorrect. Accept it. We all make a few wrong turns from time to time, but recognizing and owning up to our errors is the first step to righting the ship. If you let your pride get in the way and refuse to admit anything has gone awry, nothing will change – in fact, it will get a lot worse. Once you've established that there's a problem, you can begin to solve it.

2. Reach out to your trusted advisors.
These may include family, friends or colleagues. Ask for help, and really listen to what they have to say. Seeing things from different points of view will help you identify what needs to be done right away and what can wait. It will also allow you to see a way through a situation that you might never have thought about if you hadn't reached out and asked for help.

3. Make a plan and execute it.
Once you've heard from your trusted advisors, it's time to make that plan. Set S.M.A.R.T. (specific, measurable, attainable, relevant and time-bound) goals to outline where you want to go, how you're going to get there and what could potentially get in your way. Take the first step, and I promise you that the small acts and incremental changes that you make will add up over time.

TODAY'S ACTION ITEM

JULY 4

{ CELEBRATING INDEPENDENCE FROM YOUR BUSINESS }

I love the July 4th holiday. It's a great time to celebrate the freedom and independence we enjoy in our country.

Freedom and independence are also why most entrepreneurs strike out on their own to create their own business and become their own boss.

However, during the journey of "life, liberty and the pursuit of happiness" business owners often find themselves at a crossroad. They find they are putting in more and more hours at the office and spending less time at home with the people they love.

If you're at that point, you need to ask yourself: "Am I independent of or dependent on my business?" There's a difference, and it's an important one.

Here's a test: If you can't take one month off to travel to Italy (or to write the Great American Novel or do some other time-intensive activity), then you definitely have a dependency issue. That means you need to be there day in and day out to keep your business running, and things can't function without you.

If, on the other hand, you've developed systems and hired the right people to execute the plans you've put in place, without needing to constantly look over their shoulders, you've got an independent business. And that's when you know you can celebrate your independence!

TODAY'S ACTION ITEM

JULY 5

{ HOW TO BECOME INDEPENDENT OF YOUR BUSINESS }

When I started my first company – one that I owned for 18 years – I thought I was out of the grind of a job. After all, I owned my own business, right? I was living the dream.

But something was missing. Sure, my company was successful, but after nine years I realized I still had a job, not a business. So I made some changes, which made my next nine years vastly different – and for the better.

Do you want to make the shift from job to business and realize your dreams of independence? Here are three steps to help get you there:

1. Make a plan.
You've got to be strategic about creating a business, which means having a business plan. And once you've created the plan, you need to use it. It's best if you can define your priorities by breaking them down into daily, weekly, monthly and quarterly activities.

2. Surround yourself with the best.
You have to be intentional about surrounding yourself with great people. Use a hiring strategy to ensure you have "A-players" on your team, and then make sure to provide the guidance and training necessary for them to succeed and work independently.

3. Once you have the best, leave them alone.
Resist the temptation to micromanage your team. Warren Buffet said it best: "Hire well. Manage little." If you've succeeded with steps one and two, you've set your team up for success.

TODAY'S ACTION ITEM

JULY 6

{ THE POWER OF PURPOSE}

For entrepreneurs and leaders, starting or running a business in which your personal and professional goals are aligned with your life's purpose, well, that's the Holy Grail.

The first place to start on that journey is to ask yourself: What are your life's goals and your purpose?

Generally, a purpose falls into one of four categories:

1. Service to others.

2. Search for knowledge and truth.

3. Pursuit of beauty and excellence.

4. Desire to change the world.

Make it your mission to include in your work a focus on your life's purpose. Use it to help you lead others. Find out the motivations of the people in your organization, and work to align them with the foundations of the business.

Clearly defining a purpose is only the beginning. It should help guide you in the decisions you make, the work that you do and the way that you live. You'll discover along the way other people who align with your vision – they'll be key to growing your business beyond your wildest dreams.

Share your vision and purpose with your team. They need to know how much you care about them and the business.

TODAY'S ACTION ITEM

JULY 7

{ WHERE ARE YOU WEAKEST?}

Throughout my career coaching teams and individuals, there is one common habit I see in almost every meeting I attend: People will do almost anything to avoid talking about their weaknesses. We are motivated by praise, opportunity, goals and dreams, but none of those will come to fruition without understanding what's holding us back.

Here are two ideas for how you can seek out challenges that will help you grow:

1. Ask for the challenge.
Yep, it's that simple sometimes. Just because you are the one in charge, doesn't mean that you have all of the answers all of the time. It's vital that you find a group of people that you can discuss your weaknesses with: possibly another executive at your company, a professional development group or even your closest friends. This feedback might be uncomfortable to ask for and receive at first, but it is the only true way to learn and grow.

2. Prove to yourself that you can.
Everything we do (and don't do) is noted in our brains. This is why the power of habit is so important. If you commit to making your bed each morning, you are reinforcing that habit. Similarly, if you overcome one simple challenge, like exercising in the morning instead of pushing the snooze button, you have signaled to yourself that you can overcome small obstacles. Next time you are faced with a larger challenge, rely on the fact that you have triumphed before and are capable of doing so again.

TODAY'S ACTION ITEM

{ THE TRUTH DOESN'T HAVE TO HURT }

Guest contribution from Petra Coach Greg Eisen

In my experience, it's so important for leaders to always be open and honest with their teams.

I have observed that the quality of the culture and underlying relationships of an organization can often be judged by examining the intersection of truth and tact in that organization. Here are the four resulting types of relationships:

Constrained – High truth, low tact. People generally shut down when they are talked at instead of talked to, which limits trust and prevents open discussion. These interactions can cause company cultures and individual relationships to break down.

Superficial – High tact, low truth. These interactions are polite and cordial, but they lack substance – deep care is missing, and real issues don't get resolved. I see this situation often in bureaucratic organizations where folks don't have any stake in the outcome, nor do they feel connected to a core purpose.

Dysfunctional – Low truth, low tact. Environments where we are not honest and direct and we are tactless in our interactions generally don't produce much success or fulfillment. These cultures are toxic, and turning these environments around requires significant change from the top down.

Healthy – High truth and high tact. These relationships are where great trust and respect exist. This is the zone you want to live in, both personally and professionally.

I'd encourage you to use this matrix to score your most important relationships and your company culture as a whole. Where do you stand? What can you do to improve?

TODAY'S ACTION ITEM

JULY 9

{ DON'T CALL THEM CUSTOMERS OR DEALS }

Whenever I think back on the lessons learned in sales while I was building my first business, I often remember language being one of my first challenges as a CEO. It's a tricky part of company culture that I find afflicts more and more businesses every day – especially when it comes to sales.

You often hear people say that selling is more art than science. There's a lot of truth to that, especially when it comes to how you talk internally about the companies you are targeting to buy your product or service.

As you work to grow revenue, the words you use during the sales process will have a subconscious impact on you, your team and your potential client. Change your mindset to think more positively about sales, and increase the chance to close more deals.

Customers vs. Clients: Do you want to work with a "customer?" Great. Call them a "client," anyway. Dealing with a "customer" is a one-sided transaction that feels cold and leaves a partner feeling like just a number, whereas a "client" feels like a budding or blossoming relationship between two parties.

Deal vs. Opportunity: A "deal" is a big win, so of course the term should be used in business, right? Wrong. For one, if you tout a deal as a "win," it can put the focus on the sale, not the work involved. Using "opportunity" speaks to the positivity of landing the deal as well as the responsibility of the job moving forward.

TODAY'S ACTION ITEM

JULY 10

{ 3 HIRING LESSONS FROM A SPORTS PLAYBOOK }

I remember one time I watched my daughter at a high school volleyball tournament. As I was sitting in the stands, I noticed several people with cameras who were recording stats and furiously scribbling notes.

I realized they were recruiters who were looking ahead two or more years to find the best talent for their volleyball programs. For business leaders, the process is often flip-flopped. Executives in charge of hiring wait until a need presents itself before worrying about filling it.

Below are three lessons for leaders to take from the sports playbook to use to their advantage when hiring:

1. Think about future seasons: For sports coaches, success comes when they envision where the team will be in future seasons. Business leaders should do the same and ask questions like, "What will cause our company to add personnel and when?" and "What skills or experience will we need when this growth happens?"

2. Create a (long-term) game plan: A proactive hiring process doesn't end with just thinking about it. Businesses should build an organizational chart of what the company will look like one, two and three years in the future and design a hiring game plan based on how they project the growth of their business.

3. Build your bench: The last step is to recruit – not when positions need to be filled, but well in advance. That way you build a "virtual bench," which is exactly what it sounds like – a roster of candidates from which businesses can pull. Once you have your prospects, keep them pre-qualified and ready for whenever the need might come up.

Just like in sports, businesses need proactive preparation to get a leg up on the competition. If a college volleyball team can do it, business leaders can too.

TODAY'S ACTION ITEM

JULY 11

{ 4 LEADERSHIP LESSONS WHEN CHOOSING CLIENTS }

Our company is fortunate in that we receive phone calls, emails, texts and even Facebook messages from businesses around the world asking about our coaching services. It's very humbling, but I also have to confess: I'm picky when it comes to the business leaders with whom our company coaches.

I learned over the years that the qualities we look for in clients mirror the attributes of successful leaders who have built thriving companies. Here are those four key qualities:

1. Personal growth-oriented versus goal-oriented.
Is the organization interested in being better or just interested in accomplishing goals? When companies are personal growth-oriented, they are automatically goal-oriented, but not the other way around.

2. Willing to reproduce themselves.
Leaders have to be willing to let go of things to grow. Leadership has to be willing to reproduce itself, to share information so others can take on responsibilities. People don't get better automatically – you have to invest in them.

3. Able to commit to application.
Leaders must be willing to take what they learn and apply it immediately to themselves. They must be willing to take what we tell them to do on faith and just do it until they believe it – and until it becomes part of their culture.

4. In the right mind-set.
They have to be in at least one of two emotional states that are conducive to change: either so frustrated with their business that they're willing to do anything to change it, or fearful of missing an opportunity that can't be achieved if they keep doing what they are currently doing.

TODAY'S ACTION ITEM

JULY 12

{ THE PHRASE THAT WILL MAKE YOU A BETTER LEADER }

Contrary to what you may think, leadership isn't a trait we're born with, but one that is honed, developed and practiced throughout our entire life – much like a habit. According to research by the European Journal of Social Psychology, it takes an average of 66 days to create a habit. How many hours are you spending intentionally exercising better leadership?

If you're feeling off your leadership game lately, or looking for ways to be more of a leader on your team, consider the words you're using in your daily interactions. Here is one phrase to consider adding:

"It was me!"

If there's no such thing as a perfect person, then why are we so afraid of failure? Taking responsibility for your mistakes is not fun, but it's necessary to practicing good leadership because it reveals you care more about building your character than protecting it. Great leaders understand that it's impossible to be perfect, and by vocalizing your imperfections, you are giving others the freedom to do the same.

On the flip side, when you achieve something awesome, don't be afraid to let everyone know that you worked hard to contribute to the success of the team and the company. Finding opportunities to practice humility in both circumstances will challenge and grow your leadership skills.

TODAY'S ACTION ITEM

JULY 13

{ KEEP WORRIES AND FEARS OUT OF YOUR DAY }

Guest contribution from Petra Coach David Pierce

Do you ever have days where you wake up and instantly start worrying about the day(s) ahead of you?

You don't need me to tell you that isn't healthy, and you need to find ways to get through the day without fears and worries holding you down.

I suggest starting your day with a "grateful list." If you begin your day actively thinking about the things for which you are grateful, your mind cannot simultaneously be actively dwelling on worries or fears.

With your first cup of coffee, or during your shower or morning walk, state quietly in your mind, or even out loud, five to 10 things for which you're grateful. Doing this will start your day on a positive trajectory.

Note: Remember to do this no matter how you feel. It will be tough, but you don't have to feel grateful to be grateful.

Another coping mechanism I learned from Dale Carnegie's book, *How to Stop Worrying and Start Living*, is to live in "day-tight compartments." The premise is to shut off thinking about the yesterdays, which are gone and cannot be changed, and also shut off the future, which is full of its own anxieties.

Instead, exist in the safety of "today," where you can live, breathe and make an impact with your thoughts and actions.

It might seem a tad oversimplified, and yes, you may have to deal with past mistakes and should plan for the future, but don't give those things any right to cause you worry, fear or anxiety.

TODAY'S ACTION ITEM

JULY 14

{ WHY YOU NEED TO SURVEY YOUR TEAM }

Your team members are one of the main reasons that clients buy your product or service. Without great team members, operational execution suffers, which means your business will also suffer. It's as simple as that.

If you are not conducting surveys at least annually you are missing out on collecting invaluable information about areas of the business your team believes need improvement and where the company is excelling. Here are things to think about when you do it:

1. Keep surveys anonymous.
This is crucial because it gives team members the opportunity to provide frank and honest feedback. To grow your business, you need to know the good and the bad.

2. Share the results.
You will learn a lot about how your team views the business, so share the data. You will find out how team members view the company culture, where the business is heading and what should and should not change about the way the organization is being managed. Sharing the results will encourage discussion about next steps.

3. Act on the results.
You must be willing to act on the results – otherwise you're simply paying lip service to your team. Your team needs to see that action is being taken to address challenges and opportunities that may come to light in the survey results.

Your business is constantly in motion and employee surveys will provide you with a reality check to help you improve and achieve company goals.

TODAY'S ACTION ITEM

JULY 15

{ COLLABORATION WITHOUT MEETINGS }

Often we find ourselves meeting just for the sake of meeting. Let's nip that habit in the bud right now.

The No. 1 question to ask yourself is, "Do we really need to meet at all?"

Collaboration is important, but you don't have to have a meeting to be collaborative. Find ways to get each person's input without wasting everyone's time.

For example, send around a link to a shared document for everyone to add their input on their own time. You can still get those crowdsourced ideas, but no one has to make the stars align to get everyone in one room. Another option is to speak to each team member separately about only the things that pertain to each of them.

If you determine you do need to meet as a group, do it strategically. Do you really need every single person in that meeting? If you do, does everyone need to be there for the entire time?

Begin with the things that everyone needs to hear. Then, release people as you narrow the focus to items that involve only certain people.

It will save everyone time and keep everybody sane.

TODAY'S ACTION ITEM

JULY 16

{ BOOSTING ENGAGEMENT WITH TRIAL PROMOTIONS }

Not sure if someone is ready for a promotion? Is a team member untested in tackling new responsibilities? A test run could be the perfect solution.

Example 1: Jennifer had been with my company for years, always showed up with a positive attitude and generated consistent results in her customer service role. A customer service manager position opened, and I felt Jennifer deserved a shot since she had fulfilled her existing role so well. The only problem: Jennifer didn't have managerial experience and I didn't know if she could handle, or would even enjoy management duties.

We decided she'd take on the managerial responsibilities for three months. If she did well and enjoyed the work, she'd get the manager title and the accompanying pay raise. If the trial period didn't go well, we'd have a different conversation.

Example 2: Mandy had been with my company for a while and had been naturally promoted several times. Looking for her next challenge, Mandy identified areas in the business that could use development, such as enriching our social media influence, creating a newsletter and producing marketing brochures.

She approached me with these ideas and told me she'd like to own them, and we agreed that she could develop a three-month plan. If the three-month trial proved fruitful to the company and enjoyable to her, then she'd have the marketing position full time.

End result: Jennifer and Mandy both went above and beyond in their trial periods and were advanced to their new positions. They pursued their new roles with vigor and passion for two big reasons:

1. They earned their positions. We always value what we rightly earn.

2. They were engaged.

TODAY'S ACTION ITEM

JULY 17

{ DO YOU HAVE A DREAM LIST? }

As a new entrepreneur, it's so easy to take any client that comes along. Someone wants to pay me to do what I'm doing? Bring it on! Not so fast. The right client is always more important than just having a client, which is why building a dream sheet is so important.

Here are four steps to make your "Dream List" a reality:

1. Identify: Understand exactly what you're offering. Dig deep, and focus in on the unique benefit you provide customers that competitors don't or won't. Don't settle for just "the highest level of customer service" or "the best product" – everyone claims that. Find your sweet spot. It's what you uniquely provide that clients will pay to have. That's what you take to market.

2. Refine: Gather your team and narrow down your attribute list to 10. Have everyone discuss and vote. Your team must be in on this step. After all, they're typically at the frontlines working directly with clients.

3. Match: Research the types of business that can fulfill your attribute list. Maybe technology companies tend to have the annual revenue and the right number of employees you're searching for, plus that industry typically has a void your service or product can fill. Next, get more specific. Identify the businesses by name. Search through chamber listings and industry association member directories to pinpoint prospective "Dream List" clients. Here you can find the company's stats like revenue, size and age. Keep researching. Those companies that match your ideal attributes will make up your "Dream List."

TODAY'S ACTION ITEM

JULY 18

{ ENCOURAGE EMPLOYEES TO KEEP LEARNING }

I've noted before that a book club can benefit a company in many ways – such as inspiring creativity and generating new ideas. Another major benefit of a company book club is team building.

A strong team with engaged team members equals better work. Building relationships isn't easy, especially when you're juggling multiple interests and personalities. Book clubs create a space where individuals can come together over a shared experience and learn from each other.

Developing connections within club meetings leads to richer conversations outside of club meetings. When you open this kind of dialogue, it helps people tackle issues together and build on each other's ideas.

You're creating a community of lifelong learners who are applying their findings in the workplace. What more could you want? It doesn't matter the business, the sector or the book – when teams are on board, book clubs work.

Even with an emphasis on learning, sometimes more motivation is needed. Many companies will pay their people for each book they read. Team members choose what they want to read from a library of relevant titles for their field, they share what they've learned with fellow book club members, and then they get paid.

When companies cultivate eager readers, their teams are rewarded for the time and engagement, and everyone gets to learn and grow together. It's a win-win-win.

Whether you do a specific program or have informal meetings in the break room, figure out what kind of book club works best for your company – and start reading!

TODAY'S ACTION ITEM

JULY 19

{ LESSONS IN LEADERSHIP }

I coach entrepreneurs and their teams all around the globe. The teams that reach their goals all have one thing in common: a quality leader.

You can't grow your revenue, profits and company culture without a strong and effective leader.

Yes, leaders have a lot in common. Most are motivators, communicators and decision-makers. But outstanding leaders also embrace these three often overlooked leadership lessons:

A leader grows other leaders: Not wanting to be outshined, misguided leaders will embolden themselves by stifling others – especially those who demonstrate strong leadership potential. The truth is, when you empower others, you bolster the entire team. This furthers your company's mission and is a direct reflection of your success as a leader.

A leader knows how and when to follow: Effective leaders surround themselves with smart people who can offer unique solutions and insights. As a designated leader, you won't always know the answer – so let the person who does know lead the team through that project. Not only does this grow other leaders, it frees you to lead in other areas where you are more knowledgeable and efficient. The next time a team member steps up to tackle a project, remind yourself to follow like a leader.

A leader shows vulnerability: Team members trust successful leaders, and no one trusts an impenetrable robot. One way you can gain your team's confidence is by exposing your own vulnerabilities. Allow yourself to share your fears and concerns. Your team will relate with you and support you through the company's mission. If you're a leader, remember: Vulnerability can be your greatest strength.

TODAY'S ACTION ITEM

JULY 20

{ TEACH YOUR CHILDREN WELL – LEARNING SHOULD NEVER END }

My oldest daughter Madison says that she's had "a very unusual upbringing." You see, she was raised by a business coach (me) – a dad who spent many professional hours working with CEOs and entrepreneurs helping them learn how to be better leaders and how to make their businesses run more efficiently.

Naturally, some of those lessons and discussions made their way to the dinner table from time to time. In fact, the lesson that she remembers best is that we made each moment a learning moment.

As Madison tells it, "While I was growing up, Dad taught my sister and me that to be adaptable and successful we had to be prepared for learning moments, which might not always be comfortable. I learned that success never comes without taking risks and that there will always be surprises along the way. Dad taught me to use every experience in my life as a foundational moment, not to be stopped by adversity and to look for and learn from any situation and build from there. College is the perfect place to practice this. Whether inside or outside of class, I'm always looking for learning moments, and I welcome new experiences."

Madison is right (of course). Taking a risk will have one of two outcomes: The situation will work out positively or it won't. Either way, you'll learn something. It's true for everyone from students to leaders. Learning should never end.

TODAY'S ACTION ITEM

JULY 21

{ TACKLING TOUGH RELATIONSHIPS AT WORK }

If you work with others besides yourself for more than a month, you will inevitably find that you come across someone with whom you disagree, dislike or really just can't stand. So now what?

Here are the top three things I practice to elevate my interpersonal communication:

1. Rise above.
It's incredibly easy to let yourself react emotionally in the heat of an argument or tough situation with a toxic person. Don't. Keep in mind that reacting the same way they do makes you just as toxic as them. Keep calm and carry on – you'll always be glad that you did.

2. Set boundaries.
Boundaries are essential in both your personal and professional life. Don't feel bad about spending limited amounts of time with those who drain you of energy or positivity. If you know you're going into a challenging meeting, visualize how you're going to interact in a manner that shows poise and professionalism.

3. Accept it.
Not agreeing with or liking everyone doesn't make you a bad person, it makes you human. Take the steps to set proper boundaries, engage in tactful communication and then move forward.

TODAY'S ACTION ITEM

JULY 22
{ ADAPTING AS YOU GROW }

Any successful company is going to naturally grow as it takes on more business and sees more revenue. And with that growth comes organizational changes that have to happen.

In his book *Scaling Up*, Verne Harnish explains that after a company reaches the threshold of 50 employees, it's time to start "aligning teams around projects, product groups, industry segments and geographical regions," not just by function. He calls it a "Matrix Organization."

Harnish asserts that this structural transition will happen most smoothly if the C-suite starts to act more like coaches or advisors to the department leaders, who then become individual CEOs (of sorts) to their own units. Rather than making all the decisions, the C-suite will need to spend more time learning outside the organization and sharing those best practices with the unit leaders.

Of course, this can be hard for the C-suite leaders who are used to being the ones who make the decisions on a daily basis. They have to change their roles the most to adapt to the new structure. The key to keeping the structure together and functioning effectively is to make sure it is clearly decided who each employee is answering to. In most cases, it'll be their department or unit leads.

However, in the case of an employee who serves multiple units at once, he or she still needs to take feedback from each unit leader, rather than the organization leaders, because they need to be accessible to their immediate units first and foremost.

Harnish's final point is to remember that "your company is a living organism that needs to survive in an environment that's always changing. To thrive, it has to be able to adapt."

TODAY'S ACTION ITEM

JULY 23

{ LEAVE YOUR JOB TITLE AT THE OFFICE }

As a business owner, I work hard and am gratified that I not only get to watch my clients grow and improve, but that I also get to experience daily improvement in my own organization by using the very methods that I teach every day.

I also have a home life where I am just as intentional about practicing what I preach – so my coaching method is applicable in the boardroom and the living room.

One piece of advice I often tell leaders is to leave your job title at the door when you go home. If you're a parent, don't act like a CEO giving orders while you're sitting at the dinner table.

Lead by example.

Home is not the workplace, and you need to encourage self-motivation in your kids. Unless they can do it without you dictating every step, it's not going to work.

Instead, lead by example to foster inner drive and self-motivation. Show your family that it's possible to get a feeling of accomplishment from a job well done. Outward recognition is one thing, but when a person learns to be satisfied and motivated by their own accomplishments, that success breeds more success.

TODAY'S ACTION ITEM

JULY 24

{ GOING BEYOND THE CORE VALUES }

One of my business coaches at Petra Coach works with a large public works company based in New York City that was having a lot of trouble getting everyone aligned with the company culture the leaders wanted to have and to ensure they were lived out across all of the job sites and workers across the city, especially with a continuous influx of new employees.

Prior to starting the coaching process, the leaders developed 27 of what they call "Fundamentals," or the basic rules by which they live and work. They detailed the "Company Way" with points such as, "Think Safe, Work Safe," "Use Data to Make Decisions" and "Act Like It's Your Own."

However, those weren't being communicated to everyone on a regular basis, so the company came up with the idea to give all employees cards with those values on them. That allowed each employee to have a handy pocket-sized reminder of the values and their commitment to carrying them out.

Then, with the coach's help, the company defined its core purpose and four core values. To make sure these central tenets were ingrained in every single employee, the leaders had a "Rollout" event, where – over food, drinks and camaraderie – they revealed them to everyone in the company and generated excitement around them.

Furthermore, the company printed the core purpose and four core values on every single safety vest. It serves as a constant reminder to the team – and makes it public to anyone passing their workers on the street – who the company is, how they work and what they stand for.

Takeaway: Don't just define your company's purpose, values and intentions – share them and make them a part of everyday life at your company.

TODAY'S ACTION ITEM

JULY 25

{ 3 WAYS TO SHORTEN THE SALES CYCLE }

Entrepreneurs and CEOs play a vital role in growing revenue and profits for their companies, yet there's one important area that often gets overlooked and can have a dramatic effect on cash flow: the length of the sales cycle.

Improving and shortening the sales cycle can materially improve cash flow and the financial health of your business. Follow these tips and you'll get paid faster and improve the productivity of your sales team.

1. Create a written plan for your sales cycle.
If you don't have a written sales process, do it now. It will help your sales team stay on task as they work with prospects. While every sale is unique, the process should be repeatable and scalable. There's no silver bullet that can shorten the sales cycle, but anticipating speed bumps and having strategies to get around them will help close more clients faster.

2. Agree to a purchase timeline early in sales discussions.
Every written sales cycle should outline timelines and milestones, including deadlines for product/service delivery and, where applicable, installation, implementation and client on-boarding. Your reps should work closely with prospect decision-makers to build a timeline that all parties can agree to – and then stick to it as closely as possible.

3. Automate repetitive tasks.
List all the key tasks your team does repeatedly – such as inputting data into a CRM or preparing presentations – and look for ways to automate those activities.

The faster you produce and deliver a product or service, the quicker you get paid and can put your cash to work growing your company!

TODAY'S ACTION ITEM

{ THE CASE FOR MINI-HABITS }

Run a marathon. Lose 20 pounds. Get up before 6 a.m. Cut out soda. Get a promotion. Go on a dream vacation. Be intentional with your family. Chances are you've set out to accomplish one of these goals in your lifetime. How did that turn out?

In his book *Mini Habits: Smaller Habits, Bigger Results*, Stephen Guise argues that the problem with these goals has nothing to do with the goal itself and everything to do with how we approach them. Creating a new habit or breaking an old one doesn't happen overnight, it's all about small steps at a time, which is why I love implementing mini-habits. To put it simply, a mini-habit is a much smaller version of a new habit you want to form.

Take the goal of running a marathon, for example. If you decide to create a habit of running 14 miles per week for one month, there is still a lot of work to be done between getting out of bed each morning and finishing those 2 miles each day. One mini-habit could be setting and waking up to your alarm each morning. While this seems trivial, it's a habit that directly correlates to your successful ability to train to complete a marathon.

The power of the mini-habits system is that while you are actively doing things that contribute to achieving a goal, you are also creating a positive feedback loop in your brain, naturally increasing your willpower and self-efficacy.

What mini-habit can you implement today?

TODAY'S ACTION ITEM

JULY 27

{ 2 THINGS TO REMOVE FROM YOUR NEXT MEETING }

We've all been there. Eyes glazed over. Continuously checking the clock. When will this useless meeting ever end?!

When working on a team, meetings are unavoidable, and done right, can be a great way to keep your team aligned and moving forward towards your goals.

However, there are a few things that can suck the life out of meetings. Here are two things you need to remove from your next meeting:

1. Chairs.
Make every meeting a stand-up meeting and you'll increase the engagement and attentiveness of attendees. Standing during a long meeting is uncomfortable and the team will want to finish faster, i.e., be more productive in a shorter amount of time. This model will make any meeting short, sweet and to the point.

2. Electronics.
Electronics in meetings are my biggest pet peeve. A meeting should be free of distractions or it's a waste of time. If you're the meeting leader, pass around a bucket for everyone to throw their cell phones in or create a stack of them in the center of the table. Thirty minutes without a connection to email, texts or Facebook isn't the end of the world and enforcing such a rule will change the vibe of your meeting.

In 2019, your meetings don't have to suck. Incorporate these principles into your everyday meetings and they'll start to become a little more endurable. Your team will thank you.

TODAY'S ACTION ITEM

{ 5 LANGUAGES OF APPRECIATION IN THE WORKPLACE }

In today's workplace it is crucial for employees to feel valued. Your first thought may be, "Valued? They're employed by my company, doesn't that mean enough to them?" Well, frankly, no.

To make sure I'm properly caring for my incredible employees, I've implemented wisdom from Gary Chapman's *The 5 Languages of Appreciation in the Workplace*. He notes that what employees want most is to feel appreciated. Want motivated, harder-working employees? Just learn one of these "languages," or ways that people prefer to give and receive praise:

1. Words of Affirmation: Driven by praise for accomplishments, characteristics and personality, this person cherishes receiving sincere and specific compliments and recognition.

2. Quality Time: This person values personal, focused attention over proximity or length of time, so aim to maintain good eye contact and have frequent one-on-one meetings in a safe environment.

3. Acts of Service: True leadership requires a willingness to serve, and this person values a cheerful and careful helper. Offer to take something off of their plate or go the extra mile on a project when working together.

4. Gifts: Giving the right gift to the person who values it can be a powerful tool to show appreciation and thanks. And accompany it with a hand-written note to make it personal.

5. Physical Touch: This can be executed appropriately in the workplace. A firm handshake or high-five can nonverbally communicate respect, admiration and encouragement.

Curious about which one describes you or those around you? Take the free test at www.appreciationatwork.com.

TODAY'S ACTION ITEM

JULY 29

{ WHY YOUR COMPANY'S 'SUMMER BUCKET LIST' WON'T CUT IT }

It's hot, humid and officially summer. And with summertime comes summer bucket lists, or lofty agendas of things to accomplish before the end of the season.

For leaders, these summer bucket lists can be reminiscent of the goals and "would be nice" lists they create for their companies. At board meetings, team members scribble things like "increase revenue" and "grow customer base" on the whiteboard. After the meeting, however, little gets done toward achieving those goals. That's because making progress on bucket list ideas requires adding those activities to the company's strategy.

Here's a great example. One of your organization's goals might be something like, "Be the number one company in our market." While you may really believe this will happen, it's still just a vague statement until it has a strategy behind it. Potential strategies for this goal might include increasing the amount of advertising and marketing done in the community, expanding a product line or introducing new services.

Stop viewing bucket lists as an assortment of things that you want to do. Instead, look at how they fit into the overall strategy for your company. If your summer bucket list seems like a random assortment of activities, then it probably doesn't reflect the company's strategy that you have worked so hard to fine-tune.

TODAY'S ACTION ITEM

JULY 30

{ THE JOB SCORECARD }

There's a hiring methodology by Brad and Geoff Smart called "Topgrading," which is a surefire way to find A-players for your team.

The Smarts' posit that an A-player isn't necessarily just the person who is most qualified for the job, but rather the most qualified out of the people who are interested in your specific offer. In other words, you need to find the people who are best for the job within your company's financial means.

You do this by using what the Smarts call a "Job ScoreCard."

Rather than basing your decision on whether the candidate is qualified for the tasks that the job description outlines, base it on specific and measurable outcomes that you want to see the candidate accomplish over the first few years with the company. Then, you can evaluate whether the candidate is actually capable of achieving these results based on his or her previous achievements.

You also need to outline a list of the candidate's competencies and think about how they might match up with your culture and company initiatives. This kind of fit is more important than having the specific skills because skills can be learned and developed, but you can't change someone's personality.

The last bit of the Job Scorecard is looking at whether a candidate can help fulfill your brand promise and activities pertaining to your company's strategy. Meaning, if your brand promise is to be "Lots of Fun," you can't hire a total bump on a log.

By focusing on the "outcomes and competencies" of a potential hire, you can more accurately project how they'll perform in the job and build the ultimate A-team.

TODAY'S ACTION ITEM

JULY 31

{ WORK IS NOT THE ENEMY OF LIFE }

Why should work and life always be on opposite sides of some great cosmic balance? What are we hoping to balance? Are we all such clock watchers that every second of work must have an equal amount of "life"?

Chasing a work-life balance implies that somehow work is the enemy of life. Ask yourself this: Are you alive when you spend time working? When you're living your life, do you ever think about work? Work is a part of life. Work is responsible for much of what we have in life. Work isn't the enemy of life, it is the engine.

If you want more time for life, you need to make sure the engine is running as efficiently as possible.

Instead of chasing work-life balance, chase purpose.

If you can fire up your enthusiasm for what you're doing, it isn't so difficult to see your work as a part of your life. It should be something you're proud of. Seek out opportunities that drive your enthusiasm. If you're passionate about your work, that passion will be reflected in your life.

Don't worry as much about balancing the amount of time you spend on life vs. work. Instead, concentrate on making the most of the time available. Think about it in terms of work, family, community and personal life.

If you are efficient, plan ahead, and take control of your time, you'll discover that there is more than enough time to attain your goals *and* enjoy a purposeful and fulfilling life. Others have done it, and they worked with the same 24 hours in a day.

TODAY'S ACTION ITEM

AUGUST

{ VITAMIN B-8 }

Like the classic Beatles song "8 Days a Week,"
sometimes it can feel like you're truly working that much.
This month, build in some much-needed
"you time" to keep from burning out.

AUGUST 1

{ I'VE MADE A BUSINESS PLAN – NOW WHAT? }

Congratulations! You've completed the first step that many business owners are too afraid to do. You've created a sound business plan, but now how do you execute? There are three important steps:

1. Actually do it.
Yep, it's that simple, but also insanely difficult. Your goal will not be accomplished without someone (or multiple someones) putting in the work to make it happen. You know those daily, weekly and monthly priorities you set up for yourself? Carve out the time to complete them. How do you accomplish a goal? One step at a time.

2. Review your plan often, and revise it.
In my experience, the few business owners who actually have a plan review it annually, which is just about as useless as never reviewing it. You should review your plan monthly, or better yet, weekly. The economy changes, the market shifts, and your business needs the flexibility to respond and adapt. After all, if you're anticipating an attack from the north and receive intel the enemy is instead approaching from the south, you obviously need to reassess.

3. Don't let anything get in the way of implementing your plan.
What if Washington had given up because the weather in Valley Forge was horrible or because his adversary was better trained and equipped? I'll tell you what: We'd be singing "God Save The Queen." Don't get so busy fighting everyday battles that you lose the war. It won't be easy. In fact, few business owners can carry out a strategic plan and handle the day-to-day challenges of running a business. But those who can have an incredible competitive advantage. In fact, it is usually the difference between true business success and simply getting by.

TODAY'S ACTION ITEM

AUGUST 2

{ FIGHT OR FLIGHT: MANAGING STRESS IN BUSINESS }

We've all heard of "fight or flight." A fast heartbeat, sweaty palms and a surge of energy are our body's natural responses to a stressful situation. Whether we feel threatened, strained, or worn too thin, it happens to us all.

However, learning how to manage well during times of excessive stress or emergencies will make you a better leader.

Take control of your emotions. Whether you're anxious, scared or angry, managing the feelings that come with a tense situation is crucial when handling a crisis. Take a deep breath, or leave the room if you have to. Your team will take cues from you, and if you appear calm and collected, they will feel more at ease, too.

In a fight or flight situation, our body tends to move past rational thought and towards immediate action. These decisions are rushed, unplanned and often defensive. Taking time to stop and think about how to best proceed will inevitably lead to a more sound, considered response – and one you won't regret once the crisis is over.

How you respond is what separates good leaders from the rest.

TODAY'S ACTION ITEM

AUGUST 3

{ MAKE THE MOST OF TECHNOLOGY TO KEEP YOUR TEAM HAPPY }

Think about how important technology has become in our personal lives. Uninterrupted cable, internet and Wi-Fi access, a smartphone and a reliable computer with current software applications have become necessities rather than a luxury. And voice-activated smart home technology has made it easier than ever to do a myriad of things we didn't think imaginable 10-15 years ago.

We've come to expect – demand even – that the technology in our home work seamlessly 24/7/365. Now think about your office and how technology has become essential, even mission critical, to maximize your team's productivity.

I attribute the success of my first company largely to that fact that we had technology to handle customer relationship management, sales management, billing, etc. Because of our technology's ease and accessibility, our team was always organized and aligned, which increased our overall happiness and success.

Don't skimp on technology. With so many apps and programs, you have so much to choose from. Having outdated technology at your company is a surefire way to get your team frustrated, which in turn can lead to a lack of engagement and decreased job satisfaction. Incorporate technology into your office protocols to simplify processes for your team members' ease.

TODAY'S ACTION ITEM

AUGUST 4

{ LEADERS, DON'T ISOLATE YOURSELVES}
Guest contribution from Petra Coach Marshall Martin

In my experience coaching CEOs, I've found that many of them go through periods of loneliness when leading their organizations. This scenario always intrigues me when I come across it. How did it develop? Why do they feel isolated? Did this happen overnight, or were there warning signs? What could they have done to prevent this isolation?

When leaders feel isolated, it is most likely a result of either not building the right team along the way or overleveraging the few managers they have. Here are some contributing factors:

1. Seeking power and control.
Inexperienced leaders don't want anyone around who will challenge their authority. They want to steal the limelight, and they often view strong team members with insecurity. When leaders are scared of peers who bring significant experience to the table, it holds their companies back. It's better to give up micromanagement and give the team free reign to take ownership of their respective areas of expertise.

2. Not investing in your team.
Saving money by not investing in professional development resources that build strong leadership teams won't get anyone to the finish line. Invest heavily in your team and you'll soon see the ROI.

3. Hiring "Yes" people.
While it avoids conflict, hiring "yes" people is not the answer. Leaders need others to challenge the status quo and provide inspiration and energy to the team. Without dissent, there is no change, and change is the key to progress.

4. Not having enough diversity.
Diversity fosters better and alternative ideas in the decision-making process. Bringing different backgrounds, experiences and points of view to the management table leads to a more effective strategy.

TODAY'S ACTION ITEM

AUGUST 5

{ BE THE WORST PLAYER ON THE BEST TEAM }

My daughter played volleyball throughout middle and high school. When she was going into high school, she had to leave her younger, less-experienced group of girls behind to play with the starting varsity high school team.

My daughter is no longer one of the best players on her team. She's surrounded by a team of girls that are playing at a higher level than her. This inevitably forced her to improve.

Much like athletes, business professionals must place themselves in environments where they can improve their skills with the guidance of people that are better or more experienced.

Look around your organization and ask yourself: "Am I surrounded by people that are smarter than me, or am I the smartest one?" If you're the smartest, you're in the wrong room or you have the wrong team.

I encouraged my daughter to find a mentor – someone she wants to be like – and spend time with her so she could learn how to be a better player and teammate.

Likewise, it's crucial to find a mentor in your organization. You'd be surprised how willing others will be if you ask them to share with you. Watch, listen and learn how to improve.

TODAY'S ACTION ITEM

AUGUST 6

{ DISCIPLINE YOURSELF FIRST }

When I was building NationLink Wireless, I attended the Birthing Of Giants entrepreneurship program – based on Verne Harnish's book *Mastering the Rockefeller Habits* – at the Massachusetts Institute of Technology. I vividly remember this comment from an instructor:

"Eighty-five percent of you will leave here and do nothing. Fifteen percent of you will do something, and of that small group, only four percent of you will do everything."

That's what I call the "execution breakdown," because 96 percent of people fail to complete their goals and stick to their priorities. Pretty scary number, huh?

For many companies, the difference between success and failure often can be traced to the level of self-discipline among key players. Leaders who practice self-control and a commitment to getting the job done move a company forward, while those who don't risk the business's well-being.

Fortunately, self-discipline is a personality trait that can be learned. That's one reason that fellow entrepreneur and author Gregg Thompson believes that great leaders in business or life aren't born – they're made. They are simply more committed to becoming better each day and contributing to the growth and development of their colleagues and organization. Will Smith said it well in his inspirational video, "At the center of bringing any dream into fruition is self-discipline."

TODAY'S ACTION ITEM

AUGUST 7

{ ALWAYS MAKE TIME FOR FRIENDS AND FAMILY }

No matter how old you are or what your job is, it's important to have a full life and surround yourself with family and friends who will not only build you up but also be there when you need help or a dose of reality. They will provide real counsel to make you a better leader, family member and friend.

I can't stress this enough: **Value your friends and family, and make time for both.**

My daughter Madison said it best:

> "Luckily, I was raised by a dad who had crazy hours and an insane day-to-day schedule. People ask me, 'Why is that lucky?'
>
> "Thanks to his busy professional life, Dad had to learn how to prioritize time for himself and his family – and I see it took a lot of work. Of all the lessons I've learned from him, this is the one I remember each day. Dad put relationships first. In addition to setting aside time to make sure he was available to all of us, he made it a tradition to take my sister and me on individual father-daughter trips each year (something we still do)."

This lesson can't be overstated and I had to learn it myself: It's imperative that you don't get too caught up in business and forget to make your personal life a priority. Dedicate time for your personal well-being and for family. It might seem cumbersome in the beginning, but doing so will actually increase your productivity at the office, which is a win-win.

TODAY'S ACTION ITEM

AUGUST 8

{ DO YOU KNOW YOUR LEADERSHIP GRADE? }

Whether or not we realize it, our days are filled with assessing and measuring. We do this with our email inboxes, bank accounts and to-do lists, but how often do we appraise our leadership efforts?

It isn't a monumental thing to do, but it's extremely meaningful. Listening, accepting responsibility and giving encouragement are small acts that can add up to a big change in your leadership skills.

How often are you voicing the following sentiment to your team?

"Well done!"

When it comes to feedback, we all want it, but how much do we actually give and receive it? The results on appreciation in the workplace are astounding, with one study by Salesforce finding that employees who feel their voice is heard are 4.6 times more likely to feel empowered to perform their best work.

As leaders, it's up to us to encourage our employees to be the best they can be. See or hear someone doing something to help the team? Take a second to tell them "great job!" Reviewing a junior employee's work? Leave a positive note after your constructive criticism.

Do you have a way for employees to recognize each other at work? Consider starting a kudos board, where peers can give positive feedback to each other, and watch your office engagement soar.

TODAY'S ACTION ITEM

AUGUST 9

{ ARE YOU READY TO GO REMOTE? }

Implementing and managing a remote working policy is no easy feat, however it is becoming essential to meeting the desires of today's workforce. If you haven't heard, your employees are happier, more engaged and achieve better results when you give them the flexibility to work from home – whether that's every day or once per month.

Here are three ways to make your remote workforce the strongest it can be:

1. Establish a solid system for working remotely.
Set clear communications and expectations. Outline when, where and how many times per month your employees can work remotely. Outline the system for how to request this benefit and times you'd like them to check-in with the rest of the team, if necessary.

2. Do it yourself.
The only way this policy works is if everyone buys in, starting from the top. If you're not convinced this is the right choice for your company, ask yourself why and then ask other business leaders if they feel the same. If you make the decision to implement a remote working policy, use it yourself. Modeling to employees that you take advantage of the company benefit will give them the freedom to do so, as well.

3. Don't micromanage.
You hired your employees for a reason, now let them prove to you they are worth your trust. Once you establish your remote working ground rules, give your team space to meet and exceed them.

TODAY'S ACTION ITEM

AUGUST 10
{ GETTING LOST }

I recently read a blog post from best-selling author and speaker Seth Godin that illustrated why some entrepreneurs succeed where others fail. He wrote, "Sometimes, when we're lost, we refuse a map, even when offered. Because the map reminds us that we made a mistake. That we were wrong. But without a map, we're not just wrong, but we're also still lost. A map doesn't automatically get you home, but it will probably make you less lost. (When dealing with the unknown, it's difficult to admit that there might not be a map. In those cases, a compass is essential, a way to remind yourself of your true north...)."

Life has a lot of ups and downs. That's never going to change. However, the way you deal with those changes and the coping mechanisms you put in place to handle the challenges that come your way is totally up to you. Understand that you'll occasionally be wrong.

That's right. Just when you think you've got it all figured out, you're likely to get lost again. Keep your roadmap (see July 3) close, and make adjustments to the journey as you go. Part of being an effective leader is being humble enough to know that you can't do everything yourself and that you're not perfect. You're human, and that's a good thing. Knowing that you're going to get lost again will allow you to be better prepared each time it happens.

TODAY'S ACTION ITEM

AUGUST 11

{ WHEN YOU SHOULD HIRE A CFO }

At some point in the life cycle of a business there comes a time when it's wise to hire a chief financial officer (CFO).

For business owners, hiring a CFO is a significant financial and emotional decision for three reasons. First, it's expensive to hire talented financial pros. Second, the position does not contribute to revenue to offset the cost. Third, by hiring a CFO you are essentially ceding control and stewardship of your company's finances to another person.

The anxiety involved in hiring a finance pro is understandable, but here are three areas to review that will help you make the right call:

Revenue.
If your business has sales of $1-$2 million you probably only need a bookkeeper. Once you start pushing $5-10 million, you'll want an experienced accountant to manage the company's finances. Once you have blown past the $10 million mark, it's a safe bet that you'll also need a CFO to manage the increasingly detailed accounting transactions for the company's financial statements.

Funding.
If your business reaches the point where it requires debt or equity capital to fund future growth, you may need a CFO to ensure you raise the right amount on the right terms that make financial sense.

Complexity.
If your company sells multiple products and/or service lines, or is juggling many different customers and vendors, possibly in multiple countries, a CFO will safeguard your cash by more effectively managing accounts receivable and accounts payable.

TODAY'S ACTION ITEM

AUGUST 12
{ DON'T FEAR "THE DIP" }

A lot of factors go into growth and success, and sometimes you have to take risks, such as acquiring another company or investing in a new security technology.

But when you're investing, there can be increases as well as dips. Remember that this is a normal part of growth, and a healthy balance of both won't hinder your success, as long as the business is adapting along with industry trends and new technologies.

Make sure you are staying on top of your profit structure. With customers being as price-sensitive as they are now and competition becoming fiercer, dropping your prices may seem like the only option. Not true.

You may be tempted to increase your sales and marketing efforts and even offer deals, sales and giveaways to make your product more enticing. Not necessary.

Instead, focus on attracting clients that are willing to spend more for a high-quality product backed by the services you can provide. That will keep your profit margin more stable and ensure that your customers value your services and are willing to compensate you for them.

TODAY'S ACTION ITEM

AUGUST 13

{ REWARD HARD WORK }

We spend at least 40 hours in and around the office during a normal workweek. Add in the time spent working at home or staying late, and some team members work closer to 50, 60 or even 70 hours a week.

When people spend this much time in the office, it's important to make sure they feel appreciated; in fact, it's absolutely necessary. A survey by the American Psychological Association found that feeling valued at work is a key indicator of job performance and engagement.

I have talked about how many of the companies I coach have a "Kudos" board, or some other method of internal appreciation. It can be a wall, a corner, the chalkboard in your lobby, the fridge in your break room or any other designated space in your office to display notes of gratitude.

But I say take the appreciation one step further. Collect kudos from the board at the end of each month or quarter, and select team members that best represent each of the company's core values. Then, give those winners a tangible award.

Buy each of them lunch, or send them out on a nice date with his or her spouse. Show up at work with a bottle of wine or a gift card to their favorite ice cream place. Give them something small but thoughtful to physically show your gratitude – no one's too old to appreciate a prize, especially if its well-deserved.

Showing gratitude isn't difficult, and oftentimes can end up providing the most fun you'll have all week. Start an appreciation board today and let your team members know that their work is valued.

TODAY'S ACTION ITEM

AUGUST 14

{ YOUR BEST SALESPEOPLE MAY NOT BE WHO YOU'D EXPECT }

Guest contribution from Petra Coach Jason Rush

My wife Rhonda used to drive a small Mercedes-Benz C-Class. Despite my explaining that there were more affordable options, Rhonda always took her car to the Mercedes-Benz dealership for maintenance. Why? She insisted on the care she received from her service adviser, Barbara.

Barbara and Rhonda's visits more closely reflected old friends catching up rather than routine customer interactions. Not only did my wife enjoy chatting with Barbara, but their longstanding relationship established trust that Rhonda's prized possession was always in good hands.

Think about this in relation to your own business: Who manages the client relationships? How can you ensure that these interactions are positive?

Here are two key tips to get your company on the right track:

1. Consider each employee a part of sales.
Growing sales is a full-team sport. It cannot be left up to the people with "sales" in their title. Every interaction an employee has with a potential customer will impact the success of your sales efforts. Therefore, everyone should be trained on product knowledge and taught how to use that knowledge to inspire action.

2. Engage with clients holistically.
The interpersonal relationship between my wife and Barbara played a key role in Rhonda's openness to the dealership's sales efforts. Employees should be trained in the same way. A gesture as small as remembering a client's birthday builds a level of trust that no amount of sales effort can replace.

Barbara's training equipped her to create intentional opportunities to connect with clients based on what many people would consider "routine" work. Can your team do that?

TODAY'S ACTION ITEM

AUGUST 15

{ 3 WAYS TO EXECUTE }

Entrepreneurs and leaders all too often will make a plan but lack the discipline to see it through. It's the self-discipline to execute on daily priorities and tasks that separates successful companies from failed ones. Don't let "old habits die hard" – fight to change them and win!

Here are three ways to kick old habits to the curb and start fresh today:

1. Set priorities and identify potential roadblocks.
There's an old saying in business: "Plan your work and work your plan." The key to effective planning is identifying priorities and tasks that are required to achieve company goals. You want goals to be S.M.A.R.T. – specific, measurable, attainable, relevant and time-bound.

I recommend setting three to five quarterly priorities to avoid spreading anyone too thin – and make sure the priorities support the company's monthly, quarterly, one-year, five-year and 10-year goals.

2. Measure progress toward your goals.
Successful execution is the direct result of completing many small activities over a period of time. Every time you complete one of those tasks, check it off a list, so you can see what's done and what's left to do. My clients use a web-based software application called AlignToday.com, which tracks tasks and measures individual and group successes for the whole company to see. It's a great reminder of what needs to be done to keep the company moving in the right direction.

3. Just do it.
Yes, that's Nike's slogan, and it should be ingrained in the psyche of every entrepreneur. One of the quickest ways businesses lose momentum and trust is by not following through on commitments. Don't promise unless you are sure you can deliver.

TODAY'S ACTION ITEM

AUGUST 16

{ WORK YOUR BRAIN TO BUILD FOCUS }

We live in a world where multitasking is praised. If you can tweet, write, research and do the chicken dance at the same time, you're considered a go-getter. Here's the truth: multitasking puts stress on the brain and can actually shrink memory receptors. That's according to Dr. Gary Small, a UCLA memory specialist and author of *The Memory Prescription*.

If that's not enough, multitasking actually decreases your IQ. According to scientist Harold Pashleer, when people do two tasks at once their cognitive capacity can drop from that of a Harvard MBA to that of an eight-year-old.

Studies aside, the multitasking grind might possibly sustain you and your company's current level of success, but it will not elevate it. To rise, you must focus. Here's how:

Do the big thing first.
Identify your top priority and put on your blinders until that task is completed. Share your top priority with your team to foster accountability. Pinpoint your top priority the evening before so you are on task when you hit the office in the morning. Write your priority down – a written reminder helps you stay on track.

Purge the little things.
Sometimes our little tasks act like mental roadblocks. They make us anxious and keep us from accomplishing our top priority. Do your brain a favor and release all the little things from your mind by writing them down.

Eliminate distractions.
Turn off your phone and email, and sign off Facebook. Rings, bings and pings distract you from what's really important. When you feel like checking your texts and posts, ask yourself this question: Am I wasting my time to avoid the important?

If you're still with me, congrats – you've worked out your focus muscle!

TODAY'S ACTION ITEM

AUGUST 17

{ THE PEOPLE YOU LIKE VS. THE PEOPLE YOU NEED }

We all have one or two (or many) people in our office that can sometimes (or always) rub us the wrong way. It seems like it's for no apparent reason, but in fact, there is a perfectly good explanation.

That person is, most likely, your exact opposite in character traits.

If you're, say, determined and confident, the person who is hesitant and soft-spoken is likely to get on your nerves.

But want to know the other kicker? As David Rendall says in his book *The Freak Factor,* "The person you like the least might be the person you need the most."

He shares the example of a CEO that, before Rendall was scheduled to speak to the group, got up in front of his whole company and publicly apologized to his right-hand man for yelling at him, arguing with him and belittling him. The CEO realized that while he often struggled to work well with his counterpart, he needed that person in his life to counterbalance him.

Rendall adds, "The people with opposite characteristics can get along not through compromise, but through acceptance." The CEO ultimately accepts his colleague for who he is, even if they don't always see eye to eye, and that's how they've maintained a successful partnership.

It's a lesson we all can learn. Take a moment and catalogue those people that you have trouble with. Is it for this reason? Do they actually serve some higher purpose in your life that you didn't realize?

TODAY'S ACTION ITEM

AUGUST 18

{ HOW TO OVERCOME BAD NEWS }

Bad news is an essential part of life. However, as cliche as it sounds, it's not what happens to you, but how you react to it that will determine how the bad news affects you and your company. When bad news (inevitably) strikes, here are two things to do:

1. Determine a path forward.
It's not enough to get things out on the table. You've got to be able to move forward in a deliberate way. Once everyone has been heard, make a plan for how things are going to proceed. Whether the task is small or large, outline a way to address any underlying problems that may have caused the issue in the first place. Get buy-in from your team, and then go about executing that plan.

2. Agree that when it's over, it's over.
Bad news can't be allowed to float in the air forever. Once you've set aside the time to discuss the news and have made a plan to address any problems, you've got to put any negativity behind you and move forward in a positive way. So, ask everyone in the room to agree that you're going to discuss the issue fully, hear everyone out, determine a course of action to move forward…and then agree together that you will move on.

Bad news can send lasting reverberations throughout an organization if it's not handled correctly. Don't let that happen. If you take the time to address problems and truly move on, it's possible for a team to enter a room fractured and exit the room whole.

TODAY'S ACTION ITEM

AUGUST 19

{ HOLD TIGHT TO THOSE "A-PLAYERS" }

Failure to retain top talent is one of the biggest barriers to growth. And in today's competitive economy, it's increasingly common for companies in all industries to lose top talent.

What does it take to keep your "A-players" engaged and happy at your company?

First, build a culture of "why." Engaged team members want to clearly understand how their day-to-day tasks fit into the bigger picture of the organization. Explain how their work directly contributes to the organization's goals. When team members understand why their work is important, they feel a sense of purpose, and are therefore more motivated to do the best work possible.

Over time, give team members the opportunity to focus on activities that give them strength, rather than those that are chores and drain the life out of them. Team members who use their strengths every day are six times more likely to be engaged in the workplace, according to a Gallup survey.

Perhaps most importantly, pay them more! Don't lose your top talent to another company because you don't pay them enough. Your team members are not costs that take away from profitability; they are the engines that drive revenue growth. Invest in your top talent and give them the training (and pay) they need to grow within your company. Think about it – replacement costs for team members can range from 30 to 150 percent of an annual salary.

As you can see, you don't have to pull out all of the bells and whistles to keep your team happy. Develop a simple retention plan, and you'll be less likely to lose another "A-player." And you'll ultimately build a stronger company.

TODAY'S ACTION ITEM

AUGUST 20

{ GO WITH YOUR GUT }

While still in college, I founded a pager business. In time, it grew into a multi-million-dollar company. I knew in my gut that although pagers were all the hype, a new technology would inevitably take its place.

I didn't listen to my gut.

Instead I obstinately defended the pager business and its relevance because I linked my success directly to it.

Because of my inability to embrace new technology head on, I lost a lot of money and my business nearly perished.

Eventually and fortunately, I did make the change to mobile phones. But because I adapted slowly, I was forced to start my mobile business nearly from scratch. It was then that I promised myself I would never again ignore threats, or my instinct, in business.

Go with your gut. Instinct is a powerful tool we're all hardwired with. Use it. It will rarely fail you.

Like many of life's difficult lessons, I'm better for having experienced my defining business lesson early on. It has undoubtedly shaped my personal evolution as well.

TODAY'S ACTION ITEM

AUGUST 21

{ BE OPEN WHEN THINGS GET STRESSFUL }

In business and in life, hard times are inevitable.

That's why you need to surround yourself with a group of friends that you can turn to when things get tough. Connect with individuals who will support you, and openly share with them the struggles you're facing.

You should also add a professional to your team of confidantes. When things go awry, asking a seasoned professional for advice will almost always improve the outcome. After all, they've been in your shoes and succeeded, and probably did it with a little help, too.

With these types of support, you'll be able to face any stressful situation with the confidence needed to tackle it.

After assessing the situation with your support system and taking the time to form a response, be open to multiple solutions. The right solution may not be what you had in mind. It may not even be options "B" or "C" on your list, but it may be the necessary resolution to the issue at hand.

Be open to others' support and the options ahead, and these stressful situations might not seem that bad after all.

TODAY'S ACTION ITEM

AUGUST 22

{ THE BENEFITS OF A CLEAR MIND }

The idea of clearing one's mind isn't exactly a breakthrough. After all, there are numerous articles and studies on how meditative acts help boost creativity and performance.

According to Walter Isaacson's *The Book of Jobs*, Steve Jobs even asserted that the driving factor behind his creative inspiration was a clear mind through meditation.

As a young business owner back in the early days, I discovered the powerful effect that clearing my mind could have on my decision-making and creativity.

In 2011, I sold my business, which I started in college and grew into a successful organization.

Once the sale wrapped and I was ready for whatever my next phase of life would be, I recognized – and was invigorated by – the fear of the unknown. I made a commitment to avoid that "next phase" decision for one full year.

During that year-long recess, I paddleboarded – a lot. I made a conscious effort to keep my mind clear and open, and each time on the board, I left worry and anxiety behind.

I realized then just how crucial my head-clearing trips had been to my overall approach to my career up to that point. It was during this paddleboarding sabbatical that I came up with the idea for my next company, where I now get to share my successes and mistakes with other entrepreneurs all over the world who are looking to improve their businesses and themselves.

What can you do to clear your mind today?

TODAY'S ACTION ITEM

AUGUST 23

{ SURROUND YOURSELF WITH CRAZIES }

Leading a business is an emotional roller coaster. You may be crazy to want to do it. As a leader and entrepreneur, one of the best things you can do to help with the emotional highs and lows is to find people who are just as crazy as you are.

Here's my advice: Surround yourself with other like-minded leaders. Find a local industry organization or group and dig in – get involved with other people so you can talk to them about how running your company is affecting you and those around you, personally and professionally. When you realize others are on the same roller coaster, or better yet, jumped on the coaster before you and are now flying down the track, you'll gain confidence and feel rejuvenated.

As a business coach there is tremendous value in associating with other successful executives. You will hear new ideas that will help you improve as a leader, successfully navigate the tricky turns ahead and get you fired up about your business. There is something powerful about realizing that someone else is on the same roller coaster you're on and has succeeded!

The connections you make with other successful leaders can often lead to new business relationships. But it has to be a two-way street, so be willing to share with your new-found brethren and help them in their journey.

The ups and downs of running a business are never easy. Getting involved with fellow leaders will help you to weather the bumpy ride in your new business, conquer the uphill climb and ride that momentum to your success.

TODAY'S ACTION ITEM

AUGUST 24

{ KEEP YOUR TEAM ON TRACK }

Alignment is the key to a company's success. Without it, businesses are held back from growing and reaching their full potential. In order to seamlessly instill alignment into your organization, make sure that your company operates according to the following three characteristics:

1. Visibility: A company must have clear core values, core purpose and goals in order to be successful in the long run. A strategic plan outlining these areas of the business should be displayed in a central location that is accessible to everyone in the organization. Individual progress towards goals should also be visible to everyone in the organization. Distinctly displaying what is and what is not on track makes it easy for business leaders to pinpoint areas that need more attention. Plus, displaying this information publicly encourages accountability among team members.

2. Accountability: Accountability drives businesses. Build a work environment of people who follow through. Give team members ownership of the organization's goals, which instills pride because they know they are making an impact on the success of the business. Use a reporting system to measure performance and results. When team members are excelling, recognize them to increase motivation. If some are off course, provide them with feedback to help them get back on track.

3. Transparency: Effective communication within an organization is crucial to achieving alignment. Encourage a culture of openness and collaboration in order to build trust. When organizations transparently and honestly share information, it keeps employees connected to the big picture.

TODAY'S ACTION ITEM

AUGUST 25

{ DEALING WITH "THE DISSENTER" }

Guest contribution from Petra Coach JT Terrell (1/3)

When we engage with a new member company at Petra Coach, we start with a two-day kickoff session where we meet with the leadership team to lay out foundational "stuff" for the company (e.g., core purpose, core values, their "big hairy audacious goal" or BHAG) and get specific on the next three to five years of the firm's trajectory.

It is during the future vision session that I'll see at least one team member push back on what's possible, shoot down new ideas and generally clam up by the end of the day. Over time, I've learned to identify these folks as the ones who "aren't going to make it," such as the person I refer to as "The Dissenter."

How many times have you heard these statements from someone behind folded arms: "If it ain't broke, don't fix it." "You don't understand our industry." Or my personal favorite, "We've always done it this way."

The fact is that your team, in whatever configuration it is currently, will have to be something different to achieve long-term goals. More staff, more training, lots of effort and the will to be flexible are all critical to success.

Getting over that mental hurdle, however, is the first step in the journey, and some people can't do it.

In my experience, the best way for leaders to help these folks is to acknowledge that change is inevitable. You should commit to providing dissenters with the tools and training they'll need, so they can grow faster than the rate of the company.

Maybe then they'll be more open to the idea of change.

TODAY'S ACTION ITEM

AUGUST 26

{ DEALING WITH "THE DISRUPTOR" }
Guest contribution from Petra Coach JT Terrell (2/3)

Tell me if this sounds familiar: Plans get made and one of your productive, happy team members suddenly mutates into a problem child. Did he change his personality overnight?

I call this person "The Disruptor."

The fact is: The leaders your company has when it's doing $3 million in revenue are generally not going to be the same ones when you're at $13 million.

For example, a director of operations requires a different set of skills and experience to achieve proper margins and efficiencies at that larger scale.

When you make a decision to scale your business, watch as the "weak links" begin to see the writing on the wall. Some will either act out or disappear – neither is a good leadership strategy for growth.

To remedy this, conduct honest talent assessments with your team members (which you should be doing anyway, regardless of your plans for growth) measured against a specific scorecard for their positions.

At Petra Coach, we do this by specifying the roles, responsibilities, skills and company culture expectations on our scorecards, and then we regularly revisit them with individual team members in one-on-one meetings.

That way, we know who is fit to keep up with the growth and can figure out the next steps for potential Disruptors. Sometimes the best course of action is to help them find another job.

TODAY'S ACTION ITEM

AUGUST 27

{ DEALING WITH "THE DIFFIDENT" }

Guest contribution from Petra Coach JT Terrell (3/3)

Ever worked with someone who is too "modest" or unassertive to take the leap of faith with the rest of the company and make changes to ensure growth?

This person is the one I call "The Diffident."

As we all know: Growth, in any form, comes from getting outside of your comfort zone. But it is harder for some than others.

The quickest way to identify whether your company has become complacent over time is to look at your team members. Are they quite happy with organic growth, 10 percent or less net profit, and barely getting by? If any of these answers are "yes," then I've got news: You have Diffidents on your team, which means complacency is the status quo, and changes are going to rock the boat – hard.

And rocking the boat is good! I encourage leaders to set aggressive targets, change the processes that need updating and see who steps up to the plate to take a swing.

The team members that get up to bat may end up striking out on their first attempt, but in my experience, those individuals are the ones to get your company out of the comfort zone and on to bigger and better things.

The team members of concern are the ones who stay in the dugout. My recommendation? Trade 'em.

TODAY'S ACTION ITEM

AUGUST 28

{ HOW PETRA COACH STARTED }

From the very first day of Petra Coach's existence, I held a daily huddle (with myself, initially!), created a one-page strategic plan for the company and outlined quarterly priorities. I also created the core values that would drive my company forward. I've stayed true to these values from day one, and they've been the foundation for how I treat my team members and member companies.

There is no try! – Only do.
I want to eliminate the attitude of "trying" to do something – of thinking about it, wishing it would happen, creating a plan that doesn't get done, etc. – and, instead, actually doing it.

I've got your back, no matter what.
I knew my company would grow, and I wanted future team members to understand that we would all support each other through good times and bad.

"Please" and "Thank You" – say it and mean it.
Showing genuine appreciation for someone else has a powerful impact on clients and team members. It also has an amazing positive effect on company culture.

Everything is an experience, every time.
It's really not that difficult to be remarkable. If you create an experience – not just an event – people will talk about it.

See around the curves.
Anticipate needs and pre-fill them. Being uber-prepared to respond (not react!) to future events can be the difference between success and failure.

Be curious: Ask "Why" and improve.
Successful leaders never accept things as they are. They seek constant improvement, for themselves and the processes they put in place, to build their companies and grow their team members.

TODAY'S ACTION ITEM

AUGUST 29

{ WHO IS ON YOUR TEAM? }

Surrounding yourself with the right people in life is important, and the same goes for the workplace. If you hang with a crowd that favors negativity, it can be hard to break out of the cycle of cynicism and gossip, and that consequently hurts your level of fulfillment.

Even if the role you're currently performing isn't ideal, make an effort to maintain a positive spirit. I promise – it alone will help boost your attitude at work and will directly affect those around you.

Here are three ways to do it:

1. Seek colleagues with positive attitudes.
People are more productive when they're around happy people who have a positive outlook on life. Nothing can sink your happiness faster than being around team members who have a negative attitude. Make sure your morale is high by associating yourself with positive thinkers (and doers!).

2. Seek colleagues who are achievers.
Every company has team members who are driven to succeed who also support their co-workers. Find those people and become part of their inner circle. They can push you harder to grow and succeed, both personally and professionally.

3. Seek mentors.
Find a mentor, an experienced team member, who can provide you with guidance on your job and career. They've "been there, done that" and can share invaluable insight to help you excel in your role at the company. And remember, these veterans will also benefit from learning about your ideas.

TODAY'S ACTION ITEM

AUGUST 30

{ FINDING YOUR COMPANY'S DIAMONDS IN THE ROUGH}

Whether you realize it or not, your business has valuable assets that are not being used to their fullest potential. I'm talking about the people you already have on your payroll who work hard for you every day and most likely have talents you've never discovered before.

Before you start hiring to fill an empty position, focus on embracing and developing internal individuals with relevant skill sets. The process will be much easier – they are already there, and they know your company and what you value. Start uncovering your diamonds in the rough.

Mine for the gems by digging into your roster of existing team members. Create a company-wide survey to find people interested in taking on new initiatives, and give them the opportunity to be considered.

Hold company-wide brainstorms and invite everyone – at all levels – to contribute. See who comes up with the best ideas, and pay particular attention to those who can take the seed of an idea and grow it in a creative way.

The true innovators and idea champions (even if they're currently not in a role that's a perfect fit) know what they can bring to the table. If you give them the opportunity to shine, they'll come forward.

This process isn't a one-and-done kind of thing. Meet regularly with your people to find these hidden assets, and make this discovery a regular part of your company culture. That way, new team members will come onboard knowing that there's an opportunity to "flaunt what they've got" (even if it's not what they were originally hired to do).

TODAY'S ACTION ITEM

AUGUST 31

{ ARE YOU KEEPING UP WITH THE PACE? }

If your company isn't changing, it's dying. I work with businesses all over the globe, and I've seen that no matter the location, industry or size, companies that resist change stifle success.

"But we've always done it that way."

Maybe the old ways worked for a while. They might even work just fine now. But, if you're constantly looking in the rearview mirror, your current and future competition will eventually leave you in the dust.

Counteract this in your organizations by creating a Process and Accountability Chart, or PACe. Start today by listing all of your business's processes. You have to know exactly what your company is doing before you can start addressing why and how it's doing it. It may seem ludicrous that some business owners have never thought about their company's processes, but it happens all the time. Documenting what you have reveals which ones are done by default rather than by design.

Once you have your list, pick one and analyze it. From the starting point and on, write each step of the process down on a sticky note. Identify the people involved, the time it takes and the decisions that need to be made for each step. Put all your notes on a wall, then step back and look for where you can improve. Are there ways you can increase efficiency? Yes. Are there any unnecessary steps that are no longer needed? Probably. Are there opportunities to automate? Hopefully.

TODAY'S ACTION ITEM

SEPTEMBER

{ VITAMIN B-9 }

*Nutrients are essential for growth.
This vitamin ensures that your company has the
proper building blocks to grow into a healthy
and successful organization, including a core purpose
and core values. Make those your focus this month.*

SEPTEMBER 1

{ PLAY TO YOUR TEAM MEMBERS' STRENGTHS }

If you're a sports fan, you've undoubtedly dusted off your mini grill to get it into tailgating condition. More than that, you've probably drafted your all-star fantasy roster, picking players who are talented in their specific positions, enjoy playing those positions, complement the skills of other team members and have an overall passion for the game.

Now, I propose that you manage your business's team members like your fantasy roster. Hire team members who 1) have the necessary skills, 2) are ready to work and 3) fit the team dynamic. Then, play to their strengths.

When employees are able to operate from their strengths, they're six times more likely to be engaged in their role, according to a recent Gallup poll. To maximize productivity, give team members work they're good at and enjoy doing. In short, let your kicker kick.

For accurate identification of the strengths of your team members, I recommend using a personality assessment like DiSC. It's a series of questions used to measure an individual's proclivity toward Dominance, Influence, Steadiness or Compliance.

The object of identifying the behavioral style of individuals is not to put them in a box, but to better understand team members' comfort zones and assign them tasks that lie within that arena.

But be cautious – even individuals in the same DiSC quadrant will have varying work styles. Make sure you are working with all of your employees to ensure they are in roles where they are most productive.

TODAY'S ACTION ITEM

SEPTEMBER 2
{ ADAPT TO SURVIVE }

Darwin said: "In the struggle for survival, the fittest win out at the expense of their rivals because they succeed in adapting themselves best to their environment."

The same applies in business. Throughout my years, I've learned the hard way to adapt.

What is your adaptability grade? Examine these three practices and how often you are doing them to find out.

1. Look to the future.
Set your sights 18 months ahead of the market. So many business leaders get caught up in the day to day. This myopic approach stunts their evolution.

2. Read and network.
By educating yourself and conversing with your consumers and colleagues, you'll gain intel that you'll miss if you remain isolated in your office only reading yesterday's business reports.

3. Lead proudly.
Steve Jobs said: "Innovation distinguishes between a leader and a follower." As a business owner or leader you should always look for occasions to lead. Don't hide behind your last accomplishment.

TODAY'S ACTION ITEM

SEPTEMBER 3

{ SO YOU THINK YOU'RE THE BEST? }

Folks, let me tell you a secret: There's no such thing as "the best." You can be great and do all the right things for your business, but there's always room for improvement.

In business, you never want to get too comfortable. Just because your business is booming now doesn't mean it'll stay that way. Here are five tips to get even better:

1. Go to a bigger pond.
If at first you measured your success against your citywide competition, rank yourself against your statewide competition. After you're the best in your state, chart a plan to become the best in the nation. Keep raising your ceiling.

2. Remember your competition.
Your competition is chasing you. They're studying your every move. The game is yours to lose and theirs to win. Don't let them catch up. Instead, go faster.

3. Continue learning.
Make sure you continue to discover new techniques and tricks. Reinvent the standard so that by the time your competition masters your old winning move, you have a new one.

4. Request feedback.
When you're a leader, you need to know your shortcomings. Be open to and learn from honest feedback and constructive criticism from your team members, coaches and fans.

5. Celebrate.
As important as it is to learn from your mistakes, learn from your wins, too. If you did something well last quarter, pinpoint it, celebrate it and do it again. On the road to greatness, reward and recognize your and your team's achievements. It'll give you the information and energy to keep winning, so you can keep celebrating.

TODAY'S ACTION ITEM

SEPTEMBER 4

{ DON'T LET YOUR EGO GET IN THE WAY }

Entrepreneurs have many great qualities. They have a particular talent to see "gaps" – areas where something is needed in the marketplace but not being provided (at least not as well as they think it could be) – and to fill that gap with a product or service. In the same way, they can see gaps in other businesses and help business leaders improve and be more successful.

However, there can be a dark side to those instincts when startup founders begin to think they're bulletproof, that they have all the answers. When that happens those shortsighted entrepreneurs soon discover their team members find it tough working with them and become less engaged in the business.

One of the most important lessons I learned when running my company was how to keep my ego in check. Your ego can be your enemy. Don't let it happen. While you are the final decision maker, you're not the only person in the room – and all businesses require a wide variety of ideas and points of view to keep things fresh. The opinions of others have value. You put yourself and your business at risk if you let your ego get in the way of accepting other viewpoints.

Part of putting your ego aside is to listen to the people around you. They'll have great ideas – after all, you hired them! But you'll never find out if you don't ask for their input and then open your ears.

TODAY'S ACTION ITEM

SEPTEMBER 5

{ IMPROVING YOUR TALENT MANAGEMENT }

It's important to an organization's success to bring in sustained, fruitful, challenge-free team members who grow into leaders *and* to keep them in the door once you have them.

The first step is to avoid "stray dogs," or hires who don't fit all of an organization's hiring criteria but get picked up anyway. These team members become problematic, creating additional, unnecessary work that can bog down workflow, other co-workers and even entire teams.

To set up your talent management system the right way, develop a process of ensuring candidates meet your criteria. When deciding on the right people for a task, author and business consultant Jim Collins notes that leaders should always ask the "who" question first and foremost – rather than a "what" or "why" question.

For example, "Who do we need to do this work?" This allows you to identify the specific person for the task at hand. Your people are key to driving business results, and your job is to find the best "who" quickly by asking that question first.

But even with the right processes in place, let's face it – problems still come up. The tough "who" question – "Who is responsible?" – is a quick and efficient way to seek out the individuals who cause issues at work.

Don't hinder your organization's growth by hesitating to identify problematic team members or by repetitively making a short-term repair to issues as they spring up. Get to the root of the problem quickly, and be ready to make changes – even if that involves letting someone go.

TODAY'S ACTION ITEM

SEPTEMBER 6

{ 3 GROUND RULES FOR PRODUCTIVE TEAM MEETINGS }

For team meetings to be effective you need ground rules that everyone accepts and follows. Having rules in place fosters improved problem-solving and decision-making because they keep everyone on the team moving forward and not sidetracked by discussions or comments that detract from the goal of the meeting.

Here are three tried-and-true ground rules to bring to every meeting:

1. Don't hide your mistakes.
If you made a mistake, own it. If you hide things and lie about them, that is like a five-year old who broke mom's vase and blames the dog. If you didn't do the right thing, the only finger you should be pointing is at yourself. I guarantee your team will be much more understanding when you're honest with them.

2. Don't hide problems.
Similar to sharing your mistakes, don't be afraid to discuss issues you may be experiencing with your work or with others in the office. Share your thoughts in a way that inspires conversation and collaboration, such as in one-on-one check-in meetings. Once problems are out in the open, the team can help you take steps to correct them. Being honest about issues is also a great way to prevent those mistakes mentioned above.

3. Speak up.
Just as you shouldn't hide problems or mistakes, make sure you share your ideas with the team. Who knows, you could have the solution that no one considered. Even if you're a junior member of the team, your ideas are important. Give yourself and your colleagues the benefit of the doubt that your ideas are great and that they won't make fun of you for them.

TODAY'S ACTION ITEM

SEPTEMBER 7

{ THINGS NOT GOING YOUR WAY?
PLAY TAG. }

I fly a lot for business, and a recent flight to Fort Lauderdale reminded me of the importance of flexibility, both at work and in my personal life.

I boarded the plane beneath blue skies with my laptop in hand and was looking forward to getting a couple hours of work done before landing. But before we could take off a heavy thunderstorm moved in and delayed the flight. I knew I couldn't change the situation, I could only change the way I handled it. So while other passengers berated the flight attendant or complained to their spouses on the phone, I remembered "TAG."

> **T = Think.** When you're faced with something unexpected, the first thing to do is to stop and think. It's easy to get caught in the whirlwind of circumstances and act impulsively, but by pausing, you can ask yourself questions that will help direct your subsequent actions. "What's happening?" "Why is this happening?" "How does this affect me?" "What's the best response?"
>
> **A = Adjust.** Once you've identified what's happening and how you're involved, you can change your expectations and behavior to allow for the new circumstances. Accepting Plan B isn't always easy because it means Plan A failed. But what people don't realize is that Plan B represents a willingness to keep looking for solutions. Ultimately, you still need to get to your destination, but maybe you need to adjust how you get there.
>
> **G = Gather.** Even when you're being patient and practical and channeling your inner Yoda, a supportive shoulder to lean on is always helpful. Whether it's your family at home or your colleagues at work, gather people you know you can count on – especially when you've encountered an unexpected situation.

TODAY'S ACTION ITEM

SEPTEMBER 8
{ WILL, VALUES, RESULTS, SKILL }

A simple set of criteria that Verne Harnish suggests in his book *Scaling Up* that you can use to quickly evaluate a potential hire for how well they fit in your company is:

Will – Is the person literally *willing* to do it? Does this person want to learn, grow and succeed in this position? Is he or she passionate about it?

Values – Do the candidate's values align with your company's core values? Do they seem like a fit in your culture?

Results – Is this person capable of reaching the outcomes the company needs from this job role, based on his or her history of achievements?

Skills – Considering skills need constant updating, this is actually the least important factor. However, it's still important that the candidate has the basic skills and experience needed for the role.

Evaluating based on this criteria will give you a good basis for making a decision about a certain candidate's fitness, and could save you some wasted time and money on a bad hire.

TODAY'S ACTION ITEM

SEPTEMBER 9

{ WINNING THE BATTLE AGAINST INERTIA }

The truth is most of us are not "in the flow" all the time. Even the most seasoned leaders experience inertia from time to time. The key is to get moving – shake things up and make choices that force you out of your "state of stuck."

Follow these three steps to get your wheels rolling again:

1. Ask what might get in your way.
If you set a goal, but you don't think about potential obstacles, you're setting yourself up for failure. Get real about any hurdles that might get in the way of achieving your goal so you can work around those circumstances and find your best path to success.

2. Make yourself accountable.
It can be easy to tell yourself that you're going to do something, but if you make your intentions public, it's much tougher to make excuses and abandon your commitments.

Tell your colleagues, friends, and family about your plans. Once you've got a community of people watching – providing support and accountability – you'll be more likely to follow through and make it to the finish line.

3. Do it now!
No matter how small the first step is, make every effort to take it immediately. Demonstrate to yourself and others that you're committed to the process and you're ready to move forward. In the words of Lao Tzu, "The journey of a thousand miles begins with one step." Take that step as soon as you can.

Thinking about it won't get you anywhere. Set your goal, figure out how to meet it and really *do it*. Put in the time and effort to push past your inertia – the finish line is just around the corner.

TODAY'S ACTION ITEM

SEPTEMBER 10
{ ONBOARDING FOR KEEPS }

The first few days of employment are a trial period for a new employee, which is why you need to start them off on the right foot. When onboarding is done well, it pays off in long-term engagement and productivity.

Stop thinking about the new hire process simply as the time to fill out forms and instead as a team-building opportunity. Have new hires complete any paperwork before their first day, so their in-office time can be used toward activities that foster engagement and, ultimately, success.

You've found someone who made it through all your hoops, passed the tests and has chosen to spend a great portion of their waking hours working with you. Celebrate! Take them out to lunch. Load their desk up with company swag. Roll out the figurative (or literal) red carpet.

From the very first day, let your new team members know just how much you value them and the skills they bring.

Also, never start new hires on a Monday. Mondays are bad enough already. It's much better to start folks on a Friday when we're all generally in a better mood and have more time to focus on people.

Mentor or buddy programs are a great way to assimilate new hires onto a team. Knowing whom to turn to when you have a question is essential for mitigating some of the inevitable stress of starting a new job. Mentors or buddies can help answer the questions you can't Google and provide insights on company standards and resources.

Create systems that allow for consistent sharing, both for new team members to management and management to new team members. Starting every newbie off with good morale and engagement always pays off in the end.

TODAY'S ACTION ITEM

SEPTEMBER 11

{ THE THREE-LETTER WORD THAT'S SABOTAGING YOUR BUSINESS }

Guest contribution from Petra Coach David Pierce

Are you overly fond of buts? No, I'm not referring to that kind of "butt!" Get your mind out of the gutter.

I'm talking about the "but" that wrecks so many opportunities. The "but" that heralds your excuses for not stepping out of your comfort zone. The "but" that justifies your avoidance of risk, granting you permission to stay on the sidelines. The "but" that keeps you from becoming all you can be.

You know what I'm talking about. Remember the time you were asked to take charge of that big project that you knew could have been your breakthrough moment? However, you let your fear of failure and lack of confidence win. And now you're kicking yourself for not rising to the occasion. Yeah. That "but."

We've all uttered the "but" out of fear and lack of confidence when our backs are against the wall. Why is it that those times when we're asked to step up to the plate are almost always the same times we most harshly doubt ourselves? We become intimidated when we're faced with looming challenges or pushed to step into unfamiliar territory. Guilty as charged.

There's a fix for "but-itis." It's called "yet."

That's right – sometimes the solution lies in simply repositioning your frame of mind to allow for the possibility that saying or thinking "but" has a way of extinguishing.

If every time you're inclined to resort to your tried-and-true response, you would replace it with "yet" instead, you'd be free to explore the possibilities and visions that you sincerely want to achieve. This simple change of mindset can set you on a path to finding your true purpose and passion.

TODAY'S ACTION ITEM

SEPTEMBER 12
{ **LEAD BY EXAMPLE** }

If you see your job as a business leader contained only to business results, you're doing it wrong. Everything from how you walk down the hallway to how you react to bad news is being watched, whether you like it or not. If you want to produce a great company, it starts with you.

Dedicate yourself to showing your passion and motivation in everything you do. Pay attention to the little things. Make sure you are open to communication with your team members, show up on time for meetings, give 100 percent focus to your conversations and have a positive attitude.

Companies sustain their competitive edge when team members are actively involved with the business, share knowledge, and inspire each other – and it starts at the top. When your team sees your genuine excitement and enthusiasm they'll be much more likely to increase their energy level and get on board.

Healthy teams exude confidence and drive. As a business leader, you owe it to your team to create a work environment that's healthy, challenging and fun.

TODAY'S ACTION ITEM

SEPTEMBER 13

{ 4 WAYS TO ADVANCE TEAM MEMBERS }

There are four ways you can advance team members within your organization:

1. Annual performance boost.
The longer a team member is with your company, the more proficient and valuable he or she becomes. This is the logic behind the customary annual review pay raise.

2. Natural upward transition.
When a team member progresses, the next in line naturally advances – as his or her existing position is training ground for the next level.

3. If/Then 1 elevation.
This option comes into play when a position becomes available and the natural team member fit isn't apparent. At this point, the team leader and possible team member candidate embark on a trial period. If it's a success, then he or she is advanced.

4. If/Then 2 elevation.
This alternative arises when a team member wants to grow certain areas of the company and his or her skill set. He or she is given the opportunity to plan a new position and embark on a trial period. If it's a success, then he or she is advanced.

You're probably familiar with the first two advancement scenarios. The latter two may spontaneously occur, but aren't often defined or readily implemented. They should be though. They're the most effective team member advancement methods.

TODAY'S ACTION ITEM

SEPTEMBER 14
{ FIND BETTER FOCUS }

It's a Wednesday morning and you've just sat down to review your company's quarterly financials. Suddenly a co-worker pops in to ask to move a meeting. You are keenly aware of the non-stop buzzing of your phone on your desk, while you glance over to see an email chain come through about a deadline looming at noon.

This is all too familiar for many professionals, and it has a severe impact on your ability to find (and keep!) your focus throughout the day.

Here three lifestyle changes to make so you can improve your focus every day and actually get stuff done:

1. Tell multitasking goodbye.
Multitasking is actually not possible. It's a fantasy. People may think they're good multitaskers, but it only means they're going from one task to another at a rapid pace. There's a better, more productive way to get things done: Schedule tasks on specific times during the week to will allow your brain to focus completely on one topic for the allotted time.

2. Break and breathe.
It's imperative that you have a scheduled time in your day where your brain is responsible for doing "nothing." Not reading, writing, talking or thinking. Carving out time, even if it's just 10-15 minutes a day, will give your brain a break, allowing you to return fully present and ready to tackle anything that comes your way.

3. When in doubt, write it out.
Every day, start by ranking your tasks for the day in the order of what will have the most impact on your business. The priorities at the top of your list are the ones that will typically require the most focus, so make those your priorities for the day, and hold yourself accountable for getting them done.

TODAY'S ACTION ITEM

SEPTEMBER 15

{ KEEP IN MIND: MILLENNIALS ARE GAINING GROUND }

The millennial generation, or Generation Y, in 2016 made up approximately 30 percent of the U.S. population, according to the U.S. Census Bureau, and they are expected to surpass the number of Baby Boomers in 2019. By 2025, Brookings Institute predicts they will make up 75 percent of the workforce.

This means that Generation Y – which encompasses anyone born between 1980 and 2000 – will increasingly influence businesses over the next few years, more so than it already has.

There have been countless articles and studies about how business leaders should engage with and lead this generation, but now we have reached the point where millennials are preparing to lead companies or are already leading them.

This is not surprising since Generation Y is consumed by entrepreneurship. A study by Levit & Deloitte reported that 70 percent of young professionals around the world aspire to be their own boss.

If you are a leader from Generation X or the Baby Boomer generation, I hope you're asking yourself what you can do now to help prepare this younger generation to take on leadership roles and eventually the company reins.

The answer: Recognize that there are generational differences, but that they can be bridged with education and creativity. As business leaders, we want to see younger generations succeed, so let's make their transition into leadership as seamless as possible. And by teaching them, they will in turn learn how to teach the next generation after them.

TODAY'S ACTION ITEM

SEPTEMBER 16

{ LEADING AS AN INTROVERT }

I think people often believe the stereotype that leaders are born, not made. If someone is outgoing and a hard worker, they are automatically a leader. However, that couldn't be further from the truth. That person has some of the qualities that make up leaders, but not all. Did you know that leaders can actually be introverts?

Your personality style has less to do with leadership than your mindset and your willingness to help those around you:

- **DO show others how to lead.**
  If your goal is to expand your organization, your focus must be on growing leaders. Be a model for your team members and show them what you want to see in a leader. You must invest time and effort in your employees to help develop them, and in turn they will equip others with the same leadership potential.

- **DON'T hide the state of your business from employees.**
  If you're a naturally introverted person, it will be easy to keep this information to yourself. Challenge yourself to be open and genuine with your team members about the state of the business, including financials, struggles and successes. When your team is involved in the company's mission, they will be more passionate about helping you achieve its goals.

TODAY'S ACTION ITEM

SEPTEMBER 17

{ MAKE THE MOST OF ME TIME }

I'm admittedly fairly bad at taking a vacation. I'm extremely passionate about the people and businesses I work with, and it's truly hard to be "off the grid" while I'm away.

That said, I know that time and space away from work is a catalyst for new ideas and a fresh perspective. If you can, take two weeks off to completely unwind. This is the ideal amount of time – any less and I never fully relax.

Don't have vacation days? Get creative. Schedule an hour in the morning to drink your coffee in peace and quiet. Take the dog on a long walk the minute you get home. Build moments into your schedule, no matter how small, to step back from your business and just breathe.

Or take a hike. No, seriously. Go take a hike.

In a 2012 interview, Harvard Medical School psychiatrist John Raney said, "Exercise is the single best thing you can do for your brain in terms of mood, memory and learning."

Need more convincing? Another 2012 study by the Montreal Heart Institute reported that adults who exercised four times a week had improved cognitive abilities after just four months.

Translation: Taking a quick jog around the block before work every morning may make you a smarter and better business leader in the long run.

If you're too busy for self-care, you're too busy. Use these tactics to create a culture of self-care in your life to ensure you're constantly re-energized and ready to lead.

TODAY'S ACTION ITEM

SEPTEMBER 18

{ ACCOUNTS RECEIVABLE IS A TEAM SPORT }

When you think about running a business I'm pretty sure managing accounts receivable (A/R) isn't near the top of your list of reasons why you get fired up to go to work every morning. But I can promise you this: At some point in your career you will face a cash crisis and the first place you will turn to is your A/R team.

To use the often-quoted Boy Scouts motto, "Be prepared." Here are four ways to do that:

1. Identify key performance indicators (KPIs).
The first step is to determine which key performance indicators (KPIs) you need to monitor, how they affect each other and how they drive the financial performance of your business. The KPIs – such as A/R turnover ratio and average days delinquent – should be front and center in an A/R dashboard.

2. Educate your team.
Educate your team on the significance of each metric and how their actions affect each KPI. When your team sees how their work contributes to the business's growth, success and profitability, they'll work harder to achieve – and hopefully exceed – company goals.

3. Create written policies and procedures.
Every business needs written A/R standards by which to operate. These policies, which should be part of a larger accounting policies and procedures manual, specify how the company manages all important A/R activities.

4. Maintain accurate client account information.
This may seem like a no-brainer, but believe me, I've heard too many stories from business leaders who complain about getting paid late because billing information in the accounting system was wrong. Accurate client data is essential to having an effective A/R collections process.

TODAY'S ACTION ITEM

SEPTEMBER 19

{ WHEN IS THE LAST TIME YOU ASKED "WHY?" }

Very few companies I work with would list innovation as one of their top five strengths. In fact, most people struggle to find better ways to do things. They find comfort in doing things as they have always done them and never making a change.

Sometimes that's okay – like in the case of a favorite family recipe. If it's great, repeat it, right? But that's usually not the case when it comes to your business.

So, how do you stay ahead of the curve? It starts with one simple question: **"Why?"** Asking why can unlock conversations I bet you've never had about your business before.

The simple act of asking why will help you articulate any challenge before you and ultimately understand it.

> **Why does this challenge exist in the first place?**
>
> **Why do we see it as a challenge?**
>
> **Why has it not been addressed by someone in the past?**
>
> **Why do we keep having it happen over and over again?**

If you ask why at least three times, you'll start to get to the heart of the matter. Once you've drilled down on an issue and understand it, it's time to think outside the box and solve it at its core, so it'll stop arising – permanently.

TODAY'S ACTION ITEM

SEPTEMBER 20

{ BRAINSTORM INNOVATION }

The challenge with stagnation in business is that eventually the "same ol' thing" is bound to make you – or worse, your entire industry – irrelevant. Think about that. And in today's times, irrelevancy can happen very quickly. How do you make sure you're using innovation to stay relevant as a company? Start by asking these two questions:

1. "What if?"

I love this question, because it's a great alternative to looking at the negative side of every situation, which is where most people start. Instead of putting all the "can't" answers on the table, ask, "What if?" – which gives freedom to be creative with the solutions.

- What if we looked at this from someone else's viewpoint?

- What if we took ideas from other industries and applied them to this situation?

- What if we could solve this, and how would things look then?

It's important to see possibilities and not limitations. Thinking first about what you can't do will send you right back to your old ways. Ask, "What if?" – and innovation will find you.

2. "How?"

The next question to ask is, "How?" This question will lead you to action.

- How can I get this completed?

- How can I define the very first step towards a desired outcome?

- How would I do this if I had no constraints?

Things that previously seemed impossible can become reality once you take the time to consider what it takes to make them happen.

TODAY'S ACTION ITEM

SEPTEMBER 21

{ TIPS FOR ENTREPRENEURS }

In my book, *No Try, Only Do*, I talk about my journey as an entrepreneur. There's a lot that I did right, and a lot that could have been done better – if I'd had the tools. In fact, the lessons that I've learned along the way are what inspired me to write this book for you.

Often, the very qualities that drive people to start their own business are the ones that get in their way and make what is already a Herculean effort even more daunting. Here are two of my biggest tips for new (or veteran!) entrepreneurs:

1. Get out of your own way.
You can be an asset to your business or you can be a liability, and it all hinges on your willingness to be self-reflective enough to realize you've got blind spots. Take the time you need to think through situations and decisions using the TAG Method (see September 7). Ask for help when you need it and take advice when it's offered.

2. If necessary, change who you are.
If you want your business to reach its full potential, you need to be open not only to change around you, but also within yourself. How you act and react, your decision-making process and – most importantly – how you interact with the people around you will require adjustment along the way. Stay open and flexible. Think of yourself as a work in progress and be willing to do the work to make yourself the best you can be.

It's not going to be easy. You know that already if you're an entrepreneur. However, I assure it doesn't need to be as hard as you're making it.

TODAY'S ACTION ITEM

SEPTEMBER 22

{ ARE YOU SWEATING AND SLEEPING? }
Guest contribution from Petra Coach Greg Eisen

Yes, I'm serious. With everything we have going on in our daily lives, taking care of ourselves often shoots to the bottom of the priority list, while in fact, it should be at the very top. See if you can work with the flu – I dare you.

Both sleep and exercise are crucial components to staying healthy mentally and physically. Challenge yourself to make these practices a habit and watch your daily life improve:

1. Sweat it out.
Exercising isn't just about fitting into your old jeans. Research continues to show the mental health benefits of breaking a sweat, including improving mood, increasing memory and reducing anxiety. The combination of physical movement, endorphin release and stimulation of the prefrontal cortex (the part of your brain responsible for critical thinking) almost always work together to provide the clarity that I've been seeking.

2. Sleep on it.
If we're being honest, most of us treat sleep like exercise – it's a nice practice if we can make time for it, but hardly a necessity. However, if you let it, sleep can be your secret weapon. Doctors and researchers have found that sleeping for seven to eight hours per night can improve memory, lower heart attack risk and even spur creativity. I keep a journal next to my bed and jot down the most important decisions that are keeping me up at night, and then I let my brain do its thing during my hours of rejuvenation.

TODAY'S ACTION ITEM

SEPTEMBER 23
{ DEFINING SUCCESS }

How do you define success? Money, power, impact? You can define success however you like, just make sure you're on the path you want to be. For me, success is measured by peace of mind. What gives me peace of mind? Motivating myself to improve every day, choosing to spend my life the way I want to, and knowing that I have stability in my life.

What do I get for all of that? I'm able to seek out significance in everything I do. That's my path.

Here is the top way to get started: **Decide and define what's important in your life.**

Some say the end goal is the key, while others believe the journey itself is the best part. What I know for certain is that you need to know where you're going before you can decide how to get there.

Think about four areas in your life: wealth, relationships, health and achievements. Write down your first thoughts about where you are right now in each of those areas.

Now think about the most successful version of yourself: the Super You. Don't limit your thinking. This is a thought exercise. How would the Super You envision each of those areas? How much wealth has this Super You accumulated? What does your relationship with your family look like? How healthy are you, and how does that affect your life? What has Super You accomplished?

See the distance between where you are and where the Super You is? That's your goal. Now find your path.

TODAY'S ACTION ITEM

SEPTEMBER 24

{ WHY YOU NEED FACE TIME WITH YOUR TEAM }

Leaders must always remember that business is personal, and by that I mean face time – one-on-one, in-person communication – is essential to building and nurturing relationships with team members.

Face-to-face interaction builds leadership credibility and improves engagement with team members. It allows leaders to understand the challenges their business is facing and support their team in moving the company forward. Leaders who avoid facetime come off as unapproachable and disinterested in the well-being of team members.

In-person communication also improves performance. The Massachusetts Institute of Technology's Human Dynamics Lab analyzed hundreds of hours of data from personal interactions and found that on average 35 percent of the variation in the team's performance was due to the amount of time team members spoke face to face.

As a leader, you are the face of your business, division or department. Don't let the ease of using email, phone calls and text dilute the most powerful form of communication you have: face time with your team.

TODAY'S ACTION ITEM

SEPTEMBER 25

{ HOW A QUARTERLY THEME HELPED OUR COMPANY DURING THE GREAT RECESSION }

I've written before about the value of setting quarterly themes that tie into business goals (see May 31). One of the most compelling examples of the power of that strategy occurred during the Great Recession of 2008 when I was running NationLink Wireless.

Clients were shutting off their cellphones right and left as their companies downsized and fired employees by the thousands. Our revenue was taking a serious hit, and we needed a way to rally the troops and minimize the damage. Enter a quarterly theme we called "200 4Q Conversations."

We called or visited face-to-face each of our clients and asked the following:

- How are you doing?

- How is your industry doing?

- Are you hearing from our competitors?

- How are we doing and is there anything we need to do better?

That theme helped our business a ton. Our customers were hurting, but instead of us calling to wring more money out of them, we called to see how we they were doing and how we could help. We looked for ways to save them money, even if it hurt our profitability – because we were confident our clients could ride out the storm. And they did.

It was a win-win all around, but we wouldn't have taken those steps to build stronger relationships with our clients if we hadn't focused on the quarterly theme and made those phone calls.

TODAY'S ACTION ITEM

SEPTEMBER 26

{ STANDARDIZE YOUR HIRING PROCESS }

So you want to hire A-players, the best of the best, right? A great way to do that consistently is to create a sure-fire, works-every-time interview process.

The three basic questions are:

- Can the candidate do the job?

- Will he or she do the job?

- Does he or she fit in your company's culture?

Then, brainstorm with your team to develop a list of interview questions that will help you discover if the candidate fits all three criteria. Write them down and split them into two categories: phone or face-to-face interview questions.

A phone interview is a great 10-minute pre-screening step that will save you hours of face-to-face interviews with B and C-players.

Once a candidate progresses to the face-to-face stage, make sure he or she meets multiple members of your team. You need input to make this decision, and the candidate needs to get to know your team to make his or her decision.

The last interview phase is shadowing. Invite the candidate to follow one of your team members around for a few hours of the day. Be vague with what is expected, don't instruct or have an itinerary. An A-player will navigate his or her way through.

My bonus tip is to create a standby or bench list. Just like baseball teams have the minor leagues, build a bench of pre-qualified A players who are ready for hire as soon as a position opens up. This is especially useful in an industry with high turnover or promotion.

TODAY'S ACTION ITEM

SEPTEMBER 27

{ RECOGNIZE WHERE YOU ARE }

As leaders, it's important to always keep things in perspective.

I'm going to get a bit existential with you for a second: We're all a very small part of a very large universe. Each and every one of us matters, but not as much as we may think we do. The minute you think what you've done (or what you've got planned) is the most important thing going, you've already lost credibility.

If your company is on a successful streak, it's okay to celebrate and be excited. But don't let it go to your head, because that is the moment when leaders start to make poor choices based on their egos.

On the flip side, if you think that all your efforts are fruitless and you're a complete failure, that would also (almost always) be an overstatement. You can't single-handedly cause a company to fail. Just as building a company is a team effort, quite frankly, destroying one would be too.

So if you've come upon hard times in your business, don't blame yourself and think you're all alone in this. Your team experiences the highs and lows with you, so let them be part of the solution, whatever that may be.

Encourage your team to keep things in perspective as well. There's nothing worse than working with a bunch of egos who think every decision they make will shake the universe to its core. They'll see you as a genuine leader who has his or her priorities straight.

Recognize your realistic place in the world and the importance of the moment you are in – both can give you great insight into what comes next.

TODAY'S ACTION ITEM

SEPTEMBER 28

{ LEADERS, DO YOU HAVE COMMITMENT ISSUES? }

Guest contribution from Petra Coach Marshall Martin

As a business coach, I've seen many leaders lose focus on or motivation for their goals, either because they decided the goal wasn't important or because they quickly moved on to the next shiny object. This behavior makes the road to success extremely difficult.

Grabbing the trophy for your own business requires eliminating your commitment issues. It's not as difficult as it sounds – especially when you follow these steps:

1. Be realistic about the goal in question.
The first step is to be open and honest with team members about what you need from them to achieve the goal. Decide now that this goal will take priority over other things. Define what you are and aren't willing to do to ensure the goal stays top of mind at all times.

2. Build a plan.
Once you have full team buy-in, the next step is to figure out a plan to meet the goal. Start by clearly defining your BHAG, or "big hairy audacious goal." Then, break that big goal down into specific and measurable steps or tasks that can be divvied up among team members.

3. Accept that there will be challenges.
Even if you've set up a clear strategic plan, the road to success will not be smooth 100 percent of the time. Team members will encounter roadblocks that seem to delay overall progress.

As the leader, you must be an example for your team in setting and achieving goals. Show your team that you understand there will be difficult challenges along the way, and reinforce that it's okay for people to ask for help whenever they need it.

TODAY'S ACTION ITEM

SEPTEMBER 29
{ MAKE TIME TO MOTIVATE }

It's no secret that people respond to motivation, however, the specific type of motivation is different for everyone. Some members of my team need me to be frank, loud and a bit aggressive to give them the kick in the pants they need. However, others respond much better to a kind, but firm, conversation about their work and what they are doing to reach their goals.

Motivation can take many forms and part of being an exceptional leader is knowing how each person on your team is motivated. The most important part, however, is that you are making an effort to motivate daily. Whether it's the energy you bring to morning huddles or an encouraging sentence at the end of an email, the effort you make to motivate will show in your team's results.

The most successful entrepreneurs and business leaders know that success takes patience, hard work and – most importantly – a continued focus. As Steve Jobs once said, "If you really look closely, most overnight successes took a long time."

To maintain focus on your goals, motivate your team members daily. Continue to remind your team of the bigger picture, as this will help when times get tough in the trenches. Plus, they'll see a leader who cares enough to push them when they need it.

TODAY'S ACTION ITEM

SEPTEMBER 30

{ THE VALUE OF FORETHOUGHT IN BUSINESS }

"Build the well before you need the water."

This phrase had a profound impact on me the minute I heard it spoken at a conference. I Googled the instructions to build a well, and I realized how they apply to scaling up a business.

Step #1: Siting.
Siting refers to exploring the area for groundwater. Basically, dig a deep hole to find out how much water is accessible, whether the conditions are suitable, what kind of equipment you'll need, etc. In business, siting is perhaps the most important part of your endeavor. Determine the strengths, weaknesses, opportunities and threats (SWOT) of your idea or company. From there, you can develop goals and strategies and start drilling.

Step #2: Drilling.
For well builders, this part is self-explanatory: Pinpoint the optimal location and start digging. For executives, this is the part where you drill to the core of your company. What are you built on? Where did you start, and how did you get where you are? Evaluate your core purpose and think critically about whether it's illustrated in each facet of your organization.

Step #3: Building up.
When you've dug the well, you're ready to install a water system with a pump, filter and storage tank, and then build the surrounding wall. Within your company, think of the water system as your internal procedures. You have to install a deliberate culture that ensures alignment among leadership, outlines career development for employees and creates standards of practice that keep the whole team on the same page. Only with these elements in place can you begin laying bricks to build upward and expand your business.

TODAY'S ACTION ITEM

OCTOBER

{ VITAMIN B-10 }

*Vitamins improve the brain and central nervous system
and ensure the body functions properly. Similarly, a business
that functions well will have healthy leadership and
one system of communication that runs throughout
the organization. How is your company functioning?*

OCTOBER 1

{ YOUR BIGGEST OBSTACLE COULD BE YOU }

"Your brick wall is the mirror – shatter it." – Randy Pausch

Challenges are often described as barriers or brick walls that get in our way. I say, those blockades are your greatest opportunities.

Randy Pausch, professor and author of *The Last Lecture*, said, "The brick walls are there for a reason. The brick walls are not there to keep us out. The brick walls are there to give us a chance to show how badly we want something."

If you're like me, your brick wall is what you see when you look in the mirror – you get in the way of your own progress. You are your greatest barrier. Just like all challenges, you have an opportunity for growth when you face the barrier – or the mirror – stare it down and shatter it.

I find most business leaders have difficulty admitting that their leadership style may be their biggest barrier, and even more difficulty tearing it down for two reasons:

1. Leaders are accustomed to identifying and remediating challenges like profit margins and HR matters, but they often fail to reflect on themselves. Leaders don't want to identify as the brick walls because that's akin to identifying a weakness, and leaders can't be weak, right?

2. Leaders think admitting something's a challenge makes them look weak. But it's the opposite: Tackling a growth opportunity does not make you weak, it makes you strong. Stop limiting yourself and start becoming the best version of yourself you can be.

I truly believe we can only reach our fullest potential when we're challenged.

TODAY'S ACTION ITEM

OCTOBER 2
{ SHATTER THAT MIRROR }

When you look in the mirror, are you seeing a brick wall that is stopping your progress?

If so, here's how to shatter that mirror:

Ask.
Pose to your team members this question: What do I need to do to be a better leader? Set "Vegas-style" rules – what you say here stays here – so you create a safe zone where truth can flourish.

Yes, asking the question is simple, but the answer, especially if it's truthful, may sting. Actually, if it doesn't sting, ask again.

Listen.
When you feel the pain of the truth, don't react. Don't make excuses, tighten your fists or clench your jaw. Instead, let it sink in. Once absorbed, ensure the messenger that you appreciate his or her candor.

Professor and author Randy Pausch said, "Your critics are the ones telling you they still love you and care. Worry when you do something badly and nobody bothers to tell you."

Act.
Take the advice of your team members and act on it. This may mean a dramatic change to your leadership style is in order. This is the actionable step that will fulfill your ultimate goal of tearing down the brick wall or shattering your mirror to achieve personal and company growth.

Pausch noted, "The brick walls are there to stop the people who don't want it badly enough. They're there to stop the other people."

Many aren't strong enough to shatter their mirror, *but you are*, which is why you're going to take your business and your leadership abilities to the next level, and your competitor will not.

TODAY'S ACTION ITEM

OCTOBER 3

{ 4 QUESTIONS TO GET UNSTUCK }

Just like a football game, your business's fourth quarter is where the action happens. It separates the winners from the losers, determines the final score and sets the stage for the next game.

If you want to win, you need a game plan. It's the solid foundation of any victory.

Yeah, I know, you're too busy. That's exactly why you need to huddle up and plan. Set a date on your company calendar at least once per year (I recommend once per quarter) and mark it as a "planning day." This is a day for your company to focus on its health and its mission, so it doesn't run itself into the ground. Planning days ensure that you and your team members focus on what's important – not just what's urgent.

Proper planning requires one full day of your company's leadership – at a minimum – joining to discuss the following four areas of planning:

1. Where are we now?

2. Where do we want to go?

3. How do we get there?

4. How will we ensure our plan is executed?

In addition to the planning day, these four key questions can be used for any decision or project you're facing. Don't believe me? Give it a shot and see!

TODAY'S ACTION ITEM

OCTOBER 4

{ THE BUSINESS OF PARENTING }

I'm a proud Dad. My daughters Madison and Gracen are smart, hardworking, compassionate, independent, business-minded and yes, thrifty. I believe our girls developed many of these traits because of our "family economy plan," which is an accountability system that includes our girls in the business of running our household. We learned it from Richard Eyers, author of *Teaching Your Children Values*. We borrowed from his plan, added to it and here's what we ended up with:

Disclose: Sit down with your kids and explain your household's financial situation. Give them the unabridged cost breakdown, including money in (salaries) and money out (mortgage, taxes, utilities, cable, car payments).

Invite: Explain to the kids how they can contribute to the family's economic success (and their own) by helping with household chores and not spending their allowance on junk food or clothes.

Motivate: Each completed task is rewarded with a token, which can be cashed in at the end of the week.

Set boundaries and expectations: Explain to your kids that their "family economy money" will be taxed similar to mom and dad's salaries. Plus, show them how to save 10 percent for their future and give 10 percent to others.

Activate: Enact a system that enables follow-through both from parents and kids.

My wife, Nicole, and I believe the family economy plan is one of the best things we've done to prepare our girls for the real world and plan for their futures.

TODAY'S ACTION ITEM

OCTOBER 5

{ FOCUS ON THE WORK AND NOT THE WIN }

The process of creating and growing a company can breed some bad habits that could ultimately destroy (or at minimum stall the success of) the very business you're seeking to build.

One of those bad habits is only looking for the win and not giving enough attention to the work that gets you there. Don't let your focus on "winning" distract from the important work of the day, week or month.

This can be a tough one for any "doer" – which all entrepreneurs are by definition. We're hard-wired to go for the win. We focus on making plans, setting goals and achieving desired outcomes.

Part of focusing on the work also means focusing on the people doing it. Your people are the company's most valuable assets. If you get too caught up in getting that win, you may overlook them and make them feel less valued.

When something goes right, give credit to everyone involved. When something goes wrong, don't cast blame. Take responsibility yourself and work with the team to build a system to mitigate future issues.

Put faith in your team to help you get to those wins and get past those imminent roadblocks.

Trust and uncertainty are part of the process however uncomfortable they might make business leaders. Remember that allowing yourself to trust in outcomes does not mean that planning is not essential to the process. You must take small steps every day if you expect to move forward.

If you keep doing your work to the highest standards possible, the outcome will take care of itself.

TODAY'S ACTION ITEM

OCTOBER 6

{ COLLABORATE YOUR WAY TO SUCCESS }

There's a well-known phrase, "No man is an island," that applies to any successful company. It's a great reminder that no single person is completely self-sufficient, that they had help along the way.

It's important to remember that you can't be a success without other people – no matter how much you think you can. You're going to have to work with people, whether it's your boss, investors, clients or team members.

There are a lot of ways business owners and senior executives can make their own lives more difficult than they need to be, and not playing well with others ranks high on the list. The ability to work collaboratively with your team can often be the difference between success and failure.

Whether you're the founder of a startup or a senior executive at a large corporation, it's easy to fall into the trap of "I know what's best" and not seek the opinions of others on your team, who may know a better way to do something that can grow your business.

Think of collaboration as another way to learn more about your business and your team. Be open to new ideas and working with team members. By inviting new ideas you'll benefit personally and professionally – in your current business or whatever comes next.

TODAY'S ACTION ITEM

OCTOBER 7

{ YOUR PEOPLE ARE YOUR MOST IMPORTANT ASSET }

People. In order to scale up your business, you must first look at your people. Are you attracting A-players? Are your current team members happy in their roles? Would you rehire all of them if given the opportunity? If you answered "no" to any of these questions, you need to change your hiring process, and engage and grow your existing talent.

Here are a few of my tried and true hiring tips:

1. **Create a job scorecard:** Detail the job candidate's purpose, desired outcomes of his or her work and specific skills required to excel in the position. Immediately weed out applicants who don't fit the requirements presented in the scorecard. In the interview, ask probing questions to uncover behavioral and performance patterns that will likely repeat themselves in your workplace. The old adage "hire slow and fire fast" is so very true.

2. **Coach them:** Set your people up for success. Immediately include them in setting quarterly goals and bi-weekly tasks that are visible and reported to the entire team. Placing manageable, but firm expectations on a new team member will introduce them to your company culture and give them clear expectations from the beginning.

3. **Show appreciation:** Always show appreciation for great work. One part of developing, growing and keeping awesome team members is to coach them and play to their strengths. Plus, no one feels worse after receiving a compliment.

TODAY'S ACTION ITEM

OCTOBER 8

{ WHY GROSS MARGIN MATTERS }

When it comes to analyzing the financial performance of a company, gross margin is hands down one of the most powerful indicators of profitability.

The equation for gross margin is simple: It's gross profit divided by total sales. Because it measures how much profit a company makes after paying for the cost of goods sold (raw materials and direct labor), it also sheds light on how efficient the company is at producing its products or services. Higher gross margin equals higher production efficiency.

Business leaders need to pay close attention to gross margin because it also reflects a company's pricing strength and production costs – some of which are out of your control, such as rising labor and raw materials costs. Competition can drive down the sales price of our product or service, which will negatively affect gross margin.

Gross margin is important for another reason: It shows how much money you have left over to invest in marketing and product development and pay for the general and administrative expenses to run the business.

Understanding gross margin is one of the quickest ways to get a handle on profitability and how well positioned your business is for future growth. Don't overlook it.

TODAY'S ACTION ITEM

OCTOBER 9

{ 3 WAYS LEADERS COMMUNICATE CONSTRUCTIVELY, NOT CRITICALLY }

Fostering open and candid communication is one of the building blocks of a thriving company culture. As a leader, you can feel it when teams are communicating effectively, with healthy back-and-forth debate and discussion on how to tackle challenges and opportunities the company faces.

So how can you create effective communication in your organization? Here are three steps to get you started:

1. Create a feedback system: There needs to be a process that allows employees to share their comments or concerns openly with their managers. It can come in the form of a monthly check-in or a complaint submission platform that leads to a meeting with senior staff. It's important that team members feel encouraged to share and that their managers work with them to find a solution.

2. Create a culture of self-checking: Being part of a team means keeping one another in check. If people are comfortable enough to vent with their colleagues, those colleague should feel comfortable enough to advise them to speak up and share with the senior staff.

3. Include everyone in changing the culture: I like to remind all the member companies we coach about a quote attributed to Eleanor Roosevelt: "Great minds discuss ideas. Average minds discuss events. And small minds discuss people." At your own company, set aside time to talk about ways in which the team can avoid gossip and replace it with open dialogue.

The best way to create an effective, healthy communication system is to get everyone's input on how it should work. If everyone is involved, they'll get on board with it – which ensures communication is part of your company culture.

TODAY'S ACTION ITEM

OCTOBER 10
{ **OVERCOMING CHALLENGES**}
Guest contribution from Petra Coach JT Terrell

At Petra Coach, we often work with clients who express their business and personal goals with passion and excitement but have no plans for the path to achievement. I hear about fantasy vacation homes in the Caribbean, but no associated goals to get the dreamer there, financially or geographically.

At least a thousand times I've heard, "Someday I'm going to…." I always respond the same way: "When? What day? Show me on a calendar."

My fellow coaches and I are in the business of getting things done, and we're fascinated by people who set and accomplish BIG goals, as well as *how* they do it. Here are two of the usual challenges of everyday life and how they can be overcome:

"It seems like there isn't enough time in the day."
You're right! There are only 24 hours in a day, and a third of those hours are spent sleeping, so the clock is ticking. You need to maximize your time. A very wise man once said, "If you have more than 3-5 priorities, you don't have any." Identify only the most important priorities, and stick to them. Set time to work only on your most important goals, and get them checked off the list!

"I just don't know where to begin."
Sounds like you've set some big targets if you don't know where to start. GOOD! The only thing worse than having no goals is having weak ones. The best way to combat this challenge is to begin with the end in mind. A good coaching prompt is, "Tell me what success looks like," because it forces you to identify not only the outcome but all of the needed steps to achieve the outcome.

TODAY'S ACTION ITEM

OCTOBER 11

{ BETTER READERS, BETTER WORKERS }

When it comes to your brain, you are what you read.

If better readers make better thinkers, then why don't we encourage reading more in the workplace? Many leaders have a hard time getting team members excited about work-related reading. Or worse, they don't even discuss the benefits of picking up a book. Either way, too many companies are missing out on professional development and culture-building opportunities because they don't encourage reading.

With rapidly advancing technology changing business at an equally break-neck pace, you constantly have to be learning. But not every company has the means or opportunity to host workshops or send teams to conferences. Book clubs are an easy way to cultivate meaningful learning and growth without breaking the bank.

Reading allows you to learn something new from someone outside your company. You have access to the greatest thinkers and thoughts right on your bookshelf or tablet – take advantage of it. Book club books can be related to an industry or focused on company goals, but they can also be about literature, poetry or whatever Oprah's suggesting this month. Good books, no matter the genre, make you think. And you never know which thought or ensuing discussion will spark your company's next great idea.

Book clubs also encourage team members to learn from each other. Whether you're in constant communication with colleagues or siloed in your office, most conversations reside within a limited business context. Book clubs provide a chance to break out of that, spurring discussions and insights past that norm and learning from folks you may never interact with otherwise.

TODAY'S ACTION ITEM

OCTOBER 12

{ RIP OFF & DUPLICATE: THE OTHER R&D }

Some of the best ideas I've had for my businesses are ones I've borrowed (and modified) from others. It's called R&D, but in this case it's "rip off and duplicate," not "research and development." Pablo Picasso famously said, "Bad artists copy. Good artists steal." Follow his lead.

R&D is a powerful concept that business leaders should embrace. In my experience as an entrepreneur and coach, I've seen firsthand how ideas that are considered standard practice in one industry can be innovative when applied to another. It's about how you adapt those ideas to your business.

Ideas are everywhere, so create a file of ones you like that may be applicable to your business. Encourage your teams to do the same. Have brainstorming sessions to discuss the ideas that could generate new revenue, increase operational efficiency or improve client service.

One important word of caution: If you are simply copying what your competitors are doing, then you will lose because you are not providing a unique solution to a business problem. Instead, take the idea and make it better.

TODAY'S ACTION ITEM

OCTOBER 13

{ 4 PHRASES OF WISDOM }

Philosophers throughout history have had many different interpretations of what constitutes wisdom. In Aristotle's view, you can't be wise if you believe you are always right and that your judgment is 100 percent accurate. Here are the four wisest phrases I know:

1. I was wrong.
It takes immense courage to admit that you were wrong in a high-stress, negative situation. And I think that courage stems from true wisdom about yourself and your strengths and weaknesses.

2. I made a mistake.
Personal growth requires accepting blame for provoking a negative situation. Saying you made a mistake is taking responsibility for your actions, not just your words. It takes great wisdom to recognize that the best course of action to remedy a negative situation is to admit that you played a part in it.

3. I'm sorry.
One step further from the previous statements, have the courage and the wisdom to not only admit guilt but also to make reparations for it. Sometimes a simple, heartfelt "sorry" is all it takes to disperse the tension in a conflict.

4. I need help.
Perhaps the wisest of them all is realizing that you can't do it alone. Big-headed people who think they can handle every single situation on their own are not very wise to think that way because the truth is, every single person needs others to support them on their journey. Leaders, don't be afraid to lean on your colleagues or team.

As they say, "It takes a big person to admit shortcomings," and my definition of a "big person" is a wise person – one who understands that where there is weakness, there is strength.

TODAY'S ACTION ITEM

OCTOBER 14

{ DON'T BE AFRAID OF FEEDBACK }

As the leader of a company, it's not easy to take responsibility for the issues your company is having.

It isn't for most leaders who are deeply and emotionally invested in what they do because it means admitting you've made mistakes and opening yourself to scrutiny. But it is a necessary step to begin the process of change.

One of my company's clients wasn't sure how to get to the heart of the issues it was having and transform them into something productive.

The company decided to do a talent assessment with the executive team in which each leader "graded" one another on his or her performance. It was an opportunity to be very frank with one another about what's working and what's not.

Once those concerns were voiced, it became a lot easier for them to take the feedback and turn it into actionable steps.

Each team member came away with an action plan to make those changes, including key performance indicators (KPIs) to measure when that goal has been reached and an accountability partner to make sure each person stays on the right track.

When the team made a process to share their feedback, it became a lot easier for them to be open about it.

Takeaway: Don't shy away from getting feedback, formally or informally. Just make sure it's used constructively rather than destructively.

TODAY'S ACTION ITEM

OCTOBER 15

{ HOW MUCH ARE YOU WORTH? }

For many aspiring entrepreneurs, the dream of owning a business includes visions of taking home a nice paycheck AND earning a fat annual or quarterly dividend. Unfortunately, that's far from the case.

The reality is that you'll be working long hours for low pay until the business reaches a point where you are financially able to be paid what you're worth – and without the extra dividend. And this will go on for longer than you anticipate.

There is no magic formula for determining your compensation (salary and dividend). Variables include the development stage of the business, how it's performing financially and plans for future growth. For example, if you're in start-up mode and financing the business yourself, then you're probably sustaining operating losses and living off your hard-earned savings. On the other hand, if your business is generating consistent profits, then you can probably afford compensation within industry and regional standards.

Here are some of the guidelines I share with our coaching clients:

1. Have you historically generated reliable, stable revenue?

2. Can you predict with great accuracy future revenue?

3. Is your business profitable?

4. Have you included your salary/compensation in the company's operating budget?

If you can answer yes to those questions, then it's time to reward yourself for your hard work!

TODAY'S ACTION ITEM

OCTOBER 16

{ **TRIPLE THREAT** }

Hiring is hard. You take time to craft the perfect job description that you hope will attract your ideal candidate. However, you also have to make sure their personality is a proper fit for your team, not just their resume. Nobody is the perfect package, but there are some key attributes that I look for in my employees, no matter what position I intend for them to fill:

1. Communication.
Communication is a vital skill, not just in business, but in life. While your candidate might end up reading spreadsheets all day, the manner in which they are able to communicate will affect the way they collaborate with team members, interact with you and lead future employees.

2. Adaptability.
As every business leader knows, change is inevitable. Look for someone who has dealt with change and managed the transition well. This will demonstrate important traits like perseverance, patience and dedication.

3. Integrity.
Though many claim to have it, very few really do. You need someone who will do the right thing, stand up for their fellow team members and represent your company well both inside and outside of the office.

TODAY'S ACTION ITEM

OCTOBER 17

{ MY RULES FOR EMAIL }

Email – we love it and we hate it. What was created to be an extremely effective communication tool has morphed into a time-sucking monster for many of us. Since it's impossible to avoid email, I've set certain rules for it. Here are three of my rules that you may want to put in place for yourself:

1. Make your subject line relevant and indicate importance.
Things move quickly in my world (as I'm sure they do in yours), which means we read emails by level of importance and priority, not by chronological order. Make everyone's life easier by making your email subject line clear and indicating action, if needed. I always appreciate when the words URGENT or RESPONSE NEEDED are in the subject line so that I can get to it quickly and tackle what's needed.

2. Limit the copying.
Before copying dozens of people onto an email chain, ask yourself if it's necessary for them to be informed. If so, I'm a fan of letting each recipient know why they were copied in the email and what action is expected from them, if any.

3. Communicate kindly.
Everyone has their preferred method of communication, whether it's email, phone call, text or in-person. Before you get flustered over your email sitting too long in someone's inbox, consider another option of communication that they might prefer. A quick phone call or office chat might be more productive than you've ever considered!

TODAY'S ACTION ITEM

OCTOBER 18

{ BE MORE LIKE YODA }

If you haven't figured it out from my previous book title, *No Try, Only Do*, Yoda is one of my favorite movie characters of all time.

Over the years, he has taught me a lot about leadership and mentorship and how best to guide people toward their goals:

He is very matter-of-fact: He gets to the point with no BS (even if his syntax is a little convoluted). That's where I got my catch phrase after all. You can't be tentative about what you say or what you plan to do. You need to be direct, set the goal confidently and then perform the actions promised.

He's positive and encouraging: He recognizes Luke's potential to be a great Jedi Master, and he cultivates that by helping Luke train and giving him the guidance he needs to improve.

He's a great teacher: He doesn't do everything for Luke, but lets Luke face challenges, make his own mistakes and learn from them.

He's a great role model: Luke comes to him as an insolent teenager who thinks everything should just come easy. However, Luke goes on to master his skills and become a selfless hero because Yoda set a good example of a Jedi Knight.

Overall, he's a great mentor, and I think all leaders can take notes from him – I certainly have. So let's all be a little more like Yoda.

TODAY'S ACTION ITEM

OCTOBER 19

{ PUT YOUR PEOPLE FIRST }

It's 5 o'clock. You've had a long day at the office and can't wait to get home. You rush to the parking lot, leap into your car and gun it to the highway on-ramp.

What you see ahead is not pretty: a sea of cars parked across four lanes. The lane to your left starts to creep forward at 10 miles per hour, which looks like lightning from your vantage point. You see an opening, and since you're clearly smarter than everyone else, you stealthily change lanes. You start passing cars in your new lane and do a celebratory fist pump. Then, you see brake lights in front of you and begrudgingly come to a halt. The lane to your right begins to move forward.

You know from experience that if you maneuver to get back over, it won't solve the problem. No matter how much weaving and scheming you do, you won't get ahead.

Drivers navigating interstate traffic are like most business leaders who navigate their businesses without a plan or overarching philosophy. I want you to be among the few who take the less-traveled back roads.

Let's examine your most valuable asset: your people. Many businesses view employees as a work crew that exists to meet the needs of the business. Instead, view your team members as individuals with unique talents that are waiting to be applied and developed. Build a team of top performers who can contribute to the decision-making process and become invested in your enterprise.

When you focus on this area, your business will be a well-oiled machine that's operating with eight cylinders on the open road moving forward to accomplish your short- and long-term goals.

TODAY'S ACTION ITEM

OCTOBER 20

{ HOW TO HAVE PRODUCTIVE MEETINGS }

If you're going to have a meeting, make sure it's productive.

Don't sit down at the conference table and stare at each other or shmooze for 10 minutes before actually starting. Get in, sit down and follow the agenda.

Appoint someone to be in charge of creating the meeting agenda. Whether that's a physical paper that is printed and handed to everyone, or a quick list emailed out, make sure everyone has it before the meeting, so everyone can come prepared.

At the end of the agenda, have a WWW. I'm not talking about the internet. Have an action list – a "who, what, when." End every meeting with a list of who is going to do what by when. Designate someone who will capture the action items with owners and due dates for each meeting.

To avoid going astray:

1. Follow the agenda as closely as possible

2. Move any extraneous or new items to the "parking lot" for later.

3. Create a "no phone zone" during your meetings. People will stay focused, and over time your meetings will become shorter and more productive. (This starts with you, Mr. Leader).

4. Set a timer if you have to – just end when you say you will end. There's nothing worse than a meeting that "goes over."

Bonus Advice: If you really want to get serious, have your meetings standing up. You'll find speed in those meetings for sure!

TODAY'S ACTION ITEM

OCTOBER 21

{ BUSINESS IS PERSONAL }

"It's not personal, Sonny. It's strictly business."

Unless you're Al Pacino's character in "The Godfather" – or impersonating Al Pacino's character in "The Godfather" – you should never utter those words.

If you want to run a successful business and be a successful leader, business must be personal. The only offering that truly sets you apart from your competition is people. Other companies likely have the ability to develop your exact product, follow the same business manual and hire the same accountant, but they can't clone you or your people.

In order for your staff to feel like they can be vulnerable and personal, leaders must foster an open environment where honesty and out-of-the-box brainstorming can flourish. The best way to establish this safe zone is by exposing your own vulnerability. We are all human, which means we have flaws, embarrassing moments and skeletons in our closets. Effective leaders are open about their own personal flops and struggles.

This may sound counterintuitive; you might feel exposing your weaknesses makes you weak. I challenge you to stop pretending to be perfect in front of your team. Let them get to know you, and they'll return the favor.

By building a business that offers not only the best product or service, but also a personable and irreplaceable team, you have a winning combination – and an offer your clients can't refuse.

TODAY'S ACTION ITEM

OCTOBER 22

{ PRACTICE EMPATHY DAILY FOR BETTER LEADERSHIP }

Power, success, money, fame. That is the picture that many people associate with leadership. However, I've found that leadership is all about the small, un-sexy details. Do you make decisions for the good of your team? Do you care about knowing names?

Unfortunately, some company leaders think they are supposed to rule autonomously, voice their opinions loudly and hold back other managers and employees. It's like they're taking cues from dictators and 16th-century kings.

It's important to remember that a leader is measured by his or her influence – not his resemblance to King Henry the VIII.

Take a moment today to practice this one principle that will elevate your leadership:

Be empathetic.

Understand that, eventually, members of your team will fail. When that happens, have their backs. They need to know they're supported at their best and their worst. Further, failures are some of the most significant growth opportunities. When a member of your team fails, don't miss the teachable moment that could alter his or her outlook and development.

There are many definitions of leadership. To me, social psychologist Martin Chemers's explanation captures the often-missed essence of leadership, which centers on social dependence rather than isolated independence.

Chemers defines leadership as "a process of social influence in which one person can enlist the aid and support of others in the accomplishment of a common task." In other words, a quality leader cannot exist without a team.

TODAY'S ACTION ITEM

OCTOBER 23

{ ADDRESS FEARS HEAD-ON }

Guest contribution from Petra Coach David Pierce

One of Dale Carnegie's principles in his book *How to Stop Worrying and Start Living* is to directly address fear and worry. When struggles become realities, use this three-step formula:

1. Ask yourself: "What is the worst that can possibly happen if I can't resolve this matter?"

2. Once you've determined the worst case (which often is much better than you may have initially believed), prepare yourself mentally to accept it, if necessary.

3. Then, once you've accepted the worst case, calmly devote your time and energy to improve the scenario. Since you've already accepted the worst, any improvements you can come up with will be a victory. Stop worrying and work on a solution.

Another way to nip fears and worries in the bud is to enable a mental "stop-loss." Decide how much your current worries really matter in the grand scheme of life. The "stop-loss" is the point at which you mentally move past those worries or fears and cut your losses.

If you must deal with the fears or worries, only think about them for the time that they're worth. Once you've addressed the issues, be done with them. Sometimes they are what they are, and you may not be able to resolve them, no matter how much you might want to.

Like most things in life, our fears and worries can be controlled and conquered with commitment to a strong plan of action. Then you'll find yourself breathing easier day by day.

TODAY'S ACTION ITEM

OCTOBER 24

{ MY GOODNESS, THIS IS HARD }

I realize the habits I teach, while simple in concept, can be very difficult to execute – especially consistently.

I vividly remember a time when I was building my wireless company, NationLink Wireless, and I had recently attended Verne Harnish's "Birthing of Giants" program at the Massachusetts Institute of Technology.

I came back from that session determined that our company was going to be one of the rare few who implemented the philosophies and strategies Verne espoused. One of the first things we started was daily huddles – and I was truly surprised when I found out that no one in the company wanted to do it.

That was only the beginning. We started implementing other steps that are part of the Rockefeller Habits and I could see that they were not sinking in with our team. I was frustrated. The team was frustrated. And everyone was complaining about the new system they were being made to follow.

Determined not to let frustration hold us back, I called Verne and told him the "Habits" weren't working and that team members were not happy. He joined us on the phone during our daily morning huddle and reported back that we were "doing fine. You've just got to keep doing it. In 60 days, it will be a habit and then it will be part of your organization forever. You just can't give up on it."

It was some of the best advice I've ever received. And it was true.

Remember, if it was easy, everyone would be a leader or business owner. Don't give up on what you believe.

TODAY'S ACTION ITEM

OCTOBER 25

{ WHY YOU NEED TO MONITOR LABOR EFFICIENCY}

Nothing will affect the bottom line of your business more than the way you manage one of the largest expenses: labor.

Gross profit is a critical financial metric because it measures production costs and salaries/wages expense. Labor efficiency, on the other hand, quantifies the financial return your team earns on the sales they generated. Think of it this way: As a business owner or leader you want to know how much money your company earns on every $1 paid in salaries/wages.

Yes, I know I'm getting in the weeds, but trust me, this is important. I learned this lesson the hard way when I was scaling up my wireless company, NationLink, and had to make tough decisions on how many sales reps I needed to grow the business.

How effective and efficient your team performs will be reflected in labor efficiency. Watch it like a hawk for clues to find out how you can do more to motivate and inspire them to perform at a higher level.

(As an aside, there are some great resources on the internet if you want to take a deeper dive into labor efficiency. Verne Harnish' book *Scaling Up* provides a great, concise analysis of the topic.)

TODAY'S ACTION ITEM

OCTOBER 26

{ THE RULE OF ONE }

You've heard the saying many times: "How do you eat an elephant? One bite at a time." If we know that's true, why do so many of us hope to inhale it all at once, only to become frustrated and defeated by the effort?

When tackling a goal, dream or project, in life or business, it's essential to start with the Rule of One.

The Rule of One, as mentioned in Orna W. Drawas' book, *Perform Like a Rock Star and Still Have Time For Lunch*, is to "take one action, large or small, every day toward achieving your goal."

If you do the math, that adds up to sixty actions each quarter and 240 actions each year! Imagine all the progress you could make towards a goal if you spend that much time on it over a long period of time.

Still struggling with where to start? Grab a marker and the biggest sheet of paper you can find and start to write down everything you'll need to achieve your goal. Don't leave anything out. Once you have it all out of your brain, start breaking down each of those tasks into small steps you can accomplish and start by doing one thing each day.

Don't let the fear of failure hold you back from accomplishing your goals!

TODAY'S ACTION ITEM

OCTOBER 27

{ IT'S IMPROVE YOURSELF, NOT PROVE YOURSELF}

I'm sure you've heard this before, but I want to reiterate: Self-worth comes from within.

How you feel about yourself stems from how you perceive yourself, and outside opinions should not factor in.

However, I know this is something that everyone struggles with, especially leaders. There's a lot of pressure as a leader to prove yourself – to appear to have everything together and to be the best of the best in the eyes of those who look to you as an authority.

While it's important to build that kind of trust and respect from your team, it's equally important to give yourself that same respect and to not let others define who you are.

You know your own strengths and weaknesses – the ones you've realized about yourself, not that others have thrust upon you. If there's a weakness that you're not particularly proud of, work out a way to improve yourself.

When you are bettering yourself – learning new ideas and skills, tackling new challenges, doing new things that scare you a little – your self-esteem will automatically increase. And by the laws of social interaction, the more confidence you exude, the more others will believe in you.

So don't feel like you have to prove yourself, but strive to keep *improving* yourself. Don't focus on appearances, but on yourself, and people will perceive you as a better leader.

TODAY'S ACTION ITEM

OCTOBER 28

{ PROCRASTINATION CAN LEAD TO A NEW DESTINATION }

I found a funny meme from Tom Bilyeu that defined procrastination as "what happens when your goals don't excite you as much as your lizard brain desires to chill."

Great joke aside, he raises an interesting point. If your goals are repeatedly leaving you feeling lethargic and not making you spring immediately into action, are they the right goals for you?

Goals are supposed to be something you want whole-heartedly to achieve. They should get you out of bed in the morning ready to take on the day. If they're not, it might be time to reevaluate them.

The great thing about goals is that you can switch them up. If you start to work toward one and realize it's not going to turn out how you wanted (or not going to happen at all, for that matter), sometimes that means it's time to change the target.

Obviously, this is on an individual basis because if your team or others within your organization are relying on the current goal to be completed, then you may need to find the motivation to finish it out regardless of your feelings. That said, it may mean moving the goal post or calling on others to hold you accountable and support you in the effort to achieve the goal.

But if it's a personal goal that has no bearing on anyone else's life, you have the power to switch gears completely and find something that lights that spark. You won't have to fight with yourself nearly as much if what you're working toward truly excites you.

Forget the procrastination and find yourself a new destination.

TODAY'S ACTION ITEM

OCTOBER 29

{ 5 WAYS TO OBTAIN CLIENT FEEDBACK }

Obtaining client feedback should be an ongoing process. It's essential to find out how well your product or service is meeting the needs of the clients who are paying your bills. New market entrants and changing client needs can affect the competitive landscape, so you need the tools to stay informed about how clients perceive your company.

Here are five simple ways to get client feedback:

1. Provide client feedback forms on your website.
There are a myriad of secure, plug-in templates that are easy to add to your company's website.

2. Call your clients regularly.
Create a simple, four- or five-question verbal survey that doesn't take much time for clients to answer. The questions we used in a quarterly theme, mentioned on September 25, are a good place to start.

3. Use email surveys for new and current clients.
Again, limit the number and the complexity of the questions. To goal is to secure as many responses as possible.

4. Monitor social media channels for comments.
Clients love to post on Facebook and Twitter. There are a lot of free or inexpensive apps that will notify you when your company's name is mentioned online.

5. Use an online survey like Survey Monkey to evaluate loyalty.
We use this tool extensively at Petra. It's a go-to platform for gaining more insight about our clients.

TODAY'S ACTION ITEM

OCTOBER 30

{ STAYING ONE STEP AHEAD }

When we first moved into our house 17 years ago, we had hundreds of neighborhood trick-or-treaters. But, this year's Halloween was very different. The doorbell only rang four times. What happened?

Looking back now, it wasn't as fast a shift as I had thought. Each year, fewer and fewer of the neighborhood kids have come around on Halloween. They have gotten older and more preoccupied with group trunk-or-treats than door-to-door trick-or-treating. It's all a function of the times we live in.

Similarly, our industries are constantly evolving, usually without our knowledge. And sometimes we don't notice it until it's too late to catch up. Here are three ways that you can stay ahead of the changes in your business, so next year you won't buy candy for the trick-or-treaters that aren't going to show up:

1. Ask your team what trends are impacting your industry right now.
By asking a larger group, you will often get insights that you may have missed. Repeat this activity annually, if not more often, and review your team's feedback so you can decide what actions to take to keep yourself 18 months ahead.

2. Don't wait until it's too late.
Start reading and attending conferences to discover what's coming next.

3. Act as if your business is going to be extinct in five years.
This may be tough to do, but it reaps major positive results. If you approach your business this way, you will constantly think of new ideas to make it better than its competition. That will propel your business forward faster.

TODAY'S ACTION ITEM

OCTOBER 31

{ PRETENDING YOU'RE SOMEONE YOU'RE NOT }

Halloween is a fun holiday filled with candy and spookiness. But the best part about it is you get to – for one day only – pretend you are someone you're not. You can be Superman, a ghost or your favorite animal.

But I'll emphasize again that it's only one day a year, because I think it's important to NOT pretend to be someone other than yourself during the other 364 days of the year.

As a leader, your team members and those who look to you for guidance might have all kinds of expectations for you: what kind of leader you should be, what actions you should take, how you should make decisions, and the list goes on and on.

Before I get too existential, let me give an example about myself: I'm not a "feelings" guy – I go about my life making decisions based on logic and knowledge, rather than emotions. Yet, as a coach, I obviously have to deal with a spectrum of emotions from the business leaders I work with.

However, that doesn't mean I can just flip a switch and become a complete empath – it doesn't work that way. I need to figure out how I can be who I am, but still be a helpful, supportive coach for my charges. So I have reconciled that through helping leaders to understand logically why they are feeling the emotions they are feeling and then guiding them toward a feasible solution.

In other words, you can't change who you are, but you can find ways to work with what you've got and be an effective leader.

But today, be whomever you want. Happy Halloween!

TODAY'S ACTION ITEM

NOVEMBER

{ VITAMIN B-11 }

*Your prescription this month is to find balance –
that could mean balancing your work with distractions,
balancing your career with your personal life
or even balancing your checkbook.*

NOVEMBER 1
{ FIND YOUR "PADDLEBOARD" }

As entrepreneurs, we're always working, and we grow accustomed to thinking about our business every waking second. But people need a respite from constant mental processing in order to put groundbreaking ideas into action and achieve measurable results.

If you feel like you're getting burned out or that you're lacking the inspiration you once possessed, get out of your surroundings and clear your mind.

Paddleboarding became my hobby to do just that.

It allows me to experience soothing surroundings devoid of distracting noises. When I'm balancing on top of the water, listening to the laps of the waves and feeling the board beneath my feet, I truly clear my head – and I'm not talking about a zone-out-in-front-of-the-TV mindless stare, but a complete lack of active thought, a deep reserve of mental energy expenditure.

I realize paddleboarding may not be for everyone, so find your version of my paddleboarding affinity. Maybe it's visiting the driving range at a nearby golf course, or maybe it's setting aside time each month to build a woodworking project with your bare hands. The key here is to find something that's more muscle memory than creative thought.

To effectively free your mind from the daily distractions and stress of entrepreneurship, you've got to make your physical activity something you really enjoy and something you can do alone.

Find your "zen zone" where you can actually enjoy not thinking. This is important because, for many of us entrepreneurs, it's difficult to stop thinking.

Find your paddleboard and set aside time to clear your head of the daily stress and rigor of entrepreneurship. You'll notice a difference if you make the commitment.

TODAY'S ACTION ITEM

NOVEMBER 2
{ INSPIRING YOUR TEAM }

Not every workplace objective or company initiative is going to foster the same amount of teamwork or excitement among your team – that's the nature of work. So how do you inspire your team members to perform the work with gusto?

Be open and honest about the reality of the task at hand, and help people understand what it means to you personally and to the business. If the goal is challenging or high-risk, say so – people will respect you for your transparency, and they'll be more likely to trust you as a genuine leader.

Be the example by bringing passion to your work. Dedicate yourself to being "on fire" in everything you do. If your team doesn't see enthusiasm from you, why should they put in the energy?

If they see you express genuine excitement, and if you take the time to share your inspiration with the team, they're more likely to get on board with whatever project is at hand and join in on the mission.

But don't "back seat drive." Give your team the space to find what motivates them and help them along the way only if they need it.

And don't forget to celebrate the victories! It's what's going to keep the momentum going.

Positive energy is infectious. Spread it around and live by example. If self-motivation becomes a staple of your company culture, you'll benefit from the results every day – and create future leaders.

TODAY'S ACTION ITEM

NOVEMBER 3
{ GOING PUBLIC }

Warren Buffet famously said, "Someone's sitting in the shade today because someone planted a tree a long time ago." Mr. Buffet knows a lot about investing money, and he also understands the value of time – taking small steps towards a larger goal. The things you've dreamed of in life and in business may be just around the corner, and they are in no way beyond your reach. What's holding you back? Fear of failure? Afraid of what people might think?

The only way to overcome failure is to tackle it head on. That's right, the secret to making your success happen is to stop giving a sh*t about what people think.

Make it public.

When you overcome your fear, you take away its power.

It's easy to make private proclamations about all the things we're going to accomplish. If that's enough for you, great. But for those folks dealing with inertia, a private commitment is probably not enough. Make your plans known. Tell your friends, family and co-workers what your goal is and when it will be completed. Give yourself a community to answer to, and you'll be more likely to stick to your plan.

Remember the words of Yoda: "There is no try…only do." Don't use the word "try." Say what you "will" do and commit to it.

TODAY'S ACTION ITEM

NOVEMBER 4

{ CONTROLLING THE TECH MADNESS }

Guest contribution from Petra Coach Jason Rush

"Get off your phone!"

How many times have you or your spouse directed that phrase to your children? Between my wife and I, it's possible that my own kids have heard it close to a million times.

In an effort to stop technology from taking possession of our sons – but more importantly, to put them in control of their own decision-making process – my wife and I installed new technology rules in our house for weekday use.

Here is one key business lesson I learned from our efforts to control the tech madness:

Lay the ground rules.

When the kids get up on Monday morning, their devices are fully charged. The catch? That is the only charge they get all week until the weekend. By limiting the ability to charge, we've turned battery life into a new currency our kids can understand far beyond dollars and cents.

It may seem harsh, but my kids are in complete control of how and when they want to use up their batteries. They can choose to use it all up Monday night – but that will make for a long week with no battery life.

So, what's the business lesson here? Just as we had to be clear at the outset about the expectations for our kids, so should business leaders when delegating control of tasks to team members. Don't mince words or be vague. Instead, set clear guidelines and make sure your team members know what is expected of them.

A solid delegation strategy can teach team members responsibility and decision-making skills while positioning them to more quickly rank up within the organization.

TODAY'S ACTION ITEM

NOVEMBER 5

{ MAKE PERSONAL RELATIONSHIPS A PRIORITY}

In business, people skills are really important – for networking, working with clients and interacting with your teammates in the office. But these skills need to be developed, and you, the leader, can start by bringing those skills to your team.

The ability to build personal relationships is a "soft skill" and can be hard to refine. It's worth the effort, though. When your team members are united by personal relationships, it transfers to their client relationships.

One way to open up is to literally open your door. Stop burying yourself in your corner office with a cityscape view. This positions you as unapproachable, which stifles engagement and interaction and, in turn, undermines the concept of "team."

Leaders should also take time to walk around the office, peek into team members' offices and check in with them in a less formal way. But don't just pop your head in, half listen and leave again. Listen and be genuinely interested in their responses.

Schedule more formal check-ins every two weeks to discuss concerns, needs and priorities in more depth. This creates alignment through the business, keeps team members on track and furthers that personal connection that's so vital.

Asking team members to build an "aspiration list" is another way to open up and be vulnerable with them. I know it sounds corny, but have them write 100 bullet points listing professional and personal dreams and goals. Then, sit down with each team member and see which points you can make come true.

It's a thrill to have the opportunity to positively affect another human being, and that positivity is sure to permeate throughout the office.

TODAY'S ACTION ITEM

NOVEMBER 6

{ LIFE PLANNING: SETTING PERSONAL GOALS }

Every day I work with companies looking to accelerate growth, improve company culture and take their organizations to a new level of performance. As a coach, I help business leaders and their teams identify short- and long-term goals, figure out how they are going to accomplish them and make sure each member of the team is accountable on a daily, monthly and quarterly basis for achieving those goals.

This method, rooted in the Rockefeller Habits, has proved extremely effective in uniting their organizations with a common purpose and a roadmap for success. But, setting goals and tracking results shouldn't be limited to the workplace. After all, isn't the time you spend at home just as – if not more – valuable than the hours you spend at the office? Of course it is. That time can be just as productive as it is relaxing – if you take time to plan.

Don't get me wrong. There's nothing inherently wrong with prioritizing time to relax. In fact, I think it's important to take care of yourself. Everyone should have personal and family time away from the busywork of office life. Without moments where we reconnect with loved ones, friends and family, it's easier to become burned out and disregard the structure for a healthy and fulfilling life.

But if you're solely relying on a TV Guide as your life roadmap at home, you could be missing out on some of the same benefits you obtain when you have a plan at work.

TODAY'S ACTION ITEM

NOVEMBER 7

{ 4 RULES OF BUSINESS YOU CAN'T AFFORD TO FORGET}

It's very easy to complicate things. This is especially true in business, where we can make activities much harder than they have to be. That's why I live by and advise business owners across the country to follow what I call the "4 Rules of Business."

Rule #1: Be on time, every time.
Being on time is the simplest of responsibilities. When you are consistently tardy, it shows others that you are unreliable and lack consideration and respect for their time and the commitment you made.

Rule #2: Do what you say you will do.
One of the quickest ways to lose trust is to tell someone you'll do something and then not follow through. Next time you tell someone you'll do something, be sure that you can and will do it – or don't say it.

Rule #3: Finish what you start.
I say, "If you touch it, finish it." Power through the distractions of doing the small things before the big things and finish. Just finish.

Rule #4: Say and mean "Please" and "Thank you."
This is my favorite rule. As a society, we have lost many of the common courtesies that create loyalty between us. It's not enough to say the words. You have to mean them, too.

Four rules. Seems easy. It's not. But I'm betting that if you refer to these often, you will soon recognize your own improvement and before long will be operating in that top 10 percent of businesses – and the top 10 percent of people, for that matter.

TODAY'S ACTION ITEM

NOVEMBER 8

{ 4 STEPS TO GETTING STRONGER DURING A QUARTER }

You've heard the old adage; the definition of insanity is doing the same thing over and over again and expecting different results. What you may not have heard (because I came up with it) is the second part of that saying: Doing the same thing and expecting the same results is just as absurd.

If you want to take your business to the next level, take the advice of any fitness trainer and challenge yourself. Change your routines and set new goals because different results only come from different activities.

Here are four steps to success to get you out of your rut and get stronger:

1. Set three growth targets: These are three outcomes that you will commit to accomplishing over the quarter. Set the bar high. Only by setting and then completing those goals in small, consistent steps will you reach the next level of success.

2. Create a comprehensive list of tasks: These will lead you toward fulfilling each target. Make sure each task is clearly defined and simple enough to conquer within a couple days or weeks versus months.

3. Select a set number of tasks each week to tackle: Set a solid timeline and due date for each one. To ensure follow-through, take it a step further and enlist an accountability partner or personal trainer to coach you through your last few miles or tasks.

4. Identify potential obstacles: Think about what might keep you from completing your tasks and reaching your end goals. Pinpoint potential roadblocks and devise a plan to address them if they materialize. Complications will always arise, but if you're prepared, they won't derail your progress for long.

TODAY'S ACTION ITEM

NOVEMBER 9

{ BUILDING THE NEXT GENERATION OF LEADERS }

Regardless of what generation you are from – Baby Boomers, Gen X, Millennials or another – it's important to nurture the growth of the next generation.

Here's how:

1. Be a mentor.
Most people these days want to build a meaningful career, so act as a mentor and help people reach their goals. Also, everyone craves feedback and recognition, so telling them you believe in them and supporting them will go a long way.

2. Give them responsibility.
Those in younger generations tend to seek leadership and structure from their supervisors. They also expect their bosses to challenge them in the workplace. Trust them to take the lead on a campaign or run with an idea. Young team members will figure out the best way to get results without being micromanaged along the way. If they fail, help them figure out what they can do better next time.

3. Provide them with purpose.
For many people just starting out, work must have meaning. Once you communicate the purpose to them and help them see how their work impacts the company as a whole, they will not only feel more connected to their work, but also to the organization's mission.

4. Treat them with the same respect you expect.
This one is simple and holds true for most aspects of life. Treat others how you want to be treated. The next generation has knowledge and skills, especially in the technology sector, that others can learn from, and they deserve to be respected in the workplace.

TODAY'S ACTION ITEM

NOVEMBER 10

{ QUIET DOWN TO STEP UP }

"It is impossible to begin to learn that which one thinks one already knows."

This quote, attributed to the Greek philosopher Epictetus, is one of my favorite quotes of all time. It's an important piece of wisdom that I love to share with businesses, since it's aimed at the brains of leaders.

To be truly successful, CEOs, business owners and team leaders need to realize that "knowing it all" isn't really knowing anything at all, and there's always something to learn from those around (and below) you.

Consider these thoughts on listening and how you can put it into practice today:

Be quiet and listen.
Once you've asked for others' opinions, it's time to listen. Just as your teachers told you when you were a student, closing your mouth and opening your ears is crucial to gaining knowledge. If you've publicly requested feedback and then don't at least consider the feedback you receive, you'll have wasted everyone's time and damaged morale. Remind yourself to really listen when others are talking, and then take time to consider what you've heard before saying yes or no.

Engage emotionally.
You've got to engage emotionally if you want to build stronger relationships. What does that mean? Start by putting yourself in other people's shoes. It's not just about what they're saying. Take time to consider how they feel and what motivated them to share what they're telling you. When you connect with your team emotionally, you'll establish a deeper level of communication and a stronger relationship. This will lead to trust and ensure that you receive the most honest feedback possible.

TODAY'S ACTION ITEM

NOVEMBER 11

{ "ALL EMPLOYEES MUST WASH HANDS" }

You've seen the signs. Whenever you use the restroom at a restaurant, grocery store or any business where keeping things sanitary is a must – there it is: "All employees must wash hands before returning to work."

Now, I understand that hand-washing is in everyone's best interest, but whenever I see those signs, it gets me thinking: Is it really necessary to essentially stand over your employees' shoulders while they're in the bathroom and remind them about basic hygiene (albeit in the form of a sign)?

Maybe it is. Or maybe it's just the ultimate form of micromanagement in the workplace.

At the office, constant reminders about how we should function and behave can turn a creative person into a robot and an A-player with differing ideas into a dissatisfied employee looking for his next opportunity to leave the company.

If you want to engage your team members and get the very best out of them, you've got to cut down the rules and regulations, and stop micromanaging.

Remember that you and your team are all adults and should act like it, which means you don't shoot each other down or hide problems. It's crucial to keep communication open and professional at all times if you want to have a team that functions without monitoring their every move.

Also, be clear about expectations. If employees knows what's expected of them from the start, you won't need to provide constant reminders. And the biggest thing is to trust your team do the job you hired them to do.

Run your business without the "signs." Your team members will turn your trust into their best ideas, and your need to micromanage will disappear.

TODAY'S ACTION ITEM

NOVEMBER 12

{ THE IMPORTANCE OF MEETING RHYTHMS }

Verne Harnish and I recently put together an eBook discussing all there is to know about meeting rhythms.

We have both found in our work as entrepreneurs and coaches that meeting rhythms are crucial to a functioning company. After all, meetings are the backbone of communication for almost every single company in the world.

Your established meeting rhythm will generally include the time limit for the meeting, who is attending the meeting, how often you'll meet, the desired outcome of the meeting and solutions to problems that could incur with each meeting. These factors are an important part of shaping expectations and standards for how meetings are run.

Having a set meeting rhythm helps designate the appropriate amount of time devoted to a specific purpose and ensures that the time is used efficiently and accordingly. It also creates routine and helps teams hone in on the most important things.

It's easier to resolve issues in a timely manner when you have a system for bringing them forward because you can address them as they come up, dealing with them before they can develop further.

A good meeting rhythm is also useful in reinforcing accountability because you are designating time to check in on the progress of goals and priorities. You can also use that time to recognize positive news or accomplishments, which provides a good morale boost for the team.

Perhaps most importantly, meetings are a time to put your heads together and collaborate, but collaboration is only effective if there is an established rhythm for doing so. Otherwise, people start shooting one another down.

Maintaining these rhythms contributes significantly to overall alignment, keeping everyone informed and communicating.

TODAY'S ACTION ITEM

NOVEMBER 13

{ 4 LEADERSHIP LESSONS I LEARNED FROM THE VINEYARD }

Guest contribution from Petra Coach David Pierce

I love wine. My love for the grape has moved me to visit some of the finest wine regions of the world. Through my travels, I've come to understand the nuances of making a great bottle of wine.

There are a lot of parallels between fine winemaking and fine leadership. Here are four lessons I've learned from the vineyard that can help you become a better leader:

1. A great wine begins from great root stock.
Root stock is a part of the grape vine, typically underground, that produces new growth above ground. Each root stock delivers unique characteristics to the fruit. In the same way, leaders must possess root-stock characteristics, such as integrity, drive, passion and empathy.

2. Quality wine requires a quality environment.
Soil types, temperature zones, rain and countless other elements have a huge effect on wine quality. In the same way, leadership execution requires an environment conducive to a leader's style.

3. Vines that undergo a certain amount of stress yield the best wines.
Winemakers induce stress intentionally, knowing they risk damaging the crop if it's not managed properly. Great leaders will tell you how self-imposed stress made them better. Taking risks and moving outside comfort zones can produce exponential benefits.

4. The best wines in the world require time in the bottle.
Even under carefully managed conditions, wines only become great after years of aging. Great leaders also need time to develop and grow through real-life experiences.

Next time you pour that glass of fine cabernet, think about what went into making it, and make a toast to all the great leaders that have been a part of your life. Cheers.

TODAY'S ACTION ITEM

NOVEMBER 14

{ AS THEY SAY: SHARING IS CARING }

Entrepreneurs and leaders can be all too familiar with restless nights and stressful days spent worrying about their companies. But they usually internalize their struggles, meaning that those trials and troubles – and how they cope with them – go unnoticed by everyone else.

It's important to remember that you aren't the only one who has dealt with a history full of sacrifice and adversity. Everyone has a story, and it's likely not as straightforward as you may believe it to be. If you want to find success with your team, you need to dive a little deeper and discover the lessons to be learned from each individual's unique struggles and achievements. These kinds of conversations can ultimately lead to the development of an "appreciation culture" – a way of thinking in your organization that allows employees the opportunity to see that sharing is appreciated and expected.

Start by sharing your own story. Opening up to your employees about your own struggles and sacrifices is a great way to show transparency and build respect. This also models to your employees that it's okay to be open about both the personal and professional aspects of their lives.

Pose questions and truly listen to those answers. You'll get your team to open up more, and you'll build a mutual trust and level of understanding.

Additionally, establish that it's okay to make mistakes from time to time. Mistakes will happen, and team members shouldn't be punished for any failures, but rather rewarded for taking risks. If your employees understand that, then they will be empowered to share new ideas and explore them, which in turn could change your business for the better.

TODAY'S ACTION ITEM

NOVEMBER 15

{ WHEN IT'S TIME TO HARVEST PROFITS }

You've built a profitable, successful business. Now comes a hard decision: How much of the company profits should you put into your own bank account?

It's an age-old question entrepreneurs and business owners struggle with every year. Every business and every industry is different, but there are some guidelines that will help you in managing your company's cash. Do these things before you harvest your business's profits:

1. Pay your taxes.
This should be a no-brainer. Under no circumstance should you ever, ever, ever not pay your taxes! Need me to repeat that? Set aside the necessary funds to pay Uncle Sam. Few things are more disruptive to your business than dealing with IRS auditors who are breathing down your neck about an unpaid tax bill.

2. Pay down your debt to a manageable level.
Legendary investor Warren Buffett has some sage advice for business owners on debt: "You really don't need leverage in this world much. If you're smart, you're going to make a lot of money without borrowing." I agree. And do not use debt to finance cash flow challenges if you don't know what's causing the problem and how you are going to fix it.

3. Have enough cash to meet your business's working capital needs.
You need cash to pay the bills. Set aside at least two to four months of cash so you can keep your business humming along. Trust me on this: Scrambling to find cash – especially new sources of cash, like bringing in new investors – takes time and energy that are better put to use building the business.

TODAY'S ACTION ITEM

NOVEMBER 16

{ ARE YOU A MANAGER OR A LEADER? }

And do you know the difference? If someone were to ask you about your team, what would you say? They're fun, hard-working, talented? Great managers know their people on more than a general level. They know their strengths, weaknesses, likes, dislikes, motives and achievements.

If you struggle with appreciating the differences in your team, you may not be ready to be a leader. Great managers identify what is different about their team and capitalize on it, whereas great leaders identify what the company needs and build a common vision that people can buy into and rally around to achieve it.

If you identify more as a manager, make sure you are managing your team as best you can by scheduling one-on-one meetings with each member of your team to continue to get to know them and how you can uncover their talents.

If you are more of a leader, be mindful that you are blocking off time in your calendar each week to brainstorm and strategize about how you can best guide your team.

Ideally, companies who wish to be truly successful require both excellent leaders and managers. Take a minute today to identify which one you and your team members most align with.

TODAY'S ACTION ITEM

NOVEMBER 17

{ DON'T GET STUCK IN YOUR COMFORT ZONE}

There's a reason you hear the phrase "Break out of your comfort zone" a lot. Because – as comfortable as that "zone" can be, after a while, it begins to grow bars around it (and not the good kind).

Whether it's a job we think we can't leave or a way of doing business that's no longer innovative (but has become a habit), all of us can fall into a rut that we like to call "stability." It's completely expected from an evolutionary point of view. We have a drive to find food, shelter and security, and once we have it, we want to keep it.

The problem is that we're no longer living in caves in danger of being eaten by wild animals, and it's unlikely that our homes will be raided by a thieving horde of bandits. It's the 21st century, and we're living in a world that moves quickly.

So don't be afraid to take regular (calculated) risks. Calculated meaning well thought out (and preferably not life-threatening). I'm not suggesting you put everything on the line every day, but don't be afraid of a few losses.

If you've weighed your possible outcomes, even if things don't work out the first time around, you've learned something, and you're better off than if you hadn't risked anything at all.

Comfort zones were meant to protect us, but if we maintain a prehistoric mindset, comfort becomes our enemy and we cease to grow. We need to change and adapt – all the time – and be thoughtful about the moves we make in our lives and businesses. The beginning of that growth begins squarely outside of your comfort zone.

TODAY'S ACTION ITEM

NOVEMBER 18

{ STRATEGY, EXECUTION, CASH }

Entrepreneurship doesn't end at the startup of a company. Millions of people launch new companies, but only a select few grow them past just a few employees, and fewer yet into industry-leading organizations. As you grow – or, as we call it, scale up – your business, you must shake the startup mentality and focus on a few specific areas:

1. **Strategy:** You must have a strong sense of what your organization is and where it is going. What are your core values? What is your core purpose? Make sure everyone in the organization understands them. Once the company has its foundation, it's time to think about how you will move it out of its startup phase. Meet with senior leadership on a weekly basis to discuss these strategies, and make sure that your entire team is involved in executing them.

2. **Execution:** The key to growing a startup into an industry-leading enterprise is to execute flawlessly. This requires the entire team to be focused on a specific set of priorities, which are clearly understood throughout the company. Everyone should be involved and contributing to the growth of the company.

3. **Cash:** Growth costs cash, and the faster you grow, the more cash you need. Find ways to reduce your cash conversion cycle (CCC), or the amount of time it takes for a dollar spent to make it back into your bank account. Understanding how cash moves through the company will allow you to improve cash flow and ultimately will give you the cash to fuel the growth of your organization.

To learn more about building your company into an industry-dominating business, I highly recommend reading the book *Scaling Up* by Gazelles CEO and Entrepreneurs' Organization founder Verne Harnish.

TODAY'S ACTION ITEM

NOVEMBER 19

{ WHY YOU NEED A CHAIN OF COMMAND }

Just like in the military, rank and chain of command are essential for effective management and communication in your business. Team members report to their managers, who report to their superiors, who then report to executive leadership. Once an issue is resolved, the answer makes its way back down the chain.

Why is it important to follow the chain of command in the workplace? Here are three reasons.

1. The chain shows respect.
Do not complain to your peers in the workplace. This is essentially gossip. Likewise, do not jump over your supervisor and feed complaints directly to upper management. CEOs and COOs do not have time to take care of every complaint in the office.

Not only do these actions show disrespect to your immediate supervisor, but they also create mistrust. Both reflect poorly on you.

2. The chain creates efficiency.
When reporting problems or communicating with the team, an established chain of command saves time in deciding who to go to with complaints and spurs quick, impactful change.

Your managers are responsible for making sure you are happy and productive at work. If you have a problem, let them know, so they can take action. Your peers cannot help you when an issue arises, but your supervisor can.

3. The chain improves morale.
A complete disregard for the chain of command results in disorder. Build a strong, trusting relationship with your direct supervisor, the liaison between you and higher management, in order to develop a rhythm of effective communication. With this in place, the organization will work together more seamlessly and people will be happier, reducing confusion and turnover.

TODAY'S ACTION ITEM

NOVEMBER 20

{ FACING FAILURE }

The f-word. No entrepreneur wants to hear about it, talk about it or face it, but it's a reality, especially on the path towards success. So, how do the best of the best overcome it? Here are my top three ways to approach it:

1. Learn from your mistakes.
Every failure is a valuable opportunity to learn. Instead of shying away from the situation, roll up your sleeves and approach it with a student mindset. What did you miss? Did you misjudge market demand or audience demographics? Did you do the proper research? Be brutally honest with yourself, but don't dwell in the shame. Collect the information, and use it to make the proper adjustments that will be essential for your next steps.

2. See it as a sign you're exiting your comfort zone.
You've heard it said before: nothing grows in the comfort zone. Failure is a sign that you're doing something new and unexpected that you haven't mastered yet. The other side of this process is where you find some of your greatest knowledge and power.

3. Encourage discussion about it.
All business leaders have failed at some point during their careers. To foster a culture of smart risk-taking, encourage team members to share their highs and lows about projects where they took a chance. Make it acceptable to talk about mistakes so team members are encouraged to share their experiences and ideas. It will create a more open and creative environment and help build healthier teams.

TODAY'S ACTION ITEM

NOVEMBER 21

{ ADOPTING A STUDENT MINDSET }

Too often, leaders get caught in the familiar trap of making decisions without team input. More often than not, leaders would benefit from conferring with teammates to gather additional perspectives. This not only helps with the decision-making process but will ultimately save time and keep morale high.

As a leader, do you encourage feedback from your teams, colleagues and friends? If not, start now. Refine your communication skills over time and perfect your technique with practice with these three tips:

1. Accept that you can be better.
If you think you've got all the answers, you don't. Everyone can be better, including you. Turn your brain into a sponge for others' knowledge. If you're used to things being "your way or the highway," this could take a bit of effort. Start by being honest about your intentions with your team, and make a public call for their feedback, opinions and thoughts.

2. Find continuous learners.
Surround yourself with like-minded individuals who share your passion for learning. Encourage them to share their hobbies, passions and areas of interest. Sometimes the best ideas for your business will come from areas outside your business.

3. Keep an open-door policy.
Lastly, make time for your colleagues. That first step of making a proactive effort to go to the team with questions is important, but to truly take advantage of strong relationships with your teammates, show that you welcome conversation and mentoring moments, even if you think you may be "too busy."

Adopting a student mindset is key to setting an example in your organization, boosting your level of knowledge and becoming a stronger, more engaged leader.

TODAY'S ACTION ITEM

NOVEMBER 22

{ TAKE TIME WITH YOUR TALENT }

Nancy McCord, chief talent officer at Netflix, said, "The best thing you can do for employees – a perk better than foosball or free sushi – is hire only A-players to work alongside them."

Top talent likes to work with other top talent. Create a culture where team members challenge each other, learn together and propel the company forward. If your top talent is too busy managing disengaged, subpar workers, the work will get old very quickly. No one wants to go to work and babysit fellow team members.

To create a team of top-tier talent, focus your energy on engaging current members and improving the hiring process. Create a company scorecard for job candidates. Outline the type of person that excels in the position and the character traits that they must possess. If an applicant doesn't meet the criteria, politely decline to pursue them further.

During an interview, ask behavioral questions that will evoke answers that are less likely to be rehearsed. This may add time to your hiring process, but it will be worth it in the end to find someone that will fit in with your current team.

TODAY'S ACTION ITEM

NOVEMBER 23

{ WHY YOU NEED AN ACCOUNTS RECEIVABLE DASHBOARD }

There's a well-known saying in business that "cash is king," but it's effective accounts receivable policies and procedures that will help your team have faster access to the cash it needs to accelerate growth and achieve company goals.

Hiccups in accounts receivable (A/R) collections can have drastic consequences for a business because they put pressure on the amount of working capital required to fund operations. The company I founded, NationLink Wireless, nearly went out of business because of cash flow challenges. As a result, we had to look at every way possible to improve A/R collections so we could have enough cash to pay the bills.

One of the most valuable tools a business leader can have when managing cash is an A/R dashboard, a tool that provides you easy access to monitor and measure the cash coming into the company. The dashboard should include generally accepted key performance indicators (KPIs) such as:

- A/R turnover ratio

- Days sales outstanding

- Average days delinquent

- A/R aging by client

These are just a few important metrics to monitor; your business may require others. The important point is this: Think of your dashboard as an early warning system so you can fix any challenges that may be on the horizon and shorten your collection cycles so you can put the money to work growing your business.

TODAY'S ACTION ITEM

NOVEMBER 24

{ 2 DON'TS IN TEAM LEADERSHIP }

Effective business leaders conduct regular self-assessments – setting aside time to get honest with themselves by mapping out their strengths and weaknesses and finding ways to improve.

Here are two self-assessment questions to help you become a better leader:

Are you holding your team back?
There are two surefire ways to destroy the individual motivation among team members: One is micromanaging, and the other is being so hands-off that team members don't know what to do when problems arise. Business leaders need to find a balance between the two. Know how to give your team the freedom they need to become empowered and motivated, but stay involved so you can provide the necessary guidance if and when team members get discouraged.

Are you avoiding difficult conversations?
Business leaders know initiating a difficult conversation can be a challenge, but they also know it's part of their job. Punting is not an option. Not every conversation should be held immediately, but if it's important to your business and team members you will have to tackle it eventually – and sooner is better than later.

Having a difficult conversation can be stressful for many leaders. Before you have a difficult talk, take a moment to think about why you respect your colleagues and team members. Express your gratitude to your team member first. Then have the talk. Afterward, as part of your self-assessment check-up, make sure you treated your team member fairly and respectfully.

TODAY'S ACTION ITEM

NOVEMBER 25

{ GET AFTER GRATEFUL }

It's about this time of year when gratitude becomes the focus of conversation. You see it on social media, hear it on television and speak about it around the dinner table surrounded by turkey and rolls. So, why tap into this powerful feeling for only a few days per year? What would your life look like if you practiced gratitude every day of your life? Here are two easy ways to make it happen:

Write it down.
A piece of paper, the notes app on your phone or even an email to yourself will do. I just want you to take an intentional moment to think about 5 things you're grateful for each morning. The key here is to be specific versus broad. I know you love your family, but what else? What about that first sip of coffee in the morning? The way your son laughed at your joke last night? There are moments of gratitude all around us. We just have to recognize them.

Create some cues.
In today's world our calendars are full and our brains are even fuller. I understand that it's hard to make space to remember to be grateful, especially when, for many of us, our automatic response is pessimism instead of optimism. Make it easier on yourself by creating cues that are a part of your everyday life. For example, your house doorknob can signal a reminder to be grateful for your home and family. Similarly, your computer can spur gratitude for being employed and providing for your family.

These actions may sound trivial, but make it a habit to put these into practice, and watch your everyday happiness soar.

TODAY'S ACTION ITEM

NOVEMBER 26

{ MAKING WORK WORK FOR YOU }

Sure, it would be great if we could all go live on a tropical island and do nothing but soak up the sun and put our toes in the sand all day, but that's just not reality. Employment, the ability to work and serve others with your skill set, is something to be grateful for, even during the moments that you don't feel like it. It's exponentially easier to enjoy your work when you feel focused and productive throughout the day.

Here are my two top tips for owning your day:

Take control of your time.
One way I make my work more productive is by arranging my day in a way that I am most productive. For me, that's early in the morning, so I am up around 5 a.m., tackling my most challenging work when my brain is fully awake and functioning best. For you, that may mean from 2 p.m. - 4 p.m. or even 8 p.m. - 10 p.m. How can you adjust your to-do list to make sure you're taking advantage of your most productive times?

Break and breathe.
Trouble focusing for long periods of time? You're not alone. In the early 1900's Francesco Cirillo, a developer and author, developed the Pomodoro Method – a system to train your brain to focus for short periods of time. You can practice by setting a timer for 20 minutes and working consistently until the timer goes off. After the 20 minutes is complete, you get a five-minute break to do whatever you want before you set the timer for another 20 minutes. While it sounds silly to continually time yourself, this method was proven to help improve attention span and concentration.

TODAY'S ACTION ITEM

NOVEMBER 27

{ HOW TO GROW TO KNOW YOUR TEAM }

Open conversation is at the heart of good communication in the workplace, making the body work properly. After all, how can you really know what people are interested in or capable of unless you ask them?

Here are three steps to start those conversations – and keep them going:

1. Ask simple questions.
Too many business leaders fall into the trap of treating casual conversations with team members like a business meeting. Cut the strategy and keep it simple. Questions like "Do you have any vacation plans coming up?" or "What have you been watching on Netflix lately?" are great places to start. Small talk has the powerful ability to build trust and camaraderie over time.

2. Share your story.
When you open up and share your story, your team members can see you as more than just your title. More so, they feel invited to share their own story, which can initiate further discussion about common likes and interests. Getting personal shows that you value authenticity and want to promote the same among your team.

3. Foster friendliness.
As the leader, you set the tone for the entire workplace. If you never laugh, neither will your team. If you do nothing more than answer emails all day, you set that as the standard culture throughout your office walls. Create ways for your team to communicate with you (and each other) more often, whether that's with a weekly happy hour, visiting your team members individually or having a quarterly outing.

TODAY'S ACTION ITEM

NOVEMBER 28

{ LEARNING FIRST }

Guest contribution from Petra Coach JT Terrell

Tom Bemiller, founder and president of The Aureus Group, one of Petra Coach's member companies, has adopted a "learning first" mantra in his life and business. To help coach other leaders on the importance of learning, I asked Bemiller to describe exactly what this mantra means and the benefits he's experienced from it:

> "I set aside one day per week for reading and thinking. The day is blocked off on my calendar, and it's the same day each week. I'll generally read something related to an issue I'm processing or a project on which I'm working inside the business, and then I'll spend time brainstorming about how to apply the concepts. I've made big progress in very little time on some very important projects since making [learning] a priority in my schedule.

> "I also spend 10 minutes each morning practicing gratitude, 10 minutes reading, 10 minutes journaling and 10 minutes setting my priorities for the day. This is the first thing I do in the morning, and it gives me an opportunity to quiet my mind, gather new information and knowledge, establish a positive attitude for the day, and focus on what needs to happen that day. Since starting the ritual, I've become more efficient and effective in my work. I'm also more calm and less stressed, and I am spending more time with my family.

> "I attend three or four conferences or learning programs per year, where I pick up an enormous amount of knowledge in concentrated fashion."

And this is just one example of how you can commit to more learning in your life. Find the routine that you'll get the most out of and that works best for you. Then, stick to it.

TODAY'S ACTION ITEM

NOVEMBER 29

{ PUT LEARNING INTO YOUR SCHEDULE }

Guest contribution from Petra Coach JT Terrell

Part of the founder and president of Petra Coach member company The Aureus Group Tom Bemiller's "learning first" mantra is figuring out how to fit learning into your schedule. He says:

> "I'll be honest: I don't think I could survive without my calendar. Not only does it consist of a series of recurring events that dictate my activity all day every day, but it also helps me prioritize learning.

> "Being extremely disciplined with my schedule has also allowed me to get more work done in less time. Additionally, the routine of repeating events – e.g., always going to the office on Monday or always reading at the library on Thursday – allows me to prepare better and focus more on the specific task or meeting at hand.

> "For me, routine is absolutely necessary. It helps me to be focused, prepared and effective throughout the week. By scheduling my calendar ahead of time, I can fine-tune a routine that works for me, allowing me to be the best I can be as a father, a husband and a CEO.

> "Creating that routine sets you free from the little fires that we feel we must put out every minute of every day. If you're a leader who wants to set a strict routine for learning, I encourage you to tell the most important people in your life why [learning] is so important. They can also help keep you accountable.

> "For me, it basically comes down to self-discipline in prioritizing the important stuff over the urgent stuff. Like anything, progress didn't happen overnight; it was a series of small improvements over time that eventually added up. It just requires a commitment to self-improvement."

TODAY'S ACTION ITEM

NOVEMBER 30

{ MAKING GOALS HAPPEN }

So, you've had an awesome planning day with your team, filled with goals, ideas and dreams for the quarter. But now, how will you actually make it all happen?

Legendary NFL football coach Tom Landry says, "Setting a goal is not the main thing. It is deciding how you will go about achieving it and staying with that plan."

Use these four planning parameters to ensure your plan gets executed:

1. Limit priorities: A planning day typically involves establishing company goals, as well as individual priorities for each team member. I recommend no more than five priorities for each team member. Three is ideal. You can't achieve your priorities when you have too many of them competing with each other.

2. Delve deeper: Your goals and priorities must be specific, measurable, attainable, relevant and time-bound (S.M.A.R.T.). "I want to grow the company" isn't good enough. Instead say, "I will increase the company's revenue by X percent by Dec. 31." If your goals and priorities do not adhere to these five S.M.A.R.T. guidelines, you tremendously decrease your chances of achieving your desired outcome.

3. Review often: I recommend meeting regularly with your team to check in on priority progressions and original plan relevance. Not only do these meeting rhythms foster accountability, they ensure the original goal is still appropriate. I suggest half-day monthly, hour-long bi-weekly and five-minute daily check-in sessions.

4. Celebrate small wins: Just two percent movement toward your goal each week will get you to 100 percent in 12 months. It's all about the small, consistent strides. Celebrate your interceptions and tackles. It'll encourage and reinvigorate you and your team so you're charged to win the game.

TODAY'S ACTION ITEM

DECEMBER

{ VITAMIN B-12 }

Vitamins have the ability to create protections and support for your cells. Remember the reason why you work: to support your family and friends and have the means to protect them. Leave work at work during the upcoming holiday season, and enjoy spending time with your loved ones.

DECEMBER 1

{ WHEN YOU THINK YOU'RE THE BEST, YOU'RE NOT }

Would you rather be the best player on the worst team, or the worst player on the best team? Tough question.

Being the best player is easy – it's comfortable. Being the worst is difficult – it's uncomfortable.

The player in the uncomfortable position has an advantage, though. He or she has something to chase. There is more reason to improve.

Contrarily, the comfortable player has little reason to improve. He or she is already the best. The proverbial glass ceiling has been met, and there's nowhere to go. Comfort often ushers complacency.

Further, it's more difficult to improve when you're the best because once you're good, getting to great is in the minutiae. It takes a lot more focus and intent to bridge the gap from good to great.

Many of the business teams I've worked with for a while find themselves in the comfort category. They consistently reach the goals we set during planning sessions, and their businesses are growing.

But future success is determined by the work you do today – not what you did yesterday. Just because business is booming now, doesn't mean it will continue to do so in the future if you don't continue to think of new ways to improve.

TODAY'S ACTION ITEM

DECEMBER 2

{ ALWAYS LEARNING }

Leaders experience a variety of problems every day, some large and some small. And sometimes leaders will wait until a business coach is in the room to deal with those problems. But that's not effective or timely. The next time you are wrestling with an issue, consider these two thoughts:

1. Find solutions.
It's not enough just to acknowledge there are problems, you also need to find solutions to them. Push your company or leadership team to sit down and brainstorm together. It's the best way to get everyone talking and to get others' perspectives on what will best address each issue. These sessions shouldn't just happen on special planning days. They should be a regular part of the business's proceedings.

2. Learn continuously.
Channel your inner student and be ready to learn. When you take time to comb through the weeds, talk through problems and find solutions, those remedies can be applied to more situations down the road. It's also helpful to know what leaders are doing in other companies – read various books and articles to see how others have improved their companies. Even business coaches don't have all the answers, so take advantage of the world of resources at your fingertips to find a way around any roadblocks.

The underlying theme through each of these steps is that leaders should never stop pushing and growing. That mentality will transfer to your team – after all, they are the ones who help keep your business going.

TODAY'S ACTION ITEM

DECEMBER 3

{ CELEBRATE THE LITTLE WINS }

Slow and steady wins the race. Yes, it's an oft-used saying but it's one that entrepreneurs and leaders should take to heart. Very few business owners struck it rich fast. It takes good old-fashioned hard work, dedication and the willingness to endure failure and overcome obstacles.

Success isn't going to happen overnight or maybe even next year, so it's vital that you build momentum in your business by celebrating the small, initial victories. Leaders often lose their motivation because they get frustrated when they don't achieve big-picture goals fast enough.

So, do yourself a favor. Establish smaller, more attainable goals each week, month and quarter that will push your company forward. When you reach them, celebrate! You may be the only one at the party, but that's okay – more cake for you. You may not be able to celebrate with the finest champagne or a fancy new car, but you can reward yourself in other ways. How about three technology-free days? Or no email, texts or Excel spreadsheets for three whole days? Now there's a reward!

Motivate yourself to reach the big milestones by celebrating the smaller ones and savoring every little victory.

TODAY'S ACTION ITEM

DECEMBER 4

{ GREAT MARKETING LEADS TO GREAT HIRING}

I've talked before about how hiring from within is generally more effective and efficient than looking for new candidates, but when you come to the point where there's no one else internally to leverage, you have to know how to find the right talent.

A great hiring tip that I picked up from Verne Harnish's *Scaling Up* is that the marketing team needs to work just as hard to attract potential employees as it does to attract customers.

As he says, great candidates don't just "fall from the sky" and instantly become interested in your company. You need to attract them through creative marketing strategies.

For example, Google found that if a company does something enticing or intriguing enough, the talent will come looking for you. In their case, they put up anonymous billboards with a math riddle that tech and math enthusiasts everywhere shared virally to figure out whose ad it was. Once they did figure it out, they were on Google's radar, and Google was able to hire tons of great people – all because of the widespread hype.

While I'm not suggesting your ads have to go viral to find the best candidates, I am recommending that you think of your hiring ads just like your product ads. The social and psychological tactics are the same either way.

Great marketing ensures you'll have great employees and great customers. That sets your company up for long-term growth.

TODAY'S ACTION ITEM

DECEMBER 5

{ MAKE SELF-CARE A TOP PRIORITY }

Owning your own business and leading others can have some amazing highs and some gut-wrenching lows.

Additionally, you're often the first one to rise, the last one to leave and the go-to person for a weekend emergency. That unfortunately results in self-care being the first thing that's tossed out the window when things get stressful, or just too busy.

Contrary to popular belief, this "rise and grind" mentality could actually be harming your business. Why? The success of the organization depends on your ability to show up – physically and mentally – every day. This is impossible if you're burning yourself out with a crazy schedule.

To be the best leader you can be, start taking a proactive approach to your own health. Set aside a day or two every few months to knock out all of the doctor's appointments, testing, nutritionist check-ins, etc. that you need.

I call these "me maintenance" days. If your back has been aching for three months, or you've yet to pick up your new contacts, do your team a favor and take care of it.

If it takes more than one day, don't be afraid to use some personal time. You've built a great team, so trust them to keep things running while you take care of yourself.

When you're not in full health, or working with only half of your engines, you're ultimately hurting the team. Make an effort to schedule these days, no matter how busy you are, and set an example for the rest of your team.

TODAY'S ACTION ITEM

DECEMBER 6

{ POSITIVE COMPANY CULTURE DRIVES SUCCESS}

Guest contribution from Petra Coach David Pierce

The last time I took a trip to Disney World, it hit me that there are very specific reasons why this company is as successful as it is. Not only are its products and movies entertaining and its theme parks magical, but it also has an admirable culture.

The Walt Disney Company's core purpose is all about happiness, and if you've ever experienced Disney World then you know the company's core purpose is alive and well.

> "The mission of The Walt Disney Company is to entertain, inform and inspire people around the globe through the power of unparalleled storytelling, reflecting the iconic brands, creative minds and innovative technologies that make ours the world's premier entertainment company."

Every facet of Disney – the employees, transportation, park appearances, hotels and more – is about giving customers the best experience possible.

I often ask those I coach to name a company which has happiness as a core value, and someone always immediately says The Walt Disney Company. The power of having a core culture that is brimming with purpose and intentionality is that those characteristics are automatically attributed to you and connected to your name, just as happiness and magic are attributed to Disney.

In other words, your culture cannot be great if your purpose and values don't align with it.

A strong culture creates a business of which both employees and customers want to be a part. However, great culture doesn't just happen. It's hard work that requires continual focus and accountability, but the return on investment is astronomical.

TODAY'S ACTION ITEM

DECEMBER 7

{ TIME TO ENTER THE DISCOMFORT ZONE }

In business, you never want to get too comfortable because as soon as that happens, you're less likely to keep growing and working toward new goals. You get caught up in this so-called stability that you've fabricated for yourself.

So, I propose that rather than thinking of it as "leaving your comfort zone," think of it as "entering the discomfort zone."

Do something risky, like competing publicly. There's no greater motivator than the fear of public embarrassment, right? Well, that may be true, but the glory of public success can be a great motivator as well.

Set goals and make them known. Make it a public endeavor. It will give you accountability to rise up to the challenge and will likely compel you to exceed expectations.

Don't be afraid to test your limits. You can't keep doing the same thing over and over again and expect to improve. At work and at home, change up your routine. Look beyond what you "think" you can do. It's the only way to really find out what you're made of.

The truth is we need to keep ourselves in check. Don't get too comfortable. Don't rest on your laurels. There's a difference between taking time to smell the roses and just taking a nap in the shade at the foot of the bush. Keep moving, keep learning and your "discomfort zone" might just become your best friend.

TODAY'S ACTION ITEM

DECEMBER 8

{ DON'T BE A "BOSSHOLE" }

As I've mentioned before: You don't work for anyone, and no one works for you, because you all work for a *purpose*, not a *person*.

So how do you go about changing that mindset, and finding that purpose in what you and your company do?

For one, don't be a "bosshole." A bosshole is a leader that tells others what to do without any context or purpose. They are calling out shots from behind the lines without any awareness of what's actually happening on the front lines. No one likes to work for these kinds of people.

When you clearly define a meaning for your organization, you don't have to be a bosshole. A true leader gets out in front and leads others with a clear objective and direction.

Warning! Not everyone in your company will have the same goals as you – which means they may need to exit. This isn't as scary as it sounds. You want employees that see your company's vision and subscribe to the same purpose. That helps you develop a communal spirit within your team, which, in turn, helps you work together to meet and beat goals.

TODAY'S ACTION ITEM

DECEMBER 9

{ HOW TO STAY FOCUSED AT WORK AND HOME DURING THE HOLIDAYS }

We are in the midst of the craziest time of the year. Between holiday celebrations and year-end wrap-up reports, gift shopping and New Year goal setting, it all can seem overwhelming and, at times, even unmanageable.

You're not alone. Everyone is busy during the holidays. We all have the same amount of time in the day, week, month and so on. But, why is it that some people just get more done? Two words: They focus.

Here are three tried-and-true hacks I use every year to stay focused and manage my time better during the holidays:

1. Plan ahead.
Create a to-do list for both work and personal tasks. When you're at work, focus on your work. Likewise, when you're at home, concentrate on checking off tasks on your personal list. Don't bring work home with you and don't multitask. Stay focused and work on one project at a time, and finish what you start.

2. Eliminate distractions.
Technology aids businesses in a lot of ways, but it can also be detrimental to your productivity. If you want to have a meaningful day at work, simply unplug. Turn off alerts on your phone and email. Choose two to three times throughout the day to check them, using that time to respond to any urgent messages.

3. Don't over-commit.
We are constantly guilty of over-committing, especially during the holidays when there are countless parties and functions. Limit your engagements so you have time to complete your work.

This is a great time of the year to enjoy the things you truly care about and to participate enthusiastically in events and opportunities that matter to you.

TODAY'S ACTION ITEM

DECEMBER 10
{ ARE YOU FEARLESS? }

A satisfying career doesn't come without the fear of taking a few risks – often more than a few. Are you excited to tackle new things or take calculated risks? Or are you so scared to fail that you don't push any boundaries? If you can show your fellow team members that you've got the gumption for bold moves, you'll earn respect, foster a spirit of motivation and feel empowered.

Here are three tips to get you started on your fearless journey:

1. Invite team members to challenge you.
Surround yourself with colleagues who will challenge you to improve. Ask them to be part of your inner circle and to be brutally honest in your performance and how you can improve. You'll be surprised how much you learn about yourself and what you can do to perform at a higher level.

2. Don't be afraid to fail.
You will fail. That's virtually a given. I have failed many times and learned invaluable lessons from each experience. If you don't take risks then you'll miss out on big opportunities. If you're on the fence, reach out to the team members who you asked to push you.

3. Get out of your comfort zone and embrace change.
Setting and achieving lofty goals requires change. The person you are today will not get you to where you want to be.

Discover what you need to change in your approach to work (and life), put a plan in place and stick to it. It takes a lot of willpower to let go of old work habits, so start today to become the fearless person you want to become.

TODAY'S ACTION ITEM

DECEMBER 11

{ "DEHASSLE" RATHER THAN "DEMOTIVATE" }

I talk a lot about engagement and how it's important that your team members feel motivated and excited at work every day.

In his book *Scaling Up*, Verne Harnish counts off the best ways to keep your talent engaged, and one that stands out to me is actually a little opposite to the way most people think.

Rather than worrying so much about motivating your employees, think about ways you can remove the hassles that cause them to lose motivation or become "demotivated." These hassles can come from people or processes – both of which you, as a leader, have the power to fix.

Other hassles can be external, such as clients who are hard to work with. While the first step to success isn't to give up business left and right, if there's a client for whom you've given your all, and they still just drain everyone's energy and motivation, it might be time for your partnership to end. It's the same principle as having a "rotten egg" employee on your team – they stink everything up.

Sometimes, a company's processes or policies can also be big "demotivators" for employees. It could be something as simple as having outdated and slow computers in the office that makes it impossible to be productive, or something larger like having bad policies (or none at all) surrounding a particularly prevalent issue.

Any way that the leadership of a company can make things easier for their employees is recommended to keep your team going strong.

TODAY'S ACTION ITEM

DECEMBER 12
{ HOW TO TAKE CONTROL OF YOUR TECH }

Technology is a powerful tool that seems ingrained into every facet of our world today. From podcasts to online appointments and emails to airline miles, we use technology to keep our personal and professional worlds afloat. However, how much tech is too much?

Feeling annoyed by how much you rely on your phone? You're not alone. Keep these two tips in mind to manage the tech madness and get more done:

1. Understand its power.
There are many positives to technology, but understanding the power it has is essential to using it wisely. Contrary to popular belief, our brains aren't wired to multitask, and continuously breaking our minds away from one task to another is a productivity-killer. If you can, put your phone on silent in a drawer or (even better!) in the other room while you work. If you must have your phone nearby, use apps like OFFTIME or Flipd to block access to social media apps with the click of a button.

2. Monitor energy levels regularly.
Like a smartphone battery, a high energy level is optimal to your work, relationships and management success. Feeling drained? Take a step away from your screens and breathe. This can look like taking a walk during lunch without checking email or avoiding mindless social media scrolling after 8 p.m. Whatever boundary you set for yourself will be a welcome and much needed break for your mental and physical health.

TODAY'S ACTION ITEM

DECEMBER 13

{ ACCOUNTING FOR BEGINNERS }

Most business leaders I've met consider detailed discussions about accounting about as exciting as watching paint dry. But if you want to build a business from scratch into a profitable, multi-million dollar company that's growing revenue at double-digit rates, you will need a basic understanding of accounting, and I'm not talking about the difference between a debit and a credit.

Charlie Munger, Warren Buffett's longtime business partner, once called accounting "the language of practical business life." I agree. Accounting factors into about every decision a leader makes. You can only make smart decisions about sales and marketing, production and distribution, and employee hiring and training if you know the financial implications.

If you are not well versed in accounting, start today to understand the nuts and bolts of the profession. There are some outstanding online courses and eBooks available – for free – for beginners, such as at Coursera or Khan Academy. Those resources will help you learn the basics of accounting so you can make informed decisions as a leader or business owner.

TODAY'S ACTION ITEM

DECEMBER 14

{ SHOW YOUR CLIENTS SOME LOVE DURING THE HOLIDAYS }

The year-end holiday season presents the perfect opportunity to show your appreciation to the people who provide the cash to pay the bills: your clients! If you're a B2B company, you need to reach out to clients during the holidays to let them know how important they are to the continued success of the company.

Here are two ways to help your company stand out from the crowd during the holidays:

1. Send handwritten thank you cards.
Your clients receive enough email, so stand out from the crowd by sending a handwritten thank you note. Personalize your note and send it to client executives who are involved in the buying decision for your product or service. Don't send generic cards to company departments. The card doesn't have to be expensive, and your message doesn't have to be expansive. Just let them know you are grateful for their support.

2. Hand-deliver presents.
If you are sending gifts to clients, there's no better way to make a lasting impact than having them hand-delivered by team members. Trust me: Your clients will be impressed. For clients where you are unable to do that, having the gifts messengered over is the next best option.

Clients are the reason you have a business, so make sure you are treating them like the VIPs they are this holiday season.

TODAY'S ACTION ITEM

DECEMBER 15

{ PREPARE YOUR TEAM TO MOVE UP }

Your star players won't be around forever, no matter how loyal. Retirements and resignations happen.

Prepare team members now to fill higher positions in the future, and allow them to move up when an opening happens. That way, you've set up an internal succession plan – and you won't suddenly have to fill a position when someone leaves.

Identify key players who could be good fits for higher positions, and start delegating more responsibilities to them. Have leaders in your company train them on key functions of a role. When the time comes, they'll be able to jump in the saddle quickly and transition into a new position with less training.

Hiring from within also shows that you trust the people you've already hired – even if their skills aren't fully developed. You're invested in their success.

There's a time and place for hiring external applicants who are applying for a position in your company. Taking steps to promote your own team members, however, could be more beneficial to your company in the long run.

In the end, it's a better bet.

TODAY'S ACTION ITEM

DECEMBER 16

{ 3 BUSINESS LESSONS LEARNED IN 12 DAYS OFF THE GRID }

Guest contribution from Petra Coach JT Terrell

In June 2016, I joined my 15-year-old son and his troop on a Boy Scouts of America rite-of-passage: the Trek at Philmont Scout Ranch in Cimarron, N.M. I should note – this is not car camping. This is the kind of camping where you carry all your food, equipment, clothing, shelter and water in a 60-pound pack. And it's 12 days on the trail hiking five to 10 miles each day.

We were set to spend days hiking and climbing through some seriously remote, high-altitude peaks in the southern Rockies. But the part that scared me the most wasn't the strenuous nature of the trek. It was leaving my smartphone at base camp.

It turns out I learned a lifetime of lessons during our trek, including how to build a business and a team. Here are the three main things I learned:

Lesson 1: In a world of quick convenience and "fail fast" start-ups, sometimes the long way is the best course of action, with strategic planning, segmented growth and deliberate moves.

Lesson 2: Tiny problems can be easily fixed if you identify them quickly. Early in the trip a piece of my backpack broke, which made carrying the pack difficult. Fortunately, we were able to come up with a simple solution that prevented a disaster down the road.

Lesson 3: The more difficult the trek, the more you learn. If previously set goals are being crushed, regroup and reset more aggressive targets. If targets are missed, explore the failure for learning points and move on.

TODAY'S ACTION ITEM

DECEMBER 17

{ ENJOYING THE MOST WONDERFUL TIME OF THE YEAR }

"It's the Most Wonderful Time of the Year" is more than just a popular Christmas song. It reflects how many people think about the holiday season.

For many companies, however, it's one of the busiest and most stressful times of the year. A survey by health and wellness website Healthline found that 62 percent of respondents feel "very stressful" or "somewhat stressful" during the holidays. It's easy to see why as your team members have to balance work and family responsibilities.

Regardless of your job title, we all need time to disconnect from work and enjoy being around family. Here's how you do it:

1. Use your extra vacation days.
If you have unused vacation days, now is the time to take them. Spend a day with family or hit the mall to get your shopping done. This will give you a much-needed opportunity to refresh and recharge during this busy season.

2. Celebrate the holidays at work, too.
Don't forget about the workplace. Remember to embrace the holiday season and encourage everyone to have fun. Gather the team for a wrapping party or a spontaneous happy hour. A positive company culture helps drive your team to high performance.

Having a little time off or taking a break from work while at work during the holidays will inspire and motivate you and your team and help everyone get re-energized for the New Year. I challenge you to make the necessary changes at work and home to ensure that you and your team are highly productive and in great spirits during the holiday season.

TODAY'S ACTION ITEM

DECEMBER 18

{ WHY YOU NEED TO MEASURE YOUR WEBSITE'S TRAFFIC }

As a business leader or owner, it's essential that you understand the concept of big data as it relates to your website because it will provide clues into how your clients and prospective clients are engaging with your company.

There are some great books about the topic, and I could fill pages on which to recommend and why. But in my experience, it's best to start with a few key metrics and build from there. Here's where to start:

1. Traffic: Traffic measures the number of visitors who visit your website. You can also see how many are new visitors to your site, which is important because you want prospective clients viewing your website for product/service information, news about your company, etc.

2. Bounce rate: The bounce rate is the percentage of visitors who see only one page before leaving your site. You want visitors sticking around, so the lower the better.

3. Session duration: Session duration measures how long a visitor stayed on a page before moving on. You want visitors reading your content, so the longer the better.

4. SERP ranking: SERP stands for Search Engine Results Pages and ranks your web pages based on keyword searches used by people when surfing the web. The higher the better.

5. Pages per visit: Calculates the number of pages people are visiting when on your website. Great content will increase this metric.

6. Returning visitors: Just like you want repeat clients, you want repeat visitors.

TODAY'S ACTION ITEM

DECEMBER 19

{ A CHALLENGE WELL-DEFINED IS A CHALLENGE HALF-SOLVED }

In many of my coaching sessions, leaders will have trouble defining the biggest challenges they're facing. They get that look of terror on their faces like, "It's just so overwhelming, I don't know where to start."

You need to start like you would if you were climbing a mountain. That means that, first, you must know where the mountain is. Then, you learn about it, size up the summit, think through your strategy for scaling it, then off you go.

Those are the same steps to follow when working through any challenge, whether it's on a mountain or in the office. First, figure out what that summit is – what is the challenge that needs to be overcome.

Then, think about it as a question that you need to find the answer to. For example, you may write, "Our employee Net Promoter Scores (NPS) are lacking," which means the question becomes, "How can we increase them?" From there you can start brainstorming ways to combat the issue: You can 1) implement better health benefits, 2) host more company outings, etc.

Once you've reached this point, your dilemma is already half-solved. You've already put in the work outlining the problem and the tactics needed to overcome it. Now the plan just needs to be implemented, and it will be easier to do it since you've figured out the steps, the skills, the gear and other items needed for the climb.

My goal as a coach is to guide company leaders in their preparation for scaling the mountain, then support them as they ascend. Trust me, the magnificent view from the top will make it all worth it.

TODAY'S ACTION ITEM

DECEMBER 20

{ SHOW YOUR TEAM MEMBERS SOME LOVE DURING THE HOLIDAYS }

As a leader, there's no better time than the year-end holidays to show your gratitude to your team members for all their hard work and dedication. Clients provide the cash to pay the bills, but it's your team members who keep your clients happy and engaged.

Here's a trio of tips to show how much you value your team during the holidays:

1. Publicly recognize team members.
Everyone likes a public shout out from the boss. Show how much their effort means to you by letting the team know your feelings.

2. Make it personal.
I've written a couple of times in this book about the power of handwritten "thank you" notes. Yes, this is old school, but your team member will appreciate the time and effort you took to show how much you care.

3. Host a holiday "thank you" party.
Rather than hold a holiday party, turn it into a "thank you" party and allow team members to invite friends, spouses and significant others. Avoid talking too much about business and enjoy spending more time getting to know your team.

The holiday season is the best time of year to let your team know how much you care. It's a golden opportunity to strengthen the bond with your team and bolster morale.

TODAY'S ACTION ITEM

DECEMBER 21

{ THE ROAD TO HEAVEN }

One of the oldest adages says, "The road to heaven is a walk through hell," meaning you often have to go through hardships to get to the brighter, more joyful side.

I won't sugar-coat it: The road to heaven does go through hell, BUT you get to decide if it's a *day* trip or a *daily* trip.

There's another proverb that says, "The road to hell is paved with good intentions." While that may be true, there's a difference between good intentions and positive actions. One is the idea of doing something positive, the other is the actual act. You can intend to make a change, but never actually do it – or you can actually do it. See the difference?

Unless you are going to do something different, it's all just talk. You'll just keep floundering and doing the same things over and over again expecting to get a different result.

Isn't that what they say is the definition of madness?

Find a solution, and take the necessary steps to change things up. Sometimes those steps will be painfully hard, no doubt, but you can push through and decide to jump in and do them quickly. Or you can procrastinate and stretch everything out for so long that it's unbearable for all involved.

Start little by little if you have to, and work your way up to the bigger changes. Book yourself a one-way ticket away from the Bermuda Triangle of "what if's," and toward the heaven that it could be.

TODAY'S ACTION ITEM

DECEMBER 22

{ EXTROVERTS VS. INTROVERTS }

You may not realize it, but you may be using the terms "extrovert" and "introvert" incorrectly to describe someone who is "outgoing" or "shy," respectively. In fact, they are two completely different spectrums.

The scale of outgoing to shy is defined as how much you like being in the spotlight vs. being in the background in social situations. However, the scale of extroversion to introversion refers to how you handle being with people: Do you thrive off of the energy of other people, or are you drained by social situations?

Most people fall somewhere in the middle, but lean one way or another. For someone on the extroverted side, they tend to feel depressed and lonely when they're alone for too long, but on the flip side, an introverted person needs time alone to recoup from their time being with people.

That doesn't necessarily mean the introverted person is shy. The two scales are not mutually exclusive. So the introverted person could be very outgoing when they put forth the energy to be in social situations. They may just need more time to recover than, say, an outgoing extrovert.

The relevant point for business is: It's possible to be an introverted leader.

You just need to work with who you are and give yourself the necessary space. If the big presentation you had in the morning was completely draining, take some time to shut your office door (or put in headphones in your cubicle) and recharge your social battery.

Being introverted isn't an automatic crutch – it just takes some extra consideration and planning. Don't let who you are stop you from becoming who you want to be.

TODAY'S ACTION ITEM

DECEMBER 23

{ VISIONARY VS. INTEGRATOR }

I work with many people who have founded and lead successful businesses. These entrepreneurs produce great work and execute excellent ideas that drive their companies forward. However, sometimes the business can stall, or the founder can feel like something is missing – and there might be. Even if the entrepreneur is a great visionary, that is only one part of an exceptional company – there should also be an integrator. I learned this crucial idea from Gino Wickman and Mark C. Winters' book *Rocket Fuel*, and it's been transformational for me. Not sure which role you are or which you might be missing? Here's a breakdown:

The visionary role.
The first word that comes to mind when categorizing visionaries is passionate. They are passionate about their product, service, company or people. Visionaries typically have lots of ideas, which is one of the reasons why their companies thrive. Fitting for their name, visionaries also have the unique ability to look into the future and think strategically about company or client needs.

The integrator role.
The integrator is commonly called the glue of an organization. In contrast to visionaries who are talented at creating and forecasting ideas, integrators are specifically equipped to hold others accountable for executing these big ideas. They love running the day-to-day of the business and tackling problems as they arise. They are obsessed with organization and are often extremely detail-oriented, keeping everything and everyone on track.

Why you need both.
Like yin and yang, these complementary forces come together to form a dynamic duo that is essential to an optimal functioning organization. Which role do you identify with the most? Do you have an opposite on your leadership team?

TODAY'S ACTION ITEM

DECEMBER 24

{ 24 HOURS OF FAMILY TIME }

It's the night before Christmas, not a creature is stirring...except you on your email?

No matter what holiday you celebrate, Christmas is a special time in the U.S. because it's the only day of the year where everything stops. (Well, unless you work at a movie theater or Chinese restaurant).

Keep in mind, your clients, your boss and anyone else who might be constantly busting down your door, are also most likely not working right now. So take advantage of this time to take a pause with the rest of the country.

I challenge you to forget about work for the next 24 hours. Turn off your email, power down your phone, throw your computer out the window – whatever you need to do to cut the distractions and be present with your family.

After all, family is why you work in the first place, so make sure you enjoy this time with them and the life you've helped build for them. Whether that's spending time around the Christmas tree or going to a movie and eating Chinese food, it's valuable time to make lasting memories.

Wishing you and your loved ones a wonderful holiday time!

TODAY'S ACTION ITEM

DECEMBER 25

{ ADD GRATITUDE TO YOUR SEASON OF GIVING}

The time is here, readers. Radio stations have been playing seasonal classics, the temperature is dropping by double digits, and my kids have been dropping not-so-subtle hints about their gift wish lists.

While the ramp-up to the end of the year is always festive and exciting, this time of year also carries stress for many workers.

In fact, more than one-third of all employees are more stressed at work during the holidays than any other time of the year, according to a recent study by Accountemps. All businesses want their team members to sustain high-performance levels, no matter the season or outside conditions. To do that, team members need to feel motivated to overcome obstacles and fight off stress.

The good news is, there's one area of business that always provides some relief, motivation and positivity to stressed individuals – and no, it's not the paycheck. I'm talking about gratitude.

When I say gratitude, I'm not talking about Christmas bonuses or lively holiday parties, though both of those are fun and positive cultural components for your company. Instead, I'm talking about showing appreciation, sharing positive notes and reinforcing strong personal relationships.

During this seasonal focus on giving, I encourage business leaders to kickstart their thinking on how they can express gratitude toward their colleagues, for the rest of the current year and into the next.

The holidays don't have to create stressful work environments. Use the positivity of the season to express why gratitude is needed at your office, and explain to your team members how spreading a word of good cheer can boost business results and individual attitudes. And don't stop after the new year – gratitude is something you can encourage and enjoy all year long.

TODAY'S ACTION ITEM

DECEMBER 26

{ 2 TIPS TO BECOMING A BETTER DECISION-MAKER }

Guest contribution from Petra Coach Greg Eisen

Generally speaking, the more responsibilities you have, the more complex and taxing your choices become. Can you relate? For some people, decision-making comes naturally, but for others, every little choice is a hurdle to overcome.

As my responsibilities have increased, I've established a few rhythms that help me clear my mind and make quick decisions that have monumental impact. Here are two strategies I use to maximize my decision-making capabilities:

1. Meet about it.
I've heard it said that you are the sum of the five people you spend the most time with. Whether it's your spouse, colleague, parent or friend, it's essential to have a close network of trusted sources you can tap to ask questions – no matter how big or how small. Bonus points if this group includes those with different perspectives than you, or at least has quality listeners, which are an invaluable resource.

2. Establish rules.
Early in my career, people would come into my office asking for help, and I would give them answers and send them off to execute. Over time, this became a crutch for them that created more work for me. Eventually, I created a Three-Solutions Rule: My door is always open to help with any and all challenges – but, when a team member seeks my assistance, they must come prepared with up to three potential solutions for solving that problem. This simple change was transformative in developing our team culture, took pressure off of me and ultimately improved decision-making across our entire team.

Don't discount the stress you endure when it comes to decision-making, but know that by deploying smart strategies, it can get better. Adopting one of these tactics may just change your life, one good decision at a time.

TODAY'S ACTION ITEM

DECEMBER 27

{ IS YOUR CAREER FULFILLING? }

We spend a lot of time at our jobs – one in five full-time workers puts in more than 60 hours per week – so we should find fulfillment in our work, not just a paycheck. These are signs that you're feeling fulfilled:

1. You dare to be ambitious.
You must have a desire to succeed in your company in order to be happy. Ambition is what moves you forward, in and outside of the workplace.

2. You are not afraid to take risks.
You have to pursue success and happiness – it won't just fall into your lap. If you take the right risks in your career, it'll boost your confidence and make you stand out as a leader in your organization.

3. You are attracted to the experience.
Do not define your success by the size of your paycheck. Define your success by the value of the experiences at your job and how you achieve your goals and make a difference in your organization.

4. You don't mind the boring work.
There may be tasks that you don't want to do, but if you are passionate about what you're doing, you won't complain about them. Think of these small tasks as stepping stones to reach a larger, company-wide goal.

5. You surround yourself with like-minded individuals.
Your teammates should inspire and energize you to succeed, not make you feel like you're being drained of all your energy.

If you are not fulfilled by your job, do something about it – either find a way to be more engaged or find a new job. Life is too short, and we spend too much time at our jobs, to do anything less.

TODAY'S ACTION ITEM

DECEMBER 28

{ A GUARANTEE IS A POWERFUL MARKETING TOOL }

Recently, I bought a pair of running shoes online. Usually I buy my shoes at a sporting goods store so I can try them on, but I tried something new because the website offered me a 30-day guarantee. What did I have to lose?

A guarantee is a powerful tool. Not enough businesses use them to their advantage. If you're a reputable business, you're going to stand behind your product or service anyway.

So take advantage of that. Let people know from the beginning that they can do business with you without risk. Now, I hear you saying, "Wait a minute, I don't want people scamming me. What's to stop a customer from deciding to just not pay?"

Well, I won't say it never happens, but in 20 years of business it hasn't happened to me. If it did, though, it would be worth it for all the times someone saw that guarantee, pulled the trigger, and then became a loyal customer. They far outnumber the bad seeds, and this way the system helps weed out customers and clients you don't really want to do business with.

The bottom line is that every good company is going to do right by its customers. But not all customers are adept at recognizing a good company from a bad one. Putting a money-back guarantee out front lets them know you're one of the good ones and, even if it doesn't work out, you're both dealing in good faith. You'll see the good customers stay and the bad ones move on. I guarantee it.

TODAY'S ACTION ITEM

DECEMBER 29

{ 3 KEYS TO TIME MANAGEMENT }

The way business leaders allocate their time has a direct correlation to their effectiveness and, ultimately, the performance of their business. Leaders, because of the very nature of their role, get pulled in seemingly a million directions that steal time.

Here are three things to ask yourself if time slips away during your workday:

Are you disorganized?
Not locating documents quickly can cause frustration, decreased productivity and stress. Organize and name your computer files with easy-to-use names so you can find the quickly. Delete old files you don't use. And write down your filing system so others can find important documents if you're not at your computer.

Are you easily distracted?
Distractions can pose major challenges to getting work done. Phone calls, emails, texts and unscheduled office visits can easily divert the attention of even the most disciplined leader. Be mindful of when you are being interrupted, and develop habits to address distractions so you can concentrate on your priorities and tasks.

Are you delegating?
Delegating responsibilities is a critical skill. It requires letting go of control, yet still being responsible for the results. You hired great people. Now let them do their job.

TODAY'S ACTION ITEM

DECEMBER 30

{ TAKE CARE OF YOU IN THE NEW YEAR }

With the New Year just around the corner, now is the perfect time to hit reset on our personal priorities. If you don't take care of yourself, you can't take care of anyone else. Here are some tips that have helped me along the way on improving self-care:

1. Set a goal.
At the beginning of each year I sit down, review the different areas in my life and set goals in each area. For example, I ask myself, "What do I want for me in the new year?" "What are the good habits I can start right now?" Answers to these questions help me create an extensive, specific and actionable list of goals for the year.

2. Make a plan.
Once I determine my goals, it's time to make the actual plans. For example, if I set a goal to weigh a certain number of pounds at the end of the year, I create a nutrition plan, schedule a doctor's check-up or two and begin an exercise regimen to move closer toward my goal.

3. Get out the calendar.
Putting dates and times to your plan is critical. I've found that if I don't protect my time to ensure things happen, I'll fail.

4. Review your goals.
You must review your goals and plans often. The review process helps me recommit to them and make any adjustments if needed (rather than giving up completely).

Determine now that in the next year, you will stop the cycle of putting yourself last and start a new cycle focused on what will only push you forward.

TODAY'S ACTION ITEM

DECEMBER 31

{ STARTING THE NEW YEAR OFF ON THE RIGHT FOOT }

I'm a morning person. I love to take long walks early in the day to free my mind and get my blood flowing.

Like many people, however, I have to remind myself while I'm on my morning stroll to forget about work and enjoy the scenery. Why do we have such a hard time experiencing the moments that are right in front of us? This is our one life, and we must look up to enjoy it.

As we head into the New Year, take the time on your next walk to think about charting new paths. Here are several practical suggestions to consider. Take something from this list, and improve your own life in just one step.

- Do one thing you're afraid to do.
- Apologize for one thing you need to apologize for.
- Start one thing you've always planned to start.
- Tell one person how amazing they are.
- Offer to help one person.
- Just once, refuse to care what other people think.
- Do one thing that's not your job.
- Embrace one thing another person does.
- Do something foolish.
- Call your parents. (My dad says this should be at the top of the list.)

You have your whole life ahead of you. Who knows? After a few minutes on your morning walk you may make a decision that changes your life for the better!

TODAY'S ACTION ITEM

NO TRY, ONLY DO

FROM **ANDY BAILEY**
Amazon #1 bestseller

Detailing Andy's methodologies and the principles of Petra Coach,
No Try, Only Do is about how to avoid "the weak option,"
why entrepreneurs often fall back on it, and the lessons
Andy learned via his own bloody experiences over the years.

If you are a business owner or entrepreneur, there is no room for "try" in your vocabulary.

LET ANDY **TELL YOU WHY.**